INTO THE EAST

SABIR HUSSAIN

Readomania

Readomania
An imprint of Kurious Kind Media Private Limited
readomania.com
email: contact@readomania.com
Facebook: facebook.com/iamreadomania
Twitter: twitter.com/iamreadomania
Instagram: iamreadomania

First Published in 2022 by Readomania

ISBN: 978-93-91800-17-8

Typeset in Palatino Linotype by Shine Graphics
Printed in Delhi

Photographs: Sabir Hussain

Contents

Prologue

Riding across the Northeast was a dream that I had nursed for a long time but it had always seemed elusive. At one point I even told myself that Robert Browning must have been thinking of someone like me when he wrote:

'Ah, but a man's reach should exceed his grasp,

Or what's a heaven for?'

But then I also remembered Theodore Roosevelt's famous line, 'Believe you can and you're halfway there.' And so, in the summer of 2018, I started chasing my dream seriously. I told myself that if I could ride solo across Kashmir and Ladakh in 2013, I could do the Northeast too. The trouble was that I did not own a motorcycle in 2018.

I asked Royal Enfield if they could lend me a Himalayan for three months, and to my delight, they said yes.

Raising money for the trip was another hurdle because I had no connection with the corporate world. David Laitphlang, my ex-colleague at *Hindustan Times*, helped me get a sponsorship from Star Cement. And India's most famous classic and vintage car restoration expert, Tutu Dhawan, helped raise the rest of the fund I needed.

I was also lucky that my wife Sudha backed me for the adventure.

In 2018, the political situation was volatile in the Northeast and particularly in Assam, where the exercise for the National Register of Citizens was on and the political groundwork was being done for a new citizenship law. So, some of the remarks of strangers I met along the way may sound antagonistic now.

I hold no political brief but I felt these men simply gave vent to their angst against the government of the day and found me a sympathetic listener.

For me, what mattered in the end was that I lived my dream.

Sabir Hussain
New Delhi, 2022

1

Stranded in Siliguri

30 October 2018

The Rajdhani Express for Dibrugarh is already lined up for departure at 4 pm on October 30 when we reach the platform at the New Delhi Railway Station. My wife Sudha and son Aseem help me arrange the luggage and we sit down to talk for the last few minutes. I will be out for two months on a motorcycle expedition of Northeast India which I will be starting from Siliguri.

There are two other young men already seated in the coach. I learn one of them is named Rajiv Bagra, a software professional working in Texas who is on his way home to Dibrugarh. The second is Navin Mukhia, an Army officer who is also headed home to Darjeeling and would be getting down at New Jalpaiguri, which is also my destination. Rajiv is the more talkative one. I tell him about my bike trip and it immediately strikes a chord with him. Rajiv used to be a biker once and was a member of an online travel community called BCM Touring.

'Do you know Shahwar Hussain?' he asks.

'He is my brother. How do you know him?'

'I don't know him. But I follow him on social media. He seems to be travelling a lot on bikes across the Northeast.'

I tell him that Shahwar owns a motorcycle touring company and spends many months every year taking Indian and foreign bikers on tours to different places in the Northeast and many of them have become repeat clients.

It is time for the train to leave and Sudha and Aseem get down on the platform and we spend the last few moments together. I hug Aseem and tell him to look after his mother. 'You are the man of the house now,' I tell him. He is two months shy of his fourteenth birthday and seems to regard my advice as an onerous responsibility.

'Yes, Papa. Don't worry and ride safely,' he says.

I get on the train and it starts chugging. Seconds later, Sudha and Aseem disappear from view and I return to my seat. I discover that Rajiv and I share quite a few common interests like the history of the Second World War and the Sino-India war of 1962. He asks me about my route.

'I will head to Gangtok from Siliguri and then go to Darjeeling before heading for Assam from where I will enter Arunachal Pradesh. After I exit Arunachal Pradesh, I plan to head for Nagaland, Manipur, Mizoram and then Meghalaya and end the tour with Christmas in Shillong.'

He tells me, if possible, to visit a place called Vijaynagar in eastern Arunachal Pradesh where retired Nepalese troopers of the Assam Rifles, India's oldest paramilitary organization, had been settled many years ago. 'It's a very remote place in Changlang district and is still very poorly connected.'

My itinerary is already a lengthy one and I doubt if I will be able to include Vijaynagar in it or have the energy left to ride there. At 53, I am already pushing myself a little hard to chase a dream that had seemed elusive until a few months ago. The desire to see as much of the Northeast on a single trip was what had fired me to undertake this expedition. I also told myself that it was time to break free from my desk because I owed it to myself to do what I had set my heart on a long time ago. Although I was born in Assam, I had visited only a few parts of the Northeast and this trip would make up for all the near misses of the years gone by. I was particularly interested in meeting veterans in Arunachal Pradesh of the Sino-India War of 1962, catching a glimpse of the sunrise in India's easternmost village called Kaho on the Chinese border, and riding through erstwhile battlefronts of the Second World War in Manipur and Nagaland. Planning the trip hadn't been easy. My office was unwilling to let me go for two months so I decided to go on leave without pay and took to crowdfunding to raise money.

Rajiv talks about Silchar in southern Assam where he studied engineering and where I completed the last two and a half years of school. Major Navin is engrossed in his phone. He calls a string of young women one after another. On video call, he tells each one of them that he had been posted in a remote place in Ladakh for the last four months and couldn't call them earlier because of poor phone network.

'I missed you very much,' he tells every woman he speaks to. I can't make out if they are relatives or girlfriends but that man surely has a huge female fan following.

He coughs incessantly and tells us that he has also developed high blood pressure recently following which he was transferred to Varanasi where he has to join in a few weeks.

'Got this damn cough in Siachen and it won't go away. The doctor gave me five different cough syrups but nothing has worked.'

He has other problems too. The registration of his beloved motorcycle, a Yamaha RX 135, has expired and he can't renew its insurance.

'The problem is the bike was registered in Dehradun and they are asking me to take the bike there to renew the registration. How can I do it? The bike is in Darjeeling.'

Rajiv suggests that he write to the transport authorities.

'My motorcycle's registration has also run out.' Rajiv tells us. 'But I still ride it when I am home.'

He turns to me and asks, 'Is your bike in the luggage van of the train?'

'No. I put it in a truck five days ago. I will pick it up in Siliguri.'

He shakes his head and warns me about truckers and transporters.

'I had a very bad experience when I moved from Delhi to Pune a few years ago. They promised to deliver my goods in seven days and took two weeks to do it. And they did not pay compensation for the delay. It is as if once your goods are loaded, it is up to providence for it to reach the destination in time.'

Rajiv's warning rings an alarm bell but since I booked the motorcycle—a Royal Enfield Himalayan—with one of the country's best known transporters GATI, I tell myself that the company also has a reputation to protect and probably won't delay delivery.

I had requested Royal Enfield to lend me a Himalayan motorcycle for three months and they were gracious enough to agree. The company shipped the Himalayan to me from Chennai in the beginning of October after I told them that I needed a few weeks to get used to the motorcycle which is substantially larger than a 150 cc motorcycle that I had been riding earlier. But, when I took delivery of the bike, I discovered that it was simple to ride with a very comfortable riding position. It is a no-frills, no-nonsense adventure touring motorcycle with an attractive exhaust note. Three weeks later, I put it on a truck to Siliguri. The booking clerk wrote November 2 as delivery date but said it would reach on October 31 and the two extra days were a buffer for unforeseen developments.

The train chugs along and I doze off. By the time I wake up it is almost evening. Major Navin has climbed to the upper berth and Rajiv is stretched on the lower seat. An attendant comes to serve tea and snacks and wakes up Navin and Rajiv.

'Are you going to go to Darjeeling straight from New Jalpaiguri?' I ask Navin.

'No. I have relatives in Siliguri and I will stay with them for two days before I go to Darjeeling.'

I tell him that I would also be going to Darjeeling and would like to meet him there. He agrees. Rajiv also tells me that he would be in Dibrugarh through December and that I could check him out when I am in that city.

Night descends and the journey begins to feel monotonous. The train attendant serves dinner at 9 pm. I wake up in the morning to see that the train is passing through the countryside. At 1:30 pm, we reach New Jalpaiguri.

Major Navin asks me to follow him to the exit of the station and then guides me to the autorickshaw stand. But there are no autorickshaws there and I decide to wait for some time. The officer goes away to hail a cab. I call Alok Dubey, my contact in Siliguri, whose address I had given for the delivery of the motorcycle. Alok works with another transport company. He gives me directions to his office in Sevoke Road.

An autorickshaw finally arrives and the driver quotes an obnoxious fare of Rs 300 for the journey of about 10 km. I haggle and the driver finally agrees to halve the fare. Shortly afterwards, the road narrows and the volume of traffic suddenly increases. Siliguri, Bengal's largest city in the North, is a commercial hub that serves Northeast India, Bhutan, and parts of Nepal. Like most Indian cities, it is largely unplanned. Pavements are encroached by hawkers and every kind of business including small eateries, two-wheeler workshops, salons and Siliguri's ubiquitous tea stalls line up the roads.

Twenty minutes later I get off the autorickshaw and walk down a lane to Alok's office. Alok calls the GATI office only to be told that the truck has not arrived and to check again the next day.

I have to find a hotel and Alok volunteers to take me to one about half a kilometre from his office on Sevoke Road on the route to Gangtok. It is almost 3 pm when I check in. My room is on the fourth floor and the balcony offers a view of the main road and a small industrial area. The weather is still warm as the sun streams in through the balcony door. I take a bath and go down to the restaurant for lunch before returning to my room to rest.

I doze off and wake up around 5 pm to see that the sun is almost setting and decide to go for a walk. Opposite the hotel is an outlet of one of India's largest jewellery chains, Kalyan Jewellers, which is being readied for inauguration. A few other large buildings next to it include a supermarket, clothing shops, and large general stores. I walk towards the direction of Alok's office. A short distance from the hotel I come across a row of two-wheeler workshops where many KTM motorcycles are waiting for repairs. I am a little surprised that so many of these motorcycles are waiting at the roadside garages while there is a KTM showroom and service centre less than a hundred yards away.

A young man is standing next to his motorcycle awaiting his turn. I ask him what is wrong with his bike.

'It loses power suddenly and sometimes it drags to the left and the engine heats up,' he says.

'Why don't you go to the service centre?' I ask him.

'The service cost is high. I just got my first job, so I don't want to spend too much on repairs.'

'The heating is a common problem with performance motorcycles. But the other problems are probably freak ones because KTM bikes normally don't have such problems. Are you sure these roadside mechanics can repair it?'

'Yes. I came here on a friend's suggestion. He also gets his repairs done here.'

I learn that the KTM showroom in Siliguri is the only one in North Bengal. All the garages in that row are like shacks stuffed with spare parts that hardly leave any space inside.

The bikes are serviced on the road and they don't inspire any confidence in me. Many of the mechanics are in their late teens and certainly no expert in handling a KTM motorcycle. But many of the locals seem to have enough faith in them.

I keep walking and cross the KTM showroom as rush hour traffic swarms the road. There is a go-slow at every crossing which is often compounded by motorists jumping the lights and getting caught in oncoming traffic. Everybody honks but no one goes any faster.

Diwali is a week away and the varied shops have been spruced up and are doing brisk business. Automobile and two-wheeler showrooms have launched sales promotion drives to woo prospective customers. Restaurants along the road do roaring business. After half an hour of walking and window shopping, I return to the hotel and watch television for some time.

My school friend Rubaiyat Ali calls from Guwahati to ask if I am ready for the ride. I tell him that I am more than ready but the hitch is that my motorcycle has not arrived. He suggests a couple of places in Gangtok where I could stay and asks me my tentative date of arrival in Guwahati.

'Maybe in a week if all goes well,' I tell him. He signs off saying he will be in touch.

Rubaiyat and I had been to middle school together in Guwahati before we lost touch when my father was transferred. We eventually met again 12 years later in our first jobs in Guwahati in a newspaper called *The Sentinel*.

The temperature begins to fall and a chilly wind starts to blow and forces me to close the balcony door. At 9 pm, I eat dinner and go to sleep.

A strange bird call wakes me in the morning around 6:30. I laze around in the bed, hoping to sleep some more but the bird calls don't stop and force me to get up to check. I notice a huge tree with berries opposite my balcony along the road that leads to the industrial area. The tree is thick with leaves and orange-coloured berries and it takes me a few minutes before I can spot two Indian grey hornbills whose shade almost merge with that of the tree. I certainly did not expect to see hornbills inside a city and I seize the opportunity to observe them.

The male, which is larger than the female, is the one which woke me up. And, it is still calling out although the female is sitting on another branch nearby and eating the berries. The male gobbles a few berries then repeats his calls and the exercise goes on for some time before it flies off with heavy flapping of its wings. It returns a little later and then concentrates only on eating the fruits.

I freshen up and decide to go out for a morning walk towards the direction of Gangtok. There is a chill in the air but it is pleasant. I notice a small eatery with a signboard that says 'Tea Bar' and decide to buy a cup of tea. A few customers are already seated on two benches. I sit on the third one which is empty and ask for a cup of black tea.

'Darjeeling tea?' he asks.

'Yes. What else would I drink in Siliguri?'

'I have lots of varieties of them starting from Rs 10 a cup to Rs 150.'

I don't want fancy stuff so I tell him that I will settle for the Rs 10 variety. I know some varieties of Darjeeling tea are astronomically priced but I doubt if people with that much money to spend would stop at a nondescript shop like this one to buy a cup of tea for Rs 150. The other customers seem regulars. A couple of them are reading local papers and discussing Bengal politics.

The tea is good and I buy one more cup which prompts the shop owner to lecture me on how to make perfect tea.

'Never add milk to tea because then it is no longer tea. It simply becomes some concoction. Some tea sellers keep boiling the tea and then add milk and sugar and boil it some more. That's not tea, that's just hot syrup,' he says with utter disdain about those who make this kind of tea.

There is a regular flow of customers and I guess he probably makes at least Rs 1,500 by the end of a day which is not bad for a tea seller.

I return to my hotel, eat breakfast and wait till 10 am to call the GATI office to ask about my motorcycle. The man can't throw any light on where the truck has reached and promises to get the information by noon. I begin to get irritated but since there is nothing that I can do, I decide to check out another part of Siliguri—Hill Cart Road, where I had stayed a night almost 30 years ago on my way to Gangtok for the first time.

I take a shared electric rickshaw and get off at a tri-junction where Sevoke Road and Hill Cart Road meet. Hill Cart Road is narrower than Sevoke Road and is even more crowded and the traffic is perpetually in slow motion. There are a lot of wholesalers in Hill Cart Road for shoes, textiles, garments, and medicine and there is heavy business activity. Mini trucks line up near pavements to be loaded with consignments for different destinations.

I spend an hour in Hill Cart Road and then return to the hotel and call GATI again. They still have not been able to trace the truck and it is beginning to sound like a bad joke. I guess Rajiv Bagra was right about truckers. With nothing else to do, I call up my colleague and *Hindustan Times* correspondent in Siliguri, Pramod Giri to ask if we could meet in the evening. He agrees.

By the afternoon I notice labourers digging holes on either side of the road in front of Kalyan Jewellers and by the evening they pitch bamboos into the holes to make the frame of a gate. As the street lights switch on, the labourers end their work for the day; pick up their tools and leave. I feel like having something cold and go out of the hotel to a kiosk near its gate and buy a lemon drink. The hotel also runs a wine shop on one side of its premise and a rush is building up in front of it. An SUV stops near that gate and three men get out of it and head for the wine shop.

Soon, I hear loud voices and lot of swearing in Hindi and Bangla. The three men are being shoved around and a few other men warn them never to show up at the shop. I ask a security guard of the hotel about the fracas.

'Those three men are from Bihar and they were trying to jump the queue. Since they can't drink in their state, they come here once a month, buy a few crates and stay put here for a couple of days to finish their booze.'

'How many people from Bihar come here to drink?'

'Quite a lot of them. These three guys are satisfied with a crate. Larger groups buy three or four crates. And they return to Bihar only after the alcohol is over.'

I had heard of people from Bihar boarding trains for the nearest towns across the border in Uttar Pradesh to drink and return home ever since the Bihar government imposed prohibition in the state in April 2016. Getting drunk outside the state border was considered better than getting caught with alcohol in Bihar which entails a jail term. But I had no idea people from Bihar were also making trips to North Bengal to get high.

Pramod arrives at around 8 pm. He is in his late 40s. He asks me about my plans and I tell him about my misfortune of being stranded without the motorcycle. But I don't dwell on my bad luck and ask him about the town.

'The businesses are run mostly by Marwaris like in most of the Northeast. Others like Bengalis and Nepalis make up the government workforce and professionals. There's a lot of floating population also from Assam, Bihar, and Nepal.'

We talk about our work and he tells me about the districts that he has to cover, some of which are quite difficult to reach because of bad roads. I also learn that like in many other border towns, authorities in Siliguri too have to deal with smuggling and human trafficking. Many of the women trafficked are of Nepalese origin and many others belong to tea garden communities in the region.

'There is a woman named Rangu Souria who is doing a great job of rescuing and rehabilitating victims of trafficking, mostly women and children. She runs an NGO which is based here. You can meet her if you want. And, if you can't meet her then you can try to meet her associate Prabhat Pathak who lives here.'

He gives me their phone numbers.

Since Darjeeling is in my itinerary, I ask Pramod about the political situation in the North Bengal hills which had been rocked by violence for a few months in 2017 when the agitation for a separate Gorkhaland state erupted all over again.

'Darjeeling is cool now. The Gorkhaland agitation is almost dormant after the Gorkhaland Janamukti Morcha (GJM), which was spearheading the movement for a separate state, virtually split down the middle. The Bengal government co-opted one faction of the GJM which now runs the Gorkhaland Territorial Administration.'

The Gorkhaland Territorial Administration is a regional semi-autonomous government body set up after a tripartite agreement between the Indian government, the state of West Bengal, and the GJM in 2011. It comprises the hill divisions of Darjeeling, Kurseong, Mirik, and Kalimpong.

It is reassuring to hear Pramod's assessment because in the summer of 2017, Darjeeling and the North Bengal hills had gone through a 104-day strike peppered with violence as the GJM pushed for a separate state. The strike had badly hit the economy of the hills, particularly the tea and tourism industries.

'You can roam all over Darjeeling without any problem,' Pramod tells me. 'There are different roads to go to Darjeeling but take the one out of Siliguri which runs along the heritage train track.'

I ask him if he knows any Land Rover Defender owner in Darjeeling. I want to meet any taxi driver with a Defender because those vehicles had become synonymous with Darjeeling before they were shunted out of the town over new emission norms. As a schoolboy, I was almost obsessed with Jeeps and Land Rover Defenders. But while I learnt to drive on a Jeep, I could never get behind the wheel of a Defender.

'I doubt you will find any of those in Darjeeling. Land Rover Defenders now operate out of a place called Manebhanjyang, about 30 km from Darjeeling. It is close to the Nepal border.'

He gives me the phone number of a man named Chandan Pradhan, the President of the Land Rover Owners' Association in Manebhanjyang. 'You can call him and meet him if you want.'

Pramod leaves after an hour and I switch on the television to watch the news. And there is bad news hogging the limelight. Five Bangla-speaking men have been shot dead in the evening near Tinsukia in Upper Assam by suspected terrorists of the United Liberation Front of Asom (ULFA) that seeks a sovereign, independent Assam for the indigenous Assamese people. There is apprehension that the massacre could snowball into an Assamese-Bengali confrontation in Assam.

I switch off the television after some time. Rubaiyat calls to tell me about the murders and that the situation in Assam has suddenly become tense. He tells me to be careful during my ride to the state.

I go to bed with a prayer that the situation in my home state doesn't deteriorate.

The hornbills wake me up again in the morning. I brush and head for the tea bar near the hotel I had discovered the previous day. The owner recognizes me and asks, 'The same as yesterday?'

'Yes,' I say as I sit down.

Three high school boys with their satchels also walk in and sit at the next table and order tea and buns. It is not yet seven and I guess the boys must have left home without eating anything. They finish their tea and buns just in time as the school bus arrives and they climb into it.

There are three other customers in the shop and one of them mentions the massacre in Assam. They start debating whether the killings were indeed a solitary strike or whether more such murders would follow. There is a rage against the murders but there is no talk about retribution. Instead, they blame the government and intelligence failure for the killings. I also learn that the Trinamool Congress party which is in power in Bengal has called a rally later that afternoon in Siliguri to protest against the murders.

I drink my tea and return to the hotel and pick up a local newspaper from the reception. Expectedly, the front page carries the Tinsukia murders as the lead story. I scan the paper cursorily and see that there is no quality control over the use of photographs. A murder story carries a grotesque picture of a victim whose body was found in a drain.

There is more disappointment at 10:30 am with GATI telling me that the truck has still not arrived. I am beginning to feel that I have been taken for a ride and wish that I had ridden the motorcycle from Delhi instead of putting it on the truck. I feel totally helpless and go out for a random walk along Sevoke Road. Diwali marketing is in full swing and a man on stilts wearing a flowing red poncho with a finance company's logo is walking and handing out pamphlets to pedestrians. An autorickshaw crawls along with a loudspeaker on the roof and a recorded voice asking customers to buy lottery tickets with a jackpot prize of Rs one crore.

I spend almost a couple of hours window shopping. On the way back, I see a motorcyclist standing beside a Himalayan. The motorcycle is loaded and it is obvious that he is on a tour. I walk up to him and introduce myself. He is much younger, probably in his mid-30s, a techie from Chennai. Hemant tells me he is waiting for two other friends. The three had been to Sikkim and will be leaving for Chennai the next morning.

'Are you riding back to Chennai?'

'No, we are flying. We hired the bikes here in Siliguri.'

I ask him how his Himalayan behaved in the mountains.

'It behaved very well. Absolutely no problem,' Hemant replies. He tells me to check out North Sikkim for its lakes and mountains. 'You will need to apply for a pass in Gangtok.'

On the way back, I walk into a small restaurant opposite the tea bar and order chicken fried rice for lunch. One of the staffers tells me that he has seen me for the past three days and asks, 'Are you on business here?' I tell him that I am stranded.

'Where have you come from?'

'Delhi.'

'I worked in Delhi for three years before I returned here about a year ago.'

'What work did you do?' I ask.

'I was a cook at two dhabas. I worked in Karol Bagh and Nehru Place. But I could not make ends meet. The money was not enough because my family was here and I had to run two establishments. So I returned. At least, I don't have to pay rent now,' he says.

The fried rice arrives and I ask him if he has cooked it.

'No. There is new guy who has cooked it. I supervise the cooking.'

The rice tastes good. I wash it down with a lemon drink and return to the hotel to take a nap. I wake up late afternoon and go to the balcony. The gate that the labourers had started making the previous day is now complete. Designers have put up boards with pictures on the gate depicting Bengal's legendary filmmaker Satyajit Ray's classic movie *Pather Panchali* and electricians are fitting the lights. A little before dusk, the lights are switched on and Sevoke Road suddenly transforms into a different setting. One of the pictures shows Ray looking through a camera's viewfinder as if filming the traffic flowing through the gate.

GATI's delay gnaws at the back of my mind and I decide to check out motorcycle rental services in Siliguri as part of a back-up plan. I find a few bike rentals on the internet and shortlist two of them and decide to visit one. It takes me half an hour to walk to Nazrul Sarani from my hotel and locate the shop which operates out of a three-storeyed building.

The owner, Arpan Paul, is out visiting friends but he tells me on phone that he has TVS Apache 200, Pulsar 150, and Bullet Classic 350 that I could hire. A Himalayan is out on rent. The Apache and the Pulsar hire charges are Rs 800 a day while the Bullet Classic costs Rs 1,300 per day. I tell him I will get back to him and return to the hotel.

For dinner, I go back to the same restaurant where I had lunch and order chowmein. The waiter tells me it will take 15 minutes so I go for another walk. A short distance away from the restaurant, a small road runs perpendicular to Sevoke Road and at its entry is another gate for Diwali. This one in blue neon lights depicts a demon with horns, opening and closing its mouth. The hawker in the autorickshaw selling lottery tickets has parked near the gate and the loudspeaker is still blaring, asking people to try their luck for the jackpot.

Fifteen minutes later, I return to the restaurant for my dinner. Back at the hotel, Rubaiyat calls again to ask if the motorcycle has arrived. I tell him that I have run into bad luck.

My luck doesn't change even on the fourth day and I decide to escalate the matter. I take to Twitter and tag the company's founder about my plight. Later in the day, I get a call from GATI assuring me once again that they are trying to deliver the motorcycle at the earliest but still can't promise a definite date. And then the GATI employee tells me that the truck has been held up on the other side of the Farakka Bridge which is under maintenance with heavy regulations on the volume of traffic crossing it. I can't figure out why the truck was diverted towards Farakka when there was a direct route from Delhi to Siliguri. The GATI employee is clueless too.

I call Pramod and ask him for the phone number of Rajah Banerjee, whose family once owned one of India's oldest tea gardens—the Makaibari tea estate in Kurseong, near Darjeeling. Rajah Banerjee, whose real name is Swaraj Kumar Banerjee, sold his majority stake in the Makaibari Tea and Trading Company in 2014. In March 2018, he ended all association with the garden and gifted away his minority stake to the workers. He now lives in Siliguri.

Pramod sends me the number but warns that Banerjee may not give me an appointment. I decide to try my luck and call up the 70-year-old planter. He graciously agrees to meet me at 4 pm and sends me his coordinates. I ask the hotel receptionist for directions and leave the hotel at 2:45 pm. I hail a couple of autorickshaws but none of them wants to go to Pradhan Nagar. The shared autorickshaws are full and I lose time waiting. Eventually, I decide to walk to Pradhan Nagar which is four km away. I cross a bridge across the Mahananda river and see that preparations are on in the sandbars for Chhat puja which is celebrated mostly by people from Bihar and entails bathing in a river at dawn and dusk.

Pradhan Nagar is a relatively quieter part of Siliguri. It takes me about an hour to reach the address which turns out to be an office, but the guard at the gate tells me that Banerjee has just left. I call up the former planter but he tells me brusquely that he can't return. I guess my stars are not right and take another road to return to my hotel.

A short distance away from my hotel, a man in his mid-30s, starts walking alongside me.

'Tourist?' he asks.

There is something about the man that I don't like and ask him what he wants.

'I just wanted to know if you are interested in women. If you are, I can arrange them for you. Nepalese or Bengali women. Very beautiful.'

He takes out his phone and starts scrolling through some photographs of women. 'See the photos. You can choose.'

I stop walking. My nerves are already frayed because of the delay in the motorcycle's delivery and now I have a pimp to contend with. I tick him off, telling him I am not interested and not to bug me. But he persists.

I stop again and tell him that I have friends in the media and unless he wants to see his name and photograph in the next day's newspapers, he should leave me alone. It works like a charm and he immediately walks away.

There is a huge crowd in front of Kalyan Jewellers and traffic policemen are struggling to clear the road for motorists. It is difficult even to walk. Young men and women seem to be in equal numbers in the crowd. I stop at the kiosk near the hotel's gate and ask the shopkeeper about the crowd.

'Amitabh Bachchan and Katrina Kaif were supposed to come for the inauguration and so half of Siliguri has turned up here,' the shopkeeper tells me.

'Did they come?'

'No. Something happened. I guess they are not coming. But this crowd is not going to go away soon.'

India's love for all things filmy is well known but it is the first time I have witnessed a frenzy of this kind first hand. I buy a cold drink from the kiosk and stand until I finish it before heading to my room. The eight-km walk to and from Pradhan

Nagar has worn me out. I call room service for an early dinner and drop off to sleep after eating.

I spend three more days without any luck for my motorcycle to arrive. It is Diwali on the evening of my seventh day in Siliguri and I choose to stay in my room and watch the decorative lights along Sevoke Road. Most shops have closed early and fortunately not too many people are bursting crackers.

On the tenth day, I check out of the hotel and go to Alok's office, keep my luggage in his room and hop onto his motorcycle as he takes me to GATI's facility in a logistics hub on the outskirts of Siliguri along the highway to Guwahati. A few kilometres before our destination, Alok points to a road on the right and tells me that it leads to the Bangladesh border where there is a crossing point for trucks carrying mainly rocks and boulders.

'That place is full of Bangladeshis. They come over here and work on a daily basis. Some even stay put. If you go that side you won't even think you are in India, but very few people seem to know about it.'

We finally reach the GATI facility. The branch manager is not there so we talk to his deputy and berate him for the inordinate delay in the delivery of the motorcycle.

'I know there is a delay. The head office has been bombarding us since you raised the issue. It was supposed to be delivered today but the truck was involved in an accident this morning. The branch manager has gone to get the truck released from the police which have impounded it. It may take another two days,' the deputy manager tells us.

I feel like exploding in anger but instead take a few deep breaths to calm myself down and tell him to deliver the bike at Alok's address when it arrives. Alok tells me that he would be leaving for his home in Bihar two days later for Chhat Puja but he would leave instructions so that I can go collect the motorcycle.

I decide to hire a motorcycle and start my journey to Gangtok and ask Alok to drop me at Arpan Paul's residence. Arpan is a young man. He shows me the motorcycles but the Pulsar's rear tyre looks worn out so I settle for the red Apache. I make the payment and ride to a fuel station to fill up the tank and then go to Alok's office. He helps me load the saddle bags and tool kit and I finally start my ride at 2 pm.

2

Sikkim

9 November 2018

Gangtok is 115 km away from Siliguri and it normally takes around four hours to reach. I exit Siliguri and discover that the road is great to ride on. I cross the Mahananda Wildlife Sanctuary at Sukna and tell myself that if I hadn't wasted ten days waiting for the Himalayan I might have checked it out. I knew the sanctuary is home to many birds like different varieties of hornbill and exotic mammals like the Himalayan serow (a goat-antelope), Himalayan porcupine, Himalayan black bear, and the rare clouded leopard.

I cross a bridge over a raging Teesta river and stop at a kiosk to buy a bottle of water. I also call up Rubaiyat and tell him I have started my journey on a different motorcycle and that I would pick up the Himalayan once I return from Sikkim. The road remains good for about 30 km before potholes begin to appear and force me to reduce my speed. Sometime later the road condition worsens as an entire stretch seems to be made of patchworks to fill up potholes.

The Apache is not made for bad roads and is essentially meant for short sprints for fun and racing. The motorcycle has shorter suspension and I feel every bump on the road and I begin to miss the Himalayan which would have soaked up most of the impact of riding over potholes. I cross small hamlets and see that Star Cement, which is backing my expedition, has a large presence in the area with huge billboards in many places. Many shops in these hamlets also sport a signboard of

Star Cement although they do not deal with any construction material.

The road begins to go uphill and the gradient quickly increases. The Teesta flows along the road for some time before it changes direction and then returns to keep me company. A few SUVs overtake me but I am in no hurry and ride leisurely. On my rear-view mirror I notice an SUV labouring to climb the slope and after sometime the driver starts honking. I move towards the side of the road to let the vehicle pass but it doesn't overtake me. Instead, the driver keeps honking. I slow down further and as the SUV catches up, a passenger in the front seat leans out and gesticulates at me to stop.

'One of your saddle bags has fallen off. That's why the driver was honking,' he yells at me.

I thank him and try to turn back to look for the bag. But there are many vehicles on the way up and it takes me a few minutes before I actually start riding downhill. I look for the bag along the edge of the road but I can't find it. I retrace my route once again but there is no sign of the bag. It couldn't have fallen off the edge of the road into the Teesta because I was on the other side of the road. Fifteen minutes later I conclude that someone in one of the many vehicles that were behind me must have picked it up. I stop again and dismount and check my other belongings. Everything else is intact. But I feel it was the tool kit which I had kept on the seat and over which I laid the strap of the saddle bags was the culprit. It probably stretched the stitching of the saddle bag on the right to breaking point.

But the loss is not too much. I had put my shin guards, the Himalayan's rear view mirrors, thermal wears, socks, a couple of T-shirts, and toiletries in that bag. I decide I will buy those items in Gangtok. I rearrange my luggage and tie them securely with bungee cords and resume my journey with a prayer that this mishap was the last after the fiasco with GATI.

The scenery is a solace as I try to put the lost bag out of my mind. About two hours later I reach Melli, a small town spread across the Bengal-Sikkim border. There is a long bridge across the Teesta and I stop in the middle of it to take a few pictures. The river looks surprisingly placid at Melli. The Teesta is a relatively short river with a length of just over 300 km. It originates in the Pahunri glacier at an altitude of over 23,000 ft and flows southward through gorges and rapids in Sikkim before entering the plains of Bengal and then flowing into Bangladesh. Fed by a number of rivulets, the river descends quickly through a 100-km stretch in Sikkim that makes it a prime candidate for hydropower projects. The region's location in a high seismic zone notwithstanding, the Teesta has a major hydropower project in east Sikkim called the Teesta Stage 5 Dam.

It is close to sunset and I know I would be a little late in reaching Gangtok because the impending darkness would slow me down.

Twenty kilometres later I ride into Rangpo in Sikkim. It is already dark. The last time I was in Rangpo was in 2000 when it was still a sleepy little town, known mostly for its breweries and wine shops that used to draw tourists on the way out of Sikkim because of low prices. Now, it has grown exponentially and the highway which passes through the heart of the town is crowded with taxis, private vehicles, and mini trucks. I crawl through the traffic for some time before the road clears. Out of Rangpo, the night plunges the road and the surrounding hills into complete darkness. It is just two days after Diwali and there is no sign of the new moon and there are no street lights on the highway. The curves come in quick succession and I ride cautiously.

By 6:30 pm, I am on the outskirts of Gangtok and see signage for entry and exit roads of the town. Both are for one-way traffic. I cross the Sikkim Manipal University which has spawned a township around it to service students. A little later I am inside the town but completely flummoxed by its layout. I had intended to ride into Mahatma Gandhi Marg or MG

Marg to find a hotel but I see that the road has been blocked and turned into a promenade.

I ask a policeman for directions to find a hotel and he points to a narrow road uphill which bypasses the promenade. I take the road and crawl behind an SUV before I find myself on a road with rows of hotels on both sides. But none of the hotels has parking space and I take another road downhill that skirts MG Marg and which also has a few hotels although most of them have the same problem with parking space. I stop in front of a hotel to look if there is parking space when my phone rings.

Alok is on the line and he tells me that GATI has delivered the Himalayan at his office around 5 pm. 'I tried to call you but you phone was not connecting.'

I feel like kicking myself but tell Alok that I will complete the Sikkim leg of the tour with the Apache and return to Siliguri to pick up the Himalayan. I notice a few shops are closed and park the motorcycle in front of one of them and walk into the hotel. There is a room but it is only for a night. The manager tells me that I can put my motorcycle inside near the hotel's staircase but will have to take it out in the morning and park at a public parking nearby. I carry my bags upstairs to my room and freshen up and go out to buy toiletries which I lost. I decide to buy the thermal clothing the next day.

A cold wind is blowing and I zip up my jacket and pull my balaclava over my ears as I walk to the promenade. MG Marg is Gangtok's premier market and the promenade is lined up with different kinds of shops and restaurants. There is a festive air and tourists are sitting on the benches along the promenade and many are busy clicking selfies. At one end of MG Marg is a statue of the man after whom it is named—Mohandas Karamchand Gandhi in his trademark dhoti and walking stick.

I buy the toiletries and then go to a restaurant for dinner but it is full of customers. It is the same story with three other restaurants. I finally find one named Babumoshai where a few tables are vacant and I take one. I settle for dal and roti and then return to the hotel. My back and neck begin to hurt and I tell myself that I should have expected this since I am on a long-distance ride for the first time in more than five years after a solo expedition across Kashmir and Ladakh in 2013.

I wake up early next morning and take the motorcycle out of the hotel and ride a short distance to the public parking. On the way back, I see four motorcyclists getting ready for a ride. I ask one of them where they are heading.

'We are going to Lachung and will stay there tonight. We will return tomorrow and head back to Siliguri day after.'

Lachung in North Sikkim used to be a trading post between Sikkim and Tibet until 1950 before it was closed down. It is also on my tentative itinerary and I ask him about the timings to obtain a permit.

'You can get it till 3 pm,' he tells me.

I wish him luck and head for a restaurant on MG Marg for breakfast. The sun is shining brightly and I walk to the promenade after breakfast and sit on a bench and soak up the sun. I am about to leave after about 20 minutes when I see a young man in dark glasses with a guitar and a woman with a small sound system come and sit on a bench at one end of the promenade. The woman arranges the sound system and after some time the young man starts strumming his guitar and singing in Nepali. Soon, a crowd gathers to listen to his songs. They form a ring around the duo and I can't see them anymore.

I return to the hotel and ask the manager if he could suggest another hotel where I could shift.

'Yes. There is one nearby which also has parking space. I can take you there. But there is no hurry. You can leave after a few hours.'

I tell him that I would be visiting a few places and it would help me save time if I move early. We walk about a hundred metres to another hotel and I check in. This one has a larger room and a better view. There is also a restaurant in the hotel.

I go out again to buy thermal innerwear. The shopkeeper is a north Indian and there are two Buddhist monks buying maroon piece of cloth for their robes. A local man and a woman also walk in and ask for a dozen white silk scarves. I ask the woman if the scarves are for any religious ritual.

'No. There's a marriage in the family. And the scarves are given along with the invitation card to some special people or those closest to you.'

They quickly choose the scarves and leave. The monks take some more time to decide on the piece of cloth they want to buy. The shopkeeper then shows me three different brands of thermal wear before I choose one. I notice that there is a photograph of Union Minister Rajnath Singh with a group of men that includes the shopkeeper. I ask him if he is a Bharatiya Janata Party (BJP) member.

'No, I am just a supporter. We had gone to see Rajnath Singh when he visited this city since he is from our part of the country.'

'Does the BJP have support in this place?'

'Not much among the locals. The support is mostly among people like us.'

'Do you own this shop?'

'No. The owner is a Marwari man. I have been working in this shop for 25 years.'

I go back to the hotel to keep the packet and then call up a high school classmate, Manisha Singhi, who had settled in Gangtok after marriage. She tells me her house is on MG Marg and only a few minutes away from my hotel. We decide to meet at 11 am.

I have an hour to kill so I decide explore the Gandhi Market. A long staircase from MG Marg goes downhill through the market with small shops on either side of it. Most of the shops are selling winter wear, shoes, sunglasses, toys, and souvenirs. There are many hawkers and I notice most of them are outsiders. The prices are modest and haggling is an accepted norm. A steady traffic of tourists looking to buy souvenirs and gifts ensures that almost every shopkeeper makes money.

Gandhi Market ends at the bottom of the staircase in Lal Bazar from where a road leads to another part of the town. There are several alleys with small shops, restaurants, and bars. I see a crowd in the middle of an alley and stop to check. People have gathered to watch carrom matches being played in a large space which once could have been a godown. There are eight tables where matches are being played simultaneously. I watch a particular match between a middle-aged man and a much younger opponent for some time. The older man is very good at the game.

I ask another spectator if this is a tournament.

'No. It is just a club. Players pay to hire a board and play.'

It seems like a good idea to spend spare time. I start walking again and reach a multi-storeyed shopping complex called Khanchendzonga Shopping Complex. The first two floors, which host a sprawling vegetable and food market, make me curious. The vegetables present a riot of colours and there is even an outlet for Sikkim's much-hyped organic vegetables. The place also smells of cheese, dry fish, and spices.

The Sikkim government has been on an overdrive about organic farming and I ask a Nepali shopkeeper if everything in the market is indeed organic. He laughs.

'Where is the land to produce for the entire population of the state? Most of the vegetables come from Bengal and they are not organic.'

I tell him that I had a different impression since the government had already declared Sikkim as a 100 per cent organic state. He is not impressed.

'The government can say whatever it wants but the ground reality is different. There are pest attacks and wild animals also destroy the crops but we are not allowed to kill them to save our cultivations. My brother owns an organic farm near Pakyong and wild boars and monkeys often destroy his crops. Even otherwise, his produce has been falling since he started organic farming.'

He tells me he is a supporter of the ruling party, Sikkim Democratic Front, but is sceptical about organic farming because the output is just not enough to feed the entire state.

'It's just hype like the BJP's election campaign slogan of *Acche Din* (Good Days) in 2014. The good days never came,' he laughs.

I leave and take a circular path to MG Marg and then reach Manisha's house and meet her for the first time since we left school in 1982.

The ground floor is a menswear shop and Manisha and her husband Ashok live on the upper floor. We try to catch up on all that has transpired in the 36 years since we last met. Manisha used to be a sports enthusiast in school and was good at table tennis and athletics. Like most Marwaris, she had married young and is now the mother of two daughters. The elder one has just been married a few months ago.

The sitting room on the first floor offers a great view of the hills and the river. Ashok joins us for tea and I hear the fascinating story of his family. His grandfather, Ganpath Rai Singhi, had come to Sikkim from Rajasthan in 1895 as a 25-year-old and started working for Jethmul Bhojraj, the bankers to the Chogyal who ruled Sikkim. Ganpath Rai Singhi had two sons—Dulichand and Khyaliram. Ashok's father, Khyaliram spent the first few years of his life in Rajasthan before his father brought him to Sikkim. Dulichand was much older and by the time he stared working with Jethmul Bhojraj as a cashier, Khyaliram was only in the third standard. Dulichand died unexpectedly and Khyaliram had to drop out of school to help his father in his business because he was getting old. Khyaliram was still in his teens when his father died, leaving him to handle the family's cardamom trade. Most of his clients were from Siliguri, Kolkata, and Delhi.

'This house had a different layout in those years and my father used to tell me that often villagers who came from far to sell their cardamom used to stay here overnight. There was a kind of dormitory for them to stay without any charge. And one part of it was a general store which my father had opened and it was called Ganpath Rai Dulichand but the Chogyal, Sikkim's monarch, had named it Chotta Bank.'

His family's association with Jethmul Bhojraj also took Khyaliram close to the Sikkimese royal family. Khyaliram was also a sportsman and would take part in volleyball matches between the Chogyal's team and commoners. He also often led festive processions organized by the royal family.

His cardamom business had been good. He later diversified and expanded his business to Yatung in Tibet. Before the Nathu La route was closed in 1962 in the wake of the Sino-India War, Khyaliram Singhi was a regular user of the road from 1955 onwards.

It wasn't cardamom that he sold in Yatung but cigarettes, kerosene, and clothes. The merchandise was transported on mules. It normally took two entire days to cover the distance of less than 75 km from Gangtok.

'My father told me that when the hostilities broke out, he had to abandon the business in Yatung. He had about Rs 25,000 in a bank in Yatung which he could never withdraw after Nathu La was sealed following the war.'

Khyaliram Singhi was also a social worker and a few years after Sikkim became a part of India, the Congress asked him to join the party, but he refused. He passed away in February 2005 at the age of 84.

Ashok has been running the shop for some years now. He had graduated from Delhi and returned to Gangtok to run the business. Chotta Bank had been renamed Raj Enterprises and the business had changed from trading to retail.

I tell Ashok about the shopkeeper from whom I bought the thermal clothing and who told me that the BJP has the support of the north Indian business class in Gangtok.

'Even I am a supporter. But that's about it. The BJP even offered me a ticket to contest the assembly elections in 2014 but I am not interested in electoral politics.'

I spend almost two hours with Manisha and Ashok and then go for lunch. At 2 o'clock I go to the tourism department's office to apply for a permit for Lachung. But I run into bad luck. The counter closed at 1:30 pm and the motorcyclist who had told me that it is open till 3 pm probably didn't know the timings.

'Come back tomorrow at 8 am. The counter will be open till 10 am because it is Sunday.'

But the trouble is that the permit is not given for the same day. So I will have to spend an extra day in Gangtok. I decide to drop Lachung from my itinerary. I ask one of the employees of the tourism department the directions for Pakyong where Sikkim's first airport has just been inaugurated.

Pakyong is about 35 km away from Gangtok. About 10 km later the road begins to deteriorate. It begins with broken tarmac at a few places and worsens for long stretches without any sign of a black top road. The population is thin along this road. A variant of the Poinsettia, locally known as Christmas Flower, grows abundantly along the road. The red flower looks spectacular and is also commonly found in the local gardens.

I see a greenhouse and stop to check if it is an organic farm. It indeed is but there is no one around to talk and the gate is locked. I walk to a nearby kiosk and ask the shopkeeper about the farm owner.

'He lives up this hill but is not home today.'

'I wanted to know how this organic farm is doing,' I tell him.

'Not too good. Last week wild boars broke through the fence and destroyed a lot of the crops. And since hunting is banned in the state this man can't even kill the boars.'

It is the same thing the vegetable vendor in Gangtok had told me earlier in the morning. The road deteriorates further and the ride on a motorcycle not meant for this kind of terrain is far from pleasurable. A few cabs coming down from the airport with passengers from the last flight of the day kick up clouds of dust as they cross me. The road improves a little before the airport. The parking lot is empty as I ride in. I walk up to the airport building where operations for the day have ended and see that employees are preparing to leave.

During the inauguration of the airport I had seen stunning pictures of the runway that were probably taken using a drone camera. I want to climb an adjoining hill to see the runway. I ask a security guard for directions but he advises me against climbing it because it is close to sunset and there is a possibility of running into wild animals. It is not what I want to hear but I take his advice seriously.

I spend about ten minutes around the airport before I start the ride back to Gangtok. I cross the worst stretch of the road before it gets dark but find myself caught in rush hour traffic just outside Gangtok. I rest for a while in the hotel and then stroll out. The night is cold and most tourists are clad in heavy winter clothing. At 8 pm, I head to a restaurant for dinner, take a window seat and eat my food watching the traffic and the tourists.

I sleep well and go for a walk the next morning. Beyond MG Marg, I see four motorcyclists ready to head out of Gangtok. They are probably a group of rich men with Triumph Tiger 800 and Kawasaki Versys 1000 motorcycles. The Triumph Tiger has been my on wish list for many years and I wonder if I will ever get to own one given its prohibitive price.

I decide to head for Rumtek monastery, 22 km away. The road to Rumtek is almost as bad as the one to Pakyong. Almost an hour later, I park the motorcycle outside the gate of the monastery. On the opposite side of the road I notice a three-storeyed building from the top floor of which runs a long rope with prayer flags down to another hill. It is one of the longest stretches of prayer flags I have seen anywhere. There is also a straight view of Gangtok and it looks like an entire mountain has been filled up with concrete structures.

The Indo Tibetan Border Police or ITBP guards the monastery which had been rocked by a turf war that started in 1992 within the Karma Kagyu school of Tibetan Buddhism for the post of the Karmapa. Security is tight and every visitor has to enter their name and address in a register at the gate.

The trouble at Rumtek had begun after two rival organizations—the Tsurphu Labrang and the Karmapa Charitable Trust—claimed stewardship of the monastery. The two factions support two different candidates for the 17th Karmapa that eventually led to the fracas. While the Tsurphu Labrang supports Ogyen Tinley Dorje, the Karmapa Charitable Trust backs Trinley Thaye Dorje. Ogyen Tinley Dorje who has a majority following, lives in the Gyuto Monastery in Dharamsala in Himachal Pradesh while Trinley Thaye Dorje lives in Delhi. The central government does not allow the two contenders to visit Rumtek even as the two factions continue to fight a court case.

The Rumtek monastery was originally built under the direction of Changchub Dorje, the 12th Karmapa Lama in the mid-1700s. Set against a hill with a river below it, the monastery also offers a great view of the snow line.

It is a steep walk from the gate to the monastery. The tranquillity of the monastery makes it difficult to imagine that the monks supporting the two contending Karmapas had clashed here. I had expected the monastery to be full of monks but it is largely empty. I walk inside a cafeteria and see a monk at the counter. I introduce myself and ask him his name.

'Jimba Sherpa. I am the manager of this cafeteria.'

He is a volunteer monk so there is no pay or stipend. He had earlier volunteered for the monastery's accounts and construction work. I ask him why the monastery looks deserted.

'Most of the monks have gone to attend a function in Gaya. The others are in their hostels,' he tells me pointing towards a window from where I can see a multi-storeyed hostel.

Two other female tourists walk in, take a corner table and ask for tea. I take the table near the manager's desk and order a plate of noodles.

Jimba is from Kalimpong in North Bengal. I ask him about the ITBP guards.

'It is for the monastery's security,' he tells me and makes no mention of the factional feud. He has been at the monastery for eight years.

'What are the monks taught?' I ask him.

'We learn Buddhist scriptures. Young monks begin their monastic training with a nine-year programme which includes studying the ritual texts of the Karma Kagyu lineage. Once a student masters the texts he is certified by his teacher and by the monks' leader who confers a seal for each of the 36 texts that has been successfully memorized. Graduate monks are called acharyas and are sent to other monasteries to train young monks.'

Another monk serves me the noodles, topped with scrambled eggs. They taste good.

'Is it difficult to graduate as a monk?'

'It is hard work. After they learn the texts, the monks train intensively in all aspects of the tantric rites conducted at the monastery.'

The rites include shrine keeping, chanting, torma making (figures made mostly of flour and butter used in tantric rituals or as offerings in Tibetan Buddhism), the playing of musical instruments, construction of sand mandalas, and sacred dance.

'Each monk goes on to specialize in one of these areas. Some go on to become umdze (chant master) or chopen (ritual master) but before that they may have to study for several more years to master the intricacies of those positions,' Jimba tells me.

I finish my food, pay Jimba, and take a walk around the monastery and look at its architecture and intricate carvings. I had wanted to see the monks chant in unison but chanting is not scheduled for the day because most of the teaching staff has gone to Gaya and so I start the ride back to Gangtok.

An SUV has broken down in a particularly bad stretch of the narrow, twisty road and it sparks a traffic jam. I take more than an hour to reach Gangtok and the stop-go traffic wears me out. I lie down to rest but fall asleep and wake up late in the afternoon. I have to collect a document from Ashok Singhi and go over to his shop. Ashok is sitting on a high stool and offers me one as well.

I am surprised to notice AC vents in the showroom and ask Ashok if he actually needs air conditioning in a place like Gangtok.

'This wasn't my idea. The brand managers and area managers of the clothing company came and designed the layout of the shop and insisted that the air conditioning is part of the package to set up the showroom.'

A cousin of his walks in after some time and Ashok introduces us.

Jagat Singh Singhi is also a BJP supporter and is more active than Ashok in the party. But he seems resigned to the fact the BJP may never capture power on its own in Sikkim.

'Big national parties have no chance in a small state like Sikkim,' he tells me.

Unlike Ashok, Jagat is interested in electoral politics. 'But I don't stand a chance because after delimitation, our assembly constituency has been reserved for a Scheduled Tribe candidate.'

Ashok did not tell me earlier but I learn that one of the grouses of people like the Singhis who settled in Sikkim more than a hundred years ago is that they are not treated at par with locals when it comes to things like paying income tax. Locals are exempted from paying income tax but settlers are not.

'We are treated unfairly and I don't see why it should be that way. It is not as if we came yesterday and settled in Sikkim. Why should only the trading community, which is mostly of North Indian origin, be taxed?' Jagat rails.

Like the Singhis, many Marwari families from Rajasthan had moved to Sikkim to chart new courses for themselves and are now one of the dominant business classes in the state. These business families, also known as 'old settlers' had come to the state before 1975, the year Sikkim merged with India, but don't possess Sikkim subject certificates which exempt the holders from paying income tax. The erstwhile ruler of Sikkim had given out Sikkim subject certificates in 1961 but many including the Singhis never got them.

In 2008, the Parliament amended a law to exempt Sikkim subject certificates holders, about 95 per cent of Sikkim's population, from paying income tax following a request by the State. But it said old settlers would have to pay income tax with retrospective effect from 1991. Shortly after the law was changed, the Association of Old Settlers of Sikkim filed a petition with a Parliamentary Committee saying it was discriminatory and violated the Constitution.

In 2013, the Supreme Court stayed the recovery of income tax dues from 'old settlers of Indian origin' in Sikkim.

'Where on earth will you find such a law? Our families have been here for more than 100 years and we are counted differently when it comes to paying taxes,' says Jagat.

A few customers walk into the shop and look at the clothes. A woman helps her husband choose a pair of trousers and a blazer and they walk away happy with the purchase. I have to leave for Pelling the next morning and I also want to visit the Temi tea estate—Sikkim's largest tea garden—and ask Ashok for directions. It is past 8 o'clock and I decide to leave. I stop at a restaurant for dinner and return to my hotel and pack my bags before going to sleep.

By 8 am, I am out of the hotel. Pelling, my destination for the day, is about 120 km away to the west. The road is almost empty and I quickly exit the town. After about 15 km of downhill, the road starts going uphill. For a long stretch the road is almost a dirt track peppered with water crossings and it doesn't allow any decent speed.

The road finally improves a few kilometres away from Temi tea estate, which is 55 km from Gangtok but it takes me almost three hours to reach. The estate is a sprawling one spread across a few hills. I ride into the parking of Temi tea estate. All the hills nearby are filled with tea bushes. Cherry blossom trees in full bloom among the bushes provide a spectacular contrast. Temi's other claim to fame is that it produces completely organic tea. I walk past the factory into the office and see that the first few rooms are empty. There are a few people in another room down the corridor and I ask if I can speak to the manager.

'The manager has just left for Gangtok and the assistant manager has gone for lunch. What is it that you wanted to talk about?' a woman asks.

'I wanted to know about this tea garden. I am travelling to Pelling and I thought I would stop here for some time and learn about Temi.'

'I will get somebody to give you the information,' she tells me and goes out of the room and returns with another young man.

The young man introduces himself as Lawrence Leonarte Bhutia. He is a field assistant at Temi. We go to another empty room and sit and Lawrence asks an office boy to get two cups of tea. I learn that the Temi estate is spread across 177 hectares and it started going organic in 2005.

The garden was set up in 1966 and production began in 1969. It is run by a Tea Board set up by the Sikkim Government. There are 440 workers to pluck leaves.

'The estate is divided into different segments and plucking does not take place simultaneously in all of them. Leaves are plucked from particular segments at different times,' Lawrence tells me.

The office boy comes in with two cups of black tea. The garden fresh brew tastes great. I ask Lawrence about the production and sales.

'We produce about 80 metric tonnes of tea which are sold mostly in the domestic market but we have started exporting small quantities to Canada recently. The response has been good and there are plans to tap the US market as well. There is a demand for organic tea in Europe also, so Temi's prospects look good.'

Temi's advantage is that it has no competition in the state unlike Bengal where there are many tea estates in the north. A comparatively peaceful political situation has also ensured that there are no disturbances to hit production. The political stability is in stark contrast to the volatility in North Bengal which has often tripped production.

'Last year when the tea gardens in and around Darjeeling shut down for more than three months because of the Gorkhaland agitation, many tea industry workers who were jobless came here to look for work. We could employ only some of them.'

Lawrence tells me that Temi tea estate has also forayed into tea tourism by tying up with a private company to promote a part of the garden as a tourist resort.

I spend about an hour before I leave Temi. The road goes uphill for some time before it descends to Ravangla, 18 km away. I stop for lunch outside the town at a small, cosy resort and then start again for Pelling. By the afternoon, I see little children returning home from school, some with their mothers, some with siblings and friends. Christmas Flowers grow wild along the road.

By 4 pm, I reach another small town called Legship and an hour later I ride uphill into Pelling. The sky is getting cloudy and I pray that it doesn't rain. I find a hotel and check in. I ask the manager if I can see Mount Kanchenjunga from the hotel.

'Yes. I will give you a room with a direct view of the mountain. I hope the sky will be clear tomorrow morning,' he tells me as he takes me to my room. It is large, spacious with wooden walls and a nice view of the mountains but Kanchenjunga is still obscured by the clouds. The manager tells me that dinner won't be available because the cook has gone on leave.

The ride had been punishing in the first half of the day and I rest for some time before going out for a walk in the evening. Only a few shops are open after dark. I check out a restaurant and learn that it serves customers till 8:30 pm so I have enough time to return for dinner. Other shops along the road are beginning to close as mist begins to envelope the town.

A large van drives in when I return to the hotel and a six-member family of tourists disembarks. A woman among them has motion sickness and staggers to a corner of the parking and vomits. Her husband runs to hold her and then guides her to the hotel's reception where she sits. The manager shouts for a bell boy to give her a glass of water and asks another to unload the luggage from the van.

I start a conversation with the woman's husband and learn that they are from Gujarat.

'She is just not used to hilly roads. She had already thrown up twice while travelling today,' he tells me.

I tell him to give her the front seat the next day which will lessen the effects of motion sickness. The manager returns to usher the family to their rooms and I go to mine. I watch television for some time and then decide to go out for dinner when the manager calls to say that the cook has returned and I may eat at the hotel if I want. It saves me the bother of going out in the cold.

I eat a light dinner, sleep well and wake up early the next morning to catch a sight of Kanchenjunga at sunrise. But I am disappointed because the sky is still cloudy. An hour later the clouds over Kanchenjunga darken and I know that it is unlikely that I will get a clear sight of the mountain. I decide to check out of the hotel and see a glass skywalk in the town before heading back to Siliguri. I ask the manager about the road condition and he warns me that until Melli the road would be bad after which it would be mostly blacktop.

I ride about six kilometres away from Pelling to the skywalk. It is 8 o'clock and there are only a few tourists around. The entire structure seems like a transplant and I am not sure that it goes with the surroundings. I ask a local man if Kanchenjunga is visible from the skywalk and he nods and points to a direction. But the clouds show no sign of dispersing. The skywalk leads to the base of a massive Buddha statue which can be accessed by a long flight of stairs. The statue overlooks the surrounding area and the courtyard is decorated with mythological figures. The statue reminds me of the one in Diskit monastery in Ladakh which overlooks the sand dunes of Hunder.

About half an hour later, I head out of Pelling and stop briefly at the Sidkeong bird sanctuary in Rabdentse, a few kilometres away. There is only an SUV outside the gate and as I walk through the gate I see a man with his wife and little daughter walking along the pathway. He is prepared for the visit and a camera and a binocular are dangling from his neck.

A middle-aged park employee is sweeping the pathway and I ask him about the birds in the sanctuary. 'It is mostly different varieties of pheasants, fantail pigeons and of course lot of parakeets. If you are lucky you will get to see a lot of them at the same time.'

He tells me that the sanctuary was inaugurated in 2017 and is spread over two hectares of thick forests but there are plans to expand it to 18 hectares. I continue walking and go deeper into the forest. The park employee was right about the bird sightings and it is my lucky day. The quietness of the forest is suddenly shattered by the cacophony of parakeets as if each one of them is trying to make its voice heard over every other bird. I watch them fly from one tree to another, dive and hang from slender branches at different angles. A few of them peep out of their nests in the hollows of trees and retreat and repeat the exercise.

On the ground a short distance away from the parakeets, a few pheasants hunt for insects and berries and scatter the moment they see me. Further into the forest, a big owl sits inside the hollow of a tree with its eyes closed, probably sleeping. It is the first time I have seen an owl in a forest and I am tempted to take a photograph of the bird but I decide against it suspecting that the noise of the camera's shutter might wake it up. After 30 minutes inside the sanctuary, I turn back and head out.

A few more cars are now lined up at the parking. I straddle my motorcycle and ride mostly downhill to Legship where I stop for tea. But it turns out to be a costly halt in a way I hadn't imagined. At the exit of Legship towards Meli, I see that the traffic has been stopped because road builders are blowing off a hill to widen the highway. I stop behind a dozen small cars, dismount and walk to the front to find out how long the stoppage would be. A woman constable of the Home Guard is sitting on a plastic chair on one side of the road. Behind her chair is a small iron pole to which a rope has been tied from the opposite side of the road to stop the traffic. I ask her how long the stoppage is scheduled for.

'Not more than half an hour.'

I hear the muted sound of explosives and a cloud of dust rises from the hill before rocks and earth fall. A little later an earthmover crawls up the hill and pushes the pile of earth and rocks down on the road from where two other earthmovers push them over the edge of the road. The exercise repeats itself a few times. The queue of vehicles grows longer. A group of elderly tourists come and stand beside me to watch the road clearing exercise and one of them heads towards the side of the road to relieve himself. The constable sees him and yells, 'Not there, not there. Just cross the road and you will find a washroom. Don't mess around this place.' The man walks away sheepishly to the washroom.

Half an hour later the constable allows the traffic to move. The road is in terrible shape. Despite the earthmovers clearing the debris, there are a lot of stones on the road which has already been raked to lay new foundations. A short distance away a waterfall flows over the road, turning a long stretch slushy.

I run into three more stoppages of similar kind varying between 30 to 90 minutes. The stoppages begin to test my patience but the scenery acts as a balm to soothe my nerves. At some places, the Teesta flows like a true mountain river, full of foam and fury while small paddy fields along its banks sway in the wind. I try to make up time by riding fast along the blacktop stretches between road building sites but by the time I reach Melli, it is already 3 pm. I stop for lunch at a dhaba run by a Nepalese family and order noodles.

By late afternoon, the volume of traffic rises and slows me down and the ride becomes uncomfortable. I make one last stop of the day at a hamlet and get off the bike. My neck hurts badly and I sit on a chair on the verandah of a small shop and ask for a cold drink. As I sip the drink, I notice a stray pup sitting in front of a butcher's shop nearby hoping for a morsel. The butcher is oblivious to the puppy's presence as he chops a lamb's leg. The puppy continues to look hopefully at the shop window and doesn't notice a kitten crawling up towards him. The kitten puts its right front leg over the pup's neck as if trying to embrace it. The pup returns the compliment and the two of them start playing, jumping on each other and rolling on the ground. The innocence of the two little animals is so heartwarming that I feel much better as I resume my ride.

I eventually reach Siliguri at 5 pm and check into the same hotel at Sevoke Road, unload the luggage and then ride to Arpan's house to deposit the motorcycle. Tired after a day-long ride, I take a bath, eat an early dinner, and go to sleep.

3

Darjeeling

14 November 2018

I wake up late, bathe, eat breakfast, and then walk to Alok's office to collect the Himalayan. A couple of other employees wheel the motorcycle out of the warehouse and bring it to me. They help me remove the packing and dust it before I straddle the motorcycle and thumb the ignition. The engine growls to life at once and I am thrilled by the deep, meaty exhaust note.

I ride to a fuel station, fill up the tank and then go to buy a pair of shin guards and rear view mirrors which I had lost on the way to Gangtok when one of my bags fell off. It takes almost an hour to find a pair of good quality shin guards. I return to the hotel to check out and head for Darjeeling, about 80 km away.

It is almost noon. Sevoke Road is crowded for some distance before I turn left for the bridge over the Mahananda river. A few kilometres later as I take a right turn, the heritage rail track starts running parallel to the road. At some places, the track is almost within touching distance of homes and shops.

I ride through tea gardens and forests before the road begins to climb. This was what I was waiting to do with the Himalayan. The road is narrower than the one to Gangtok and the curves come quicker. It doesn't allow a rider to ride very fast but I maintain a steady speed. The bass of the exhaust note thrills me and fuels my adrenaline but I curb all impulse to ride faster. The air is crisp and invigorating.

I begin to feel hungry and stop for snacks at a small settlement with just a couple of eateries. I head for one but the woman tells me that she can serve only tea. Snacks are still not ready and I see her husband and daughter stuff minced chicken into momos but I know it will take at least half an hour to cook some of them. I settle for the tea and open a packet of biscuits from my bag. Like most people in the hills of North Bengal, this family is of Nepalese origin.

'What time do the trains cross this stretch?' I ask the man.

'The one to Darjeeling crossed about 30 minutes ago. But you will be able to catch it on the way. The train to Siliguri will cross in the afternoon. '

Four young men on two motorcycles—a KTM 200 and a Bajaj Dominar 400—ride in and stop at the next eatery. None of them is wearing a helmet. The four of them buy cold drinks, gulp them down and speed off as if their shirt tails are on fire. In the eatery where I am drinking tea, the man stops stuffing the momos and takes a look at the four men riding away and shakes his head.

'They will spend more than a lakh to buy a motorcycle but won't spend a thousand rupees to buy a helmet. Such idiots.' I agree completely with the man.

I finish the tea and get on the motorcycle. The landscape begins to change and the temperature drops as the gradient rises. The mountains are more spread out and the scenery is fabulous. Even in November the mountains are lush green. The rail track changes elevation sometimes but stays close to the road for the most part. I take a curve and see an open straight stretch of road and just as I turn the throttle the loud horn of a train startles me. I stop and scan the track which is now on both sides of the road at different elevations. For some time I can only hear the sound of the train before it comes into view exiting a station on the track below the road. It is a three-coach train hauled by a diesel engine. On the edge of the road a gangman is sitting with red and green flags in his hands. I rush to him and ask to confirm if this indeed is the train heading for Darjeeling.

'Yes. It will climb up that curve before it reaches here,' he tells me pointing to the track slightly above the road.

I scramble to take my camera out of the bag and wait for it to come into view and shoot few frames before the train disappears into the next curve. The gangman is standing near my motorcycle. I ask him how long he has been in the job.

'Almost 30 years. I am going to retire next year.'

'What exactly is your job?' I ask him.

'I have to ensure that there is no problem on the track like landslide or any other obstruction. Since the track curves a lot, the driver can't see much and it is my job to give the all clear signal. Twice a day I do the job. I report for work at this station below this road.'

I had assumed that his was a monotonous job, standing with two flags to wave depending on the situation but his explanation gives me a completely different perspective about the vital work that anonymous men like him do. I learn that like him there are other men attached to every station on the route.

'Have you had major problems in your line of work?'

'Not really. Landslides used to be a problem once, but not anymore. Now it is an occasional tree which falls on the track from the slopes but that can be removed easily.'

'What will you do after retirement?'

'I don't know, but most probably I will be into full time farming. But I am going to miss this although sometimes I think I never really could make enough money in this job. I love these trains. They have been a part of me for most of my life.' He sounds wistful.

We shake hands and I start the motorcycle.

'You will overtake this train in 15 minutes at the most and you will reach Darjeeling before it does,' he tells me. I smile and wave at him and leave.

A little later I am amazed by the gangman's prediction. On the motorcycle's dashboard I check the time to see that it has been 15 minutes since I resumed my ride when I see the train again on my rear-view mirrors descending from a slope. A little ahead the road and the track merge into a single entity ahead of another station and there is no level crossing on the road. I am confused whether to go ahead or stop to let the train pass. If I let the train pass me, it would mean I would have to wait for more than 10 minutes before it leaves the station.

I decide I will be better off without waiting and ride on. For about a hundred metres I ride through the rail track and bump over the wooden sleepers. It is the first time I have done so but for motorists and motorcyclists on this road, it is a daily affair.

Five km ahead of Kurseong, the weather begins to change, the clouds begin to get thicker and the sun is no longer visible. A cold wind begins to blow and my neck and back begin to ache. I stop, dismount and massage my neck and sit down on a pillar among a row that forms a barrier of sorts to prevent a motorist or two-wheeler rider from plunging off the road. Below the pillar, I see an old man smoking a bidi climbing up a flight of stairs to the road. He is wearing a tweed coat and a Nepali cap and comes and stands near me and smiles.

'This is a famous place. Do you know why?' he asks me.

I tell him that I have no idea and that I have stopped only because of a bad back.

'That song in that film *Aradhana* with Rajesh Khanna driving a Jeep and Sharmila Tagore on a train was shot here,' he tells me. 'Did you watch that film?'

Like most Indians of my generation I too have seen this movie that was made in 1969. The song remains an iconic one and I can still hum it but my memory is foggy and I try to visualize the sequence of Rajesh Khanna driving along the winding road wooing his heroine.

'Yes. I have watched that movie. How old were you when this song was shot?'

'I was 25. That song was such a rage.' And then he sighs. 'Poor chap. He died.'

'Where are you going?'

'Kurseong. A friend of mine is not well and I want to see him.'

He offers me a bidi which I politely refuse and straddle the bike again.

A little later I ride into Kurseong. The narrow road which runs through the heart of the town is crowded. Cars and bikes are parked along the side of the road, narrowing it down further. Pedestrians jostle on narrow pavements in front of rows of shops. I see a couple of restaurants but there is no place to park the motorcycle. Despite being ravenous, I decide it won't be worth the while to park the motorcycle at a random place and run the risk of it being towed away by the traffic police which would mean needlessly losing money and time. I decide to ride on to my destination Darjeeling which is another 30 km away.

The weather beings to worsen and a light fog rolls in. I zip up my riding jacket up to my neck and ride on. A few SUVs overtake me but I am in no mood to race with anybody. Twenty km short of Darjeeling, I run into a traffic jam and resist the temptation of squeezing through other vehicles to the top of the line. A truck convoy from the other side has narrowed the road to such an extent that some of the trucks drive with their left wheels on the rail track and the right wheels on the road.

As I wait for the jam to clear, another motorcyclist draws parallel to me and stops. He is a foreigner on a Royal Enfield Bullet 350. He looks at me, smiles and gives a thumbs-up sign before he asks, 'What bike?'

'Himalayan. Royal Enfield.'

'I didn't know Royal Enfield makes bikes like this one. I would have hired it if I knew. Are you Indian?'

'Yes. I live in Delhi.'

'I also started from Delhi. I hired the bike there. I visited Rajasthan and Himachal Pradesh before I headed for Agra and Kanpur and now I am here. '

'Where will you be staying in Darjeeling?'

'I have a booking at a youth hostel.'

Simon, almost half my age at 27, is a Swiss national. A techie, he has a pleasant demeanour. He tells me he would be going to Gangtok from Darjeeling before returning to Delhi.

The jam clears after 15 minutes and we are on our way again. We cross Ghoom rail station, the penultimate of the route, 14 km from Darjeeling. On the outskirts of Darjeeling, the weather clears a little and I can see the sun getting close to the horizon. I stop to take a picture and Simon stops too. We take a couple of selfies before riding away in different directions. Inside Darjeeling, the road is narrow and almost all streets are for one-way traffic.

I cross the rail station and take a road only to realize after some time that I am heading the wrong way on a one-way street and make a U-turn. I ask a traffic policeman about hotels and he points towards a road uphill. I ride up the road and see that there are hotels but they have no space for parking. I ride on and cross the Himalayan Mountaineering Institute at Jawahar Parvat. Outside the gate of the institute, a life-size statue of Tenzing Norgay, one of the first two men to climb Mount Everest, stares from a replica of the world's highest peak.

The road then goes downhill. I see a Bengal Tourism Department hotel and ride in only to discover that the room rents are quite high which I wasn't willing to pay for two days. There are no other hotels downhill and I turn back and take another road that brings me back to the approach to Darjeeling when I see a hotel with a garage for parking and check in.

'You are a Muslim,' the manager tells me as I fill up the guest register.

'So?' I ask him.

'Nothing. I meant to say I am a Muslim too. I am from Islampur in Uttar Dinajpur district.'

The name of the place rings a bell. Islampur in North Bengal had been rocked by violence for two days in September 2018 over the appointment of two teachers in a government school. Trouble had started over the appointment of the teachers for Urdu and Sanskrit while the students insisted that they needed teachers for science and literature. The discontent snowballed into mob violence and police had to be called in to stop the rioting. Two young men were killed in firing incidents but the police had denied opening fire.

The violence also took political colour with the ruling Trinamool Congress accusing the BJP of engineering the violence. The BJP in turn accused the government of irregularities in the appointment of teachers.

I ask the manager if the situation in Islampur has normalized.

'No it hasn't. There is peace now but there is an undercurrent of hostility in the town. The BJP brings everything down to Hindus versus Muslims which is just not the case.'

'So, are you a supporter of Trinamool Congress?'

'No. That's also a party of goons but still not half as dangerous as the BJP. I am in the final year of graduation and came here to earn some money during the holidays before the exams. I didn't want to get sucked into any law and order situation in Islampur.'

'So, when do you study for the exams?'

'At night after we close.'

That's a tough life. I wish him luck for his exams and hand over the register to him. It is 4:30 pm. A bell boy carries some of my luggage to my room on the second floor and pulls away the curtains to reveal a beautiful sight through the windows. It is still cloudy but a part of the sky is clear and reveals the orange glow in the aftermath of sunset. The slopes of the hills start twinkling with lights as darkness envelops the town. I order tea and snacks and move out of the hotel an hour later. It is very cold outside.

I walk into the railway station, take a look at the toy trains parked there and buy some souvenirs. I explore a part of the town lined with old shops, restaurants, and bars. Pramod Giri was right. Darjeeling is peaceful and there is a glut of tourists, a majority of them from the plains of Bengal. Shopping for winter wear seems to be a favourite tourist activity. Along the narrow pavements, hawkers sell tea and momos and much of the area smells of food. I spend an hour exploring the market before I decide to return to the hotel.

Near the hotel, I see the headlight of an approaching train and stop to watch it as it goes past me. It is the train I had passed on my way earlier in the afternoon. Passengers are getting up from their seats and heading for the doors as it approaches the station. A few minutes later, another train, pulled by a vintage steam engine, approaches. This one is the tourist train that runs between Darjeeling and Ghoom.

Back at the hotel I call Tenzing Norgay's son Jamling Tenzing and ask him if I could meet him the next day.

'Yes, but call me once around 2 pm because I will be free only during the second half of the day. I have just returned from a trek a little while ago.'

I had sent a message to Jamling when I was in Siliguri, asking if I could meet him on November 5 according to my original schedule. He had replied that it would not be possible as he was out of Darjeeling but did not mention a date when he would return. So the delay in the delivery of my motorcycle in Siliguri turned out to be a blessing in disguise.

I try to call Major Navin Mukhia, the army officer I had met on the train, but his phone doesn't connect. There is a knock on the door and I open it to see the manager standing outside.

'I came to tell you that if you want to eat here I will send your dinner to the room. The restaurant has been booked for a party so we are serving guests in their rooms,' he tells me.

'That's okay. I will have chicken fried rice.'

He goes back and my dinner arrives 15 minutes later. The party at the restaurant is raging with the DJ playing old Hindi film songs. Fortunately, the music is not loud. I eat well and go off to sleep. I wake up to a foggy morning and nothing is visible outside the window.

I take a bath and go out for breakfast and then stop at a small general store to buy cigarettes. The shopkeeper looks at my jacket and asks, 'Are you on a motorcycle?'

'Yes,' I tell him.

He is an outsider and I ask him his place of origin.

'We are from Bareilly in Uttar Pradesh. My father came here 50 years ago.'

'What has happened to the demand for Gorkhaland?'

'It is dormant now. And you never know what will spark it again. It was terrible last year with the strikes and shutdowns.'

I had always wondered how the residents of Darjeeling coped with the three-month long shutdown and I ask if he had actually shut his shop for the entire duration of the strike.

'The shutters at the front were closed for almost every shop. But everybody sold stuff through the rear windows or doors. You just can't shut down like that. People need stuff like grocery to survive.'

On the other side of the road I see taxi drivers line up their SUVs at a designated taxi stand and talk among themselves.

I cross the road to reach the taxi stand and ask one of the drivers if he would know the owner of any Land Rover Defender in Darjeeling whom I can speak to. The iconic British vehicles which once plied as taxis have been replaced by modern SUVs built by Mahindra and Tata, two of India's biggest automakers.

'I am not sure there is any Landy running in Darjeeling. Most of them were taken to Manebhanjyang near the Nepal border. They still run there and you can go see them and talk to their owners. There would be collectors in Darjeeling but it will be easier if you talk to someone who drives a Defender daily instead of a car enthusiast.'

It sounds like a good idea because I want to know why some people would still drive vehicles built in the 1950s, not for pleasure but to make a living. A round trip of 60 km means I can go and return from Manebhanjyang without stress.

I keep walking and on the opposite side of the railway station I see three steam engines in their shed. About half a dozen men are attending to one particular engine. I walk into the shed. Electricians and welders are at work in one corner of the shed while others are working on another engine. The tracks are on a ramp and one man is standing below the locomotive to check the wheels. The air smells of coal and takes me back to my first memories of train rides in the early 1970s in Assam when Northeast Frontier Railway used steam engines to haul the coaches.

I ask a man supervising the crew if this is a daily routine or emergency repair work.

'We do it every morning before this engine goes out on its first trip.'

'Is it possible to talk to the driver of this train? Do I need to take the station master's permission?' I ask him.

'Yes, you can speak to the driver and you don't need to take anyone's permission. Come with me.'

He takes me to a small cabin on the edge of the shed and we climb a flight of wooden stairs that leads to a small room with two tables where two men are checking two registers. He introduces me to the third man in the room who is the driver.

'I will speak to you but please give me a few minutes to complete some paperwork here.'

'I will wait,' I tell him.

I stand by the window and watch a few tourists including foreigners walk into the station. A diesel locomotive is shunting a couple of coaches from one track to another. On the road below the window, there is a steady outbound traffic, mostly tourists. And the sky is still gloomy. Five minutes later the driver gets up and tells me that he is done and that we can talk.

We go down the stairs and walk to the locomotive being serviced. He tells me his name is Anand Lama. A short, stocky man in his 50s, he has worked his way up to become a steam engine driver.

'I started as a cleaner and became a driver 11 years ago. It had always been my dream to be a steam engine driver. I have five more years before I retire,' he tells me proudly.

But while he achieved his dream of becoming a steam engine driver, the length of the train's route was slashed.

'My father was also a steam engine driver. But he was luckier because he got to drive the train from Siliguri to Darjeeling. This train now does only the tourist circuit from Darjeeling to Ghoom and back.'

The maintenance crew is working furiously to get Lama's locomotive ready for the first ride of the day at 10:30 am. He gives me a guided tour of the locomotive and shows me the furnace where a fireman shoves coal and the place where another fireman sits to push the coal down from a cavity on the roof. Lama himself has a square place to stand to operate the engine. At the front, a crew member is cleaning a large chamber of soot and carbon to make it free for the steam to exit smoothly out of the chimney. The worker finally closes the door of the chamber which resembles the hatch of a submarine.

'The 30-km round trip needs 650 kg of coal. The engine is serviced every morning before the first trip and I make three trips a day.'

It is a punishing job but Lama obviously loves it, and any occasional praise from a tourist makes his day.

I ask Lama about the summer of 2017 when the agitation for Gorkhaland had shut down North Bengal for three months.

'Those were terrible days. We just stayed home because the service was suspended. It was heartbreaking spending the days doing nothing. I hope something like that doesn't happen again.'

It is almost time for him to take the locomotive to the station for the day's first trip. I return to the hotel and decide to leave for Batasia Loop where there is a memorial to fallen Gorkha soldiers and where the toy train makes a brief stop. I reach Batasia Loop in less than 10 minutes and spend five more minutes looking for a place to park my motorcycle. I eventually find one about 100 metres away from the stairs leading to Batasia Loop. I buy a ticket and walk in.

The memorial to Gorkha soldiers is built on a raised plot of land in Batasia Loop which is also a circular garden with the rail track around its circumference. The statue of a Gorkha soldier standing with a reversed rifle and head bowed in front of a tall concrete column and the tricolour flying on his left makes for a poignant setting. But the sobriety of a memorial to fallen soldiers is lost on many tourists who pose for photographs against the monument wearing local costumes. At some places hawkers sit on the ground near the track and sell winter clothing, toys, and souvenirs.

I hear the whistle of a steam engine and remember that it is Anand Lama's first trip of the day. I rush to the edge of the garden and look down to see the train climbing up. But the trees on the slope don't allow a clear sight to take a picture. So I wait for it to show up for its scheduled stoppage at Batasia Loop. Thick black smoke and bursts of steam herald the arrival of the train and it stops with a hissing noise after covering three-fourths of the circular track.

Passengers from the two coaches disembark and start taking photographs of the train and their selfies. A young couple walking ahead of me decides to make the most of the train's stoppage. The two of them take endless pictures of each other against the train and the man constantly tells his wife how to pose.

'Get on the coach, stand at the door and look out,' he tells her. She obliges. 'Okay, now go take a window seat.' And then, 'Now come down and stand against the door.' It goes on and on and I am exasperated because I want to take a picture of the train from the rear but the couple shows no sign that they are done with their shoots. They finally move away after what seems to be an eternity and I get the frame I want.

I cross the two coaches and reach the engine which is attached to the first coach in the reverse direction. Lama is supervising a young man who is tightening some screws with a big wrench. He sees me and waves. I ask him if there is any problem. 'No, it is just part of the routine drill to check nuts and bolts at this stop.'

I wait at the exit to take a photograph as the train leaves Batasia Loop. I decide to move on to Manebhanjyang to see Land Rover Defenders and talk to their owners. A few minutes later I overtake the train and take a turn at Ghoom for Manebhanjyang. Out of Ghoom, the road is a pleasure to ride on but the fog starts to play spoilsport. In a matter of minutes, visibility falls drastically and I keep my eyes focused on the white marks that divide the road. I switch on the headlight but it doesn't help much. Cars move with hazard lights on. The fog finally lifts about six km away from

Manebhanjyang but the road then turns really bad. Much of it is broken and resembles a dirt track but it is on this kind of road that the Himalayan shows its pedigree. The bike stays steady as I ride over craters, rocks, and puddles. A few women walk with loads of firewood on their heads. Others take their cows out to pasture.

I see the first Land Rover Defender soon enough in Manebhanjyang. A military green Defender is stationed in front of a garage. It is standing on a jack with the left front wheel taken off. Another white one with a Nepalese registration is a little distance away. None of the owners is around and I ask a mechanic where I can find Chandan Pradhan. The mechanic gives me the direction. I take out my phone to call Chandan but there is no signal. The road to Chandan's house is atrocious and I rock and roll before I find it. A local man points out Chandan's house to me. On the other side of the road is the taxi stand where Land Rover Defenders are lined up.

The front portion of the ground floor is a shop and the family lives in the rear portion and the first floor of the building. Chandan's wife is at the shop and tells me that he has gone to a school to attend a function and would be back soon. She offers me a stool to sit and asks her daughter to make a cup of tea for me.

'What do you want to meet Chandan for?' she asks.

'To talk about Land Rovers.'

'Oh! He just sold his sometime ago to buy that one,' she says pointing to a Mahindra Thar 4x4 SUV.

She gets talking about her elder daughter who is studying in Mumbai and how difficult life is in Manebhanjyang.

'The road has never been good here. During the monsoon the rains destroy it and in the winter the snow damages it although it hasn't snowed for a couple of years now. Phones don't always connect and despite being just 30 km away from Darjeeling, this place seems to belong to a different world.'

Chandan arrives after sometime and we get talking. I ask why taxi owners in Manebhanjyang lapped up the Defenders which were phased out in Darjeeling over pollution concerns.

'That's because no one will invest in a new vehicle here to run as a taxi. The road to the Nepal border is so bad that a vehicle wears out quickly if it is used regularly. But Land Rover Defenders are tough guys among SUVs. They will go anywhere and don't need much care. A lot of them have changed their engines though.'

'What have they put?' I ask.

'Mostly Mahindra engines. But quite a few of them still run on original engines. Like that white one in the corner. That one is a 1956 model and the engine hasn't given any trouble.'

We walk over to the taxi stand and I check out that particular Defender. Chandan points to two others and tells me that they have Mahindra engines. Drivers sit inside the vehicles and wait for passengers. I learn that they pack seven passengers in a single trip so comfort would be last thing a passenger should expect on a ride to the Nepal border in a Landy.

The Defender became a legend because of its simplicity and workhorse capability. It has been called the automobile equivalent of the Russian AK-47 rifle because it can be repaired easily and can run virtually on any terrain. Off road, very little can touch it. On road there is very little to recommend it, mainly because of lack of comfort. But here in Manebhanjyang, the only road is perpetually off road, so nothing can yet touch the Defender. There are around 40 Defenders in Manebhanjyang and it is potentially a collector's goldmine. Chandan probably knows it. I ask him how much would a Defender cost.

'A minimum of Rs 10 lakh,' he replies without batting an eye.

The price seems preposterous to pay for a ragged Landy. But vintage has its value and you can't really put a price on it.

'Are you planning to buy one?' he asks.

'Not unless I rob a bank first,' I tell him and he bursts out laughing.

It is time for me to leave. I take a few photographs of the Land Rover Defenders and then get on my motorcycle and head back for Darjeeling. On the main road, the fog has thickened. The curves become visible at the last moment and I ride slowly. The fog stays till Ghoom beyond which the sky is clear.

I park at the hotel and go out for lunch to an eatery which sells biriyani. It is 2 pm by the time I finish my lunch. I call Jamling and he tells me to show up by 3 pm. He gives me the direction to his house and then says, 'Or you can just ask someone on the road for Tenzing Norgay's house.'

I discover that his house is a little beyond my hotel. I backtrack, cross my hotel and ask a shopkeeper for directions. 'You can keep walking on this road and it will take you uphill to the next loop where Jamling lives. Or you can take a shortcut through those stairs over there which will open right at his gate,' he tells me pointing to the other side of the road.

The second option sounds better and I take the stairs. But they are steep and by the time I reach the road above I am completely breathless. I stop for a few minutes to catch my breath and look at the house. It is a palatial residence built on the slope of a hill. I open the gate, walk in and climb a short flight of stairs when a huge black dog chained to a railing on a balcony lunges at me and starts barking. A woman opens the door and commands the dog to fall silent which it does. She introduces herself as Jamling's wife Soyang and ushers me into his office.

It is a modest office with a desk and a couple of chairs in front of it and a sofa at one end above which hangs a photograph of Jamling at the Everest summit in an expedition in 1996. That expedition was made into a documentary called *Everest*. We shake hands and start talking.

'What dog is that?

'Tibetan Mastiff. I picked it up as a pup in Nepal. Would you like to have tea or coffee?'

'I will have tea.'

I tell him that I am on a solo motorcycle expedition of the Northeast and that Darjeeling is my second port of call after Sikkim.

'That's quite commendable,' he tells me.

He is as old as I am, and like me, Jamling is lightly built but slightly shorter. I ask him about the 1996 summit which remains his only Everest conquest.

'I am done with climbing. And besides, my family doesn't let me climb anymore. It is a dangerous calling because there is almost a 50 per cent chance of getting killed. My daughters who are studying in the United Sates are completely against my climbing.'

Also, 1996 was the worst year in the history of Everest expeditions with a dozen climbers of different teams dying in blizzards and accidents. Jamling's expedition was there during those frightening days of May. His team comprised six climbers and 25 Sherpas.

'We brought down two dozen climbers who were stuck on the upper reaches of Mount Everest.'

Jamling now focuses on running his trekking company that his father had set up. He deeply reveres his father.

'My father was uneducated and so he became a Sherpa to make ends meet. But he insisted that all his children went to college because he did not want any of us to become Sherpas and for that I am eternally grateful to him.'

'Do you go on treks regularly?'

'Not often unless it is a signature trek like the last one I did. I have other guides who take clients around Darjeeling, Sikkim, and Bhutan.'

He is also a motivational speaker on leadership issues and is much sought after by the corporate world. I ask him how corporate people from a completely different background relate to a mountaineer like him.

'Actually, it is not very different. It is just that their setting is different. I make Power Point presentations of mountainous terrains then include things like crevasses, glaciers, avalanches, and vertical walls and compare them to work situations in the corporate world. I tell them about the importance and need for discipline, team work, dedication, and determination and to know when to persist and when to retreat.'

'Does it connect with your clients?'

'Oh yes. I have had people come up to me after my lectures and tell me that I have given a new perspective on how to look at problems or situations and solve them.'

Jamling, who has quite a following among the Sherpa community in Nepal, has also been an outspoken advocate for better pay for Sherpas and he feels that they can be paid 25 per cent more than what they are being paid now.

'Things have improved now. We are setting up a foundation for Sherpas in Nepal which aims to take care of compensation for a family if a Sherpa loses his life during an expedition. It used to be pretty bad earlier when Sherpas were treated shabbily by foreign expeditions.'

He mourns the fact there is very little support for a sport like mountaineering in India, either from the government or the corporate world. 'It is a costly activity and many young climbers give up because they can't afford the gear and the associated costs. Tata Steel is an exception in grooming mountaineers but that's just a blip for a country of India's size.'

He wants to show me a small museum he has set up in his father's memory. It is spread across a sprawling room next to his office and a floor above. There is a small bronze statue of Tenzing Norgay, his climbing gear, camping gear, medals, cameras, photographs of various expeditions, and citations meticulously arranged. Jamling tells me that his father had built this part of the house while he built the other part where the dog is tied.

What strikes me most about Jamling is his humility and modesty. A famous son of a famous father, he seems firmly rooted to the ground and has no airs about him. I leave his house and take the stairs to the road below and walk to a market in a different part of the town. It is dusk and droves of tourists are returning to their hotels. There are a few shops in a row selling tea leaves and I check out some of them. Some of the shopkeepers have a 'take it or leave it' attitude. I find a store where the shopkeeper is willing to talk and tell me why a particular quality of tea is better than others. He suggests a brand of tea because it is the freshest of the lot in his shop. I end up buying three packets.

I roam around for some more time before I go to a restaurant for an early dinner and return to my hotel. I pack my bags for my exit the next morning and sleep. I am thrilled to see the sun shining brightly and quickly get ready. I am planning to ride as far as possible beyond Siliguri. There is little traffic in the morning and the ride is smooth. I take a slightly different route on the return trip because I want to see one of India's oldest tea gardens—Makaibari—near Kurseong. Inside Kurseong, I run into a major traffic snarl which costs me about 20 minutes.

Shortly after Kurseong, the road to Makaibari descends in a sharp gradient with hairpin bends. The estate is spread across slopes of the hills. After several curves, I see the gate of Makaibari tea estate and ride in and park outside the factory. There are several people standing outside the factory and I ask one of them if the manager is around. He tells me that the manager is out to inspect the estate since morning and won't be back until 1 pm. I can't wait for two hours so I ask him if there is anybody else I can speak to about the garden. He points to a small shop near the gate and tells me that the man running the shop can tell me about the garden's history.

I walk in and introduce myself to the man who is in his late 30s. His name is Pronoy Bhujal. The shop is full of packets of tea of different sizes and prices. Pronoy tells me it is Makaibari's own outlet for tourists who drop in. He goes on to give me the statistics. The garden which was established in 1859 is spread across 650 acres in the hills and produces 300 kg of tea daily. One hundred and eighty workers work for eight hours a day plucking tea in different parts of the garden.

Pronoy has been employed in Makaibari for eight years. I ask him if there has been any difference in the way it is run since Rajah Banerjee sold the garden.

'There has been no drastic change yet. Maybe the new management will introduce the changes gradually.'

Rajah Banerjee was famous for a personal touch to his management and was often seen riding a horse through different parts of the garden and talking to workers.

'Does something like that still happen?' I ask.

'No. That was his signature style. I don't think anyone will copy that. The new management is more corporate in its outlook and interactions with workers are becoming structured,' Pronoy tells me.

'Do you regret that Banerjee sold the garden?'

'Yes, in some ways. He was a nice man. But maybe he had his compulsions. He certainly wasn't the same man after his bungalow was burnt down during the Gorkhaland agitation.'

That bungalow wasn't just the tea baron's residence. It was a treasure trove that contained priceless paintings, photographs, and hunting trophies among other things. Nothing could be saved. The incident happened at the height of the agitation for Gorkhaland in 2017 and I ask Pronoy if the garden was affected.

'Yes. And it was very bad. We lost the entire second flush in the Gorkhaland agitation.'

I buy a packet of Makaibari's famed black tea and ask him about the different varieties on sale. Patiently, he reels off the prices before he points to the last stack of packets.

'That's Silver Tip Imperial. It is premium quality and costs Rs 1.3 lakh a kilo. The leaves are plucked only on full moon nights. This variety is mostly exported to Europe.'

I decide to resume my journey and head for Siliguri. The road continues to go downhill with Makaibari's gardens spread across the slopes above and below the road. Around 11 am, I stop for brunch at a restaurant.

I remember that Pramod had told me that Rangu Souriya lives somewhere nearby and I call to ask if we could meet to talk about her work. But she tells me that she is travelling beyond Kurseong and would reach Siliguri the next day.

'If you are in Siliguri tomorrow we can meet.'

'I am leaving Siliguri today.'

'In that case you can meet Prabhat Pathak in Siliguri. He works with me and he can tell you what you want to know.'

That sounds good enough and I start riding again and soon descend to the foothills. Tea gardens continue to flank the road on either side and sometime later I cross the picturesque Sukna cantonment. I stop on the outskirts of Siliguri and call Prabhat Pathak to ask if we can meet. Fortunately, he is home and gives me the direction for his residence in Pradhan Nagar.

It is past noon and traffic is heavy on the highway near Pradhan Nagar. I see Prabhat waiting for me on the road outside his house as I ride in. We shake hands and he takes me inside his house. As I sit in his drawing room, his dog comes rushing at me, jumps on the sofa, and starts licking my face and hands as if he has seen me after a long time. I pat the dog and it calms down and curls up on the sofa.

Prabhat had been a journalist with a vernacular newspaper before he teamed up with Rangu Souriya who founded a non-government organization called Kanchanjungha Uddhar Kendra Welfare Society to check human trafficking. He now works full time with the NGO. He tells me that they organize awareness camps and sensitise stakeholders in the fight against trafficking.

'We arrange awareness camps in tea gardens and schools so that young girls and women don't fall in the trap of traffickers. We have partners in Kolkata, Mumbai, and Delhi who facilitate the rescue of trafficked women once we identify them.'

'How bad is the trafficking now?' I ask.

'It has come down from the high of 2003–2004. We have opened a home for rescued women who can't go back to their families for various reasons. The shelter can accommodate 50 women and it was largely crowd funded.'

Prabhat tells me that poverty of the victims makes it easier for traffickers to lure them. 'Many tea gardens are sick or closed. Many of the workers are paid Rs 170 per day and it is impossible to run a family which is often more than four people. Young girls are also vulnerable because they watch television a lot and want to acquire materialistic things they see in movies or TV soaps. Traffickers cash in on the dreams of these poor girls.'

I had assumed that all women who are trafficked are pushed into the flesh trade but Prabhat tells me that it is not always the case.

'Some are packed off as domestic servants and in most cases it is actually a form of slavery. But yes, a lot of them are pushed into prostitution and we have rescued girls from brothels in Mumbai, Pune, Delhi, Kolkata and different places in Bihar, Uttar Pradesh, and Haryana.'

I ask him about Rangu and he is effusive in his praise for her. 'She has received death threats, has been pressured to drop cases in court and offered bribes to withdraw cases, but she is relentless in her mission.'

I learn that her work has earned her a clutch of awards including the Federation of Indian Chambers of Commerce and Industry's Women Achievers' Award in 2009, the Godfrey Phillips Social Bravery Award in 2011, and the Prestigious 100 Women Awards given by the President of India in 2016.

The fight against human trafficking is a constant uphill battle. 'Sometimes government apathy, collusion of policemen with traffickers, and lack of funds become obstacles to launch rescue efforts but we have been persistent and have been largely successful in our mission.'

By any yardstick, Rangu and Prabhat are doing a great job. Their NGO, almost nondescript, has surely punched much above its weight to take on well-oiled traffickers whom even the police are not always keen to antagonize. I have no doubt that the country can surely do with more people like Rangu and Prabhat.

I leave Prabhat's house at 2 pm hoping to get as close to Assam as possible by the end of the day. My destination is my maternal grandmother's place in Gauripur, just over 200 km away but it is unlikely I will make it. My suspicion is reinforced as Siliguri's notorious traffic extracts an hour out of me while exiting the city. The highway to Assam is in good condition for barely 50 km before I run into a massive road building exercise which entails traffic diversions through unpaved roads at regular intervals. I stop for a late lunch at a dhaba at 3:30 pm and ask its owner how long would it take for me to reach Cooch Behar.

'You won't reach before 7 pm because this road will slow you down.'

By 4:30 pm the sun begins to set and a brief twilight quickly gives way to darkness. There are no lights on much of the highway. There are temporary lights on some of the stretches where the road is being built. Road rollers move over those stretches flattening the earth and stones before the road can be tarred. On every such stretch, traffic piles up and I lose more time riding slowly.

I cross a couple of small towns and stop for tea in one of them and Cooch Behar suddenly seems a city too far. My neck begins to hurt again. I see a small hotel which tempts me to break my journey but I decide to push on. A thin fog sets in. At 7 pm, like the dhaba owner said, I am on the outskirts of Cooch Behar. A little later, I stop at the first hotel I see.

The rooms are small and there is no ventilation but I am too tired to go hunting for another hotel after riding for almost 12 hours. I tell myself that since I would be leaving early morning I can put up with the inconvenience. I carry my bags to the second floor and lie down which helps ease the pain in my back and neck. An hour later, I go downstairs for dinner and return to sleep.

4

Elephant Tales

17 November 2018

I get up at six in the morning, take a bath and get ready to leave. But when I reach the lobby I see that there is thick fog outside and decide to wait. The fog clears in another hour and I start for Gauripur which is just over 50 km away. I travel about 10 km from Cooch Behar when the fog returns as the countryside begins and it is colder than what it was inside the city.

The helmet visor gets clouded and I am forced to raise it and ride. The fog gets thicker and I can't ride faster than 20 km per hour. Cows wandering on the highway become visible at the last moment and I decide that there is no point in moving at snail's pace and run the risk of running into a bovine which could possibly mean an altercation with locals and more delay. I stop on the edge of the highway in a small hamlet and leave the motorcycle's indicators on as I dismount. There is a weekly market a little below the road.

I walk to the market and look for a shop to buy breakfast. I see a woman cooking in a shop and ask her for a cup of tea.

'I don't sell tea. I am cooking rice, dal, and vegetables for lunch,' she tells me.

It is only 7.30 am and I wonder who would be eating lunch at this hour and ask her as much.

'These traders,' she says pointing to a group of men sitting on the other side of the shop and selling their goods. 'They come from distant villages early morning without breakfast and since they are here more than half the day they want something heavy to eat. Rice, dal, and vegetables see them through the day. There are other shops down the market which sell tea and you can buy it from there.'

On the other side, there is cacophony as the vegetable sellers and fishmongers shout at the top of their voices to draw customers. I find a tea stall and buy a cup and two boiled eggs. The road ahead disappears into the fog. A little later a bus comes and stops after crossing my motorcycle and passengers troop out and head for other tea stalls.

'Where are you going?' the tea stall owner asks when I pay him.

'Gauripur,' I tell him.

'It is too foggy to ride. You should wait for some time. This bus is heading for Dhubri and has to go through Gauripur. It will start in 15 minutes and you can ride behind it if you want.'

It sounds like a good suggestion and I take it up. Fifteen minutes later the bus resumes its journey and I start following it. A few kilometres later the fog begins to lift and the sun comes out. The bus driver speeds up and the vehicle is soon out of sight. I make no effort to keep up with the bus and ride leisurely and soak up the beauty of the countryside dotted with paddy fields, small villages, and ponds. The road is largely good and I enter Assam in less than an hour.

Outside a small town called Golakganj, I stop again for tea at a shop made of bamboo with a tin roof. There are two bamboo benches in front of the shop facing each other. I sit on one and wait for the shopkeeper to make the tea. Another man is sitting on the other bench sipping tea and smoking. There is a bicycle behind him loaded with goods that a travelling salesman sells in villages. He asks me where I am going. I tell him.

'I am Rehman,' he says introducing himself. 'I am from Murshidabad in Bengal but I stay here on rent. I sell these things that you see on the bicycle.'

I am not keen on a conversation but Rehman is garrulous. A motorcyclist with two pillion riders crosses the shop. None of them is wearing a helmet and Rehman makes an issue of it.

'In Bengal, you can't do this. Traffic authorities have become very strict with all kinds of vehicles after a couple of bus accidents in the fog last winter. Mamata Banerjee's government has done good work in the state. She has wide support among all sections of the people.'

The shopkeeper serves me tea. Half a dozen colourful chicken are rummaging in the grass on one side of the shop and the shopkeeper throws a fistful of rice at them. I ask him how much the chicken cost.

'Normally about Rs 180 a kilo, but it goes up during Eid when prices range between Rs 250 to Rs 300.'

Rehman butts in. 'In Murshidabad, dressed local chicken sells for Rs 130 a kilo.'

A truck stops and the driver comes down and asks for tea. Rehman is unstoppable. 'At the most, it goes up to Rs 150 per kg during Eid. But that's it. Inflation is under control in Bengal. I tell you, Mamata Banerjee is really doing a good job.'

'What is Rs 150 a kilo?' the truck driver asks.

'These chicken in Murshidabad,' Rehman tells him.

'What nonsense! I roam all over Bengal in my truck and I have never seen local chicken being sold for anything below a minimum of Rs 200 a kilo,' the truck driver retorts.

'Come with me to Murshidabad. I will get as many chicken as you want for less than Rs 150 a kilo,' Rehman tells him, his voice rising.

The truck driver is equally belligerent. 'I don't have to go to Murshidabad to buy chicken. You go and eat them. What are you doing here?'

'If you haven't seen it, don't talk about it. Just because you drive in Bengal doesn't mean you know everything about the state.'

'I know every street in Murshidabad. I know the market where they sell chicken. So don't just argue for the sake of argument,' the truck driver tells him.

I am absolutely flummoxed that my innocuous query about the price of chicken has become a catalyst in a fierce argument between two strangers. I tell the two men that since neither of them is going to eat chicken right away, they should stop fighting over its price.

I leave the shop wondering if the salesman and the driver would depart peacefully. Half an hour later, I ride into Gauripur skirting the railway station which is still as quaint as it was when I was a child. It is the second last railway station in western Assam before the track ends eight km away in Dhubri. As I enter the town I notice that traffic has increased exponentially. Once upon a time, traffic meant a few city buses between Gauripur and Dhubri, a few trucks, long-distance buses in the morning and night, a handful of private vehicles and rickshaws. Now, the highway which runs through the town seems to be too narrow to accommodate an unending rush of all kinds of vehicles.

The scenery on one side of the highway, along which the Gadadhar river flows for a short distance, has remained the same though. People on the other side of the river still use boats or cross a bamboo bridge built in the winter when the river shrinks, to reach Gauripur. At the edge of the town square, shops have come up on every plot that had been empty. Further down the road, a large brick and wooden house tilted on one side seemingly at a dangerous angle, still stands. It has remained like that for at least 40 years, impervious to monsoon storms, floods, and earthquakes. A small temple with wooden walls and a tin roof dedicated to Goddess Kali also looks like it has been frozen in time.

So much construction has taken place along the highway that I almost miss the turn to my granny's house. I finally turn right from the highway and ride over an uneven brick road. It used to be a sparsely populated locality with just a handful of houses and large tracts of agricultural lands. But many people have sold their paddy fields to outsiders who have settled in the locality and built their houses.

Out of the two huge mango trees in front of granny's house, one has died. The surviving tree is where I had learnt how to climb as a child. Its mangoes were so tasty that I used to slip out of the house to climb it or use a thin bamboo to pick the fruits when my grandmother slept after lunch. I park outside the house and walk to my grandmother's grave to offer prayers before I walk into the house where my uncle and aunt welcome me warmly. We sit and talk and catch up on all that has happened in the years since we last met. Time flies.

Around a 30-km radius of Gauripur are Assam's oldest mosque and gurudwara. The mosque is at Panbari, 20 km to the east and the gurudwara is 8 km west at Dhubri. I decide to visit both the places. I also want to meet a man named Prabir Barua, one of the sons of the erstwhile zamindar of Gauripur, Prakritish Barua, who was one of India's most famous elephant experts. Prakritish Barua, who was better known as Lalji, was more interested in wildlife than in zamindari. I call Prabir and he agrees to meet me 4:30 pm.

After lunch, I head for Panbari on the road to Guwahati through which I will be travelling the next day. The road is atrocious for some time before it gets better. Twenty minutes later I cross a camp of the Border Security Force in a forested area and shortly after that the town of Panbari appears. The mosque is along the highway. I stop the motorcycle and park it along the boundary wall of the beautiful three-domed mosque with a single minaret and walk into a sprawling compound which doubles up as an idgah for offering Eid namaz.

The mosque's exact history is not known but it is widely believed to have been built between 1493 and 1519 by Alauddin Hussain Shah, the Sultan of Bengal. After conquering the kingdom of Kamatapur, the sultan is believed to have commissioned the mosque in Panbari to celebrate the victory and to offer prayers.

There is another story about the mosque which says that it was built in 1662 when Mir Jumla, a powerful subedar or governor of Bengal under Mughal emperor Aurangzeb, invaded Assam. On one side of the idgah there is a deep well with thick brick wall. It was once thought to be a secret escape route. At some point of time, the entire complex had fallen into disuse and was overtaken by foliage before local people discovered it about 200 years ago.

Part of the mosque is under repair and scaffoldings have been erected for the work. The white paint of the domes has worn off and they now look dark grey, almost begging for a coat of paint. Beyond the mosque is a madrasa complex with boarding facility for boys. A few men are sitting on plastic chairs under a tree near the well.

I learn that a group of men run the affairs of the mosque. There is also a small office of the mosque committee where a few men are sitting including two from the committee. I introduce myself and ask them about the repairs that are being carried out.

'The Archaeological Survey of India carries out the repairs and renovation. We are not allowed to repair the main mosque on our own because it is a protected monument. We can repair the boundary wall and the madrasa if there is a need,' one of the committee members tells me.

He also tells me that about 150 people can pray together in the mosque. But on Eid a few thousand people fill up the idgah for prayers. I ask him how they run the affairs of the mosque.

'We raise funds from the public. There are many regular contributors and so we are able to pay the Imam, the muezzin (one who gives the azaan or call to prayers), a couple of caretakers, and power charges. There is a surge in donations during Ramzan and for the rest of the year the funds remain stable.'

He sounds confident that the number of contributors will continue to increase and that the mosque will be taken care of. I prepare to leave and take a walk around the mosque. A large patch outside the mosque has sandstone flooring. The classes in the madrasa are over and the boys of different age groups run out to play cricket and football.

A few minutes later I ride back to Gauripur and head for the riverfront in Dhubri. As I exit Gauripur, the rail track starts to run parallel with the road. I notice that it has been upgraded from metre gauge to a broad gauge line. I have endearing memories of the train from Guwahati that we used to take to come to Gauripur during the holidays. A steam engine used to haul the coaches on the metre gauge track that ran through forests, farmland and over many rivers. By the time we used to reach Gauripur in the morning, our hair had a layer of coal dust and needed to be shampooed.

On the outskirts of Dhubri, the track changes direction towards the station while the road goes to the riverfront. Dhubri is named after a mythological washerwoman, Netai Dhubuni, who used to wash the clothes of Hindu gods and goddesses on the banks of the Brahmaputra. I stop near the river bank outside an old park bearing Netai's name which has been spruced up with new paint on the walls, iron railings, and the gate. There is a statue of the washerwoman and her son Dhananjay and another character called Bewla-Lakhindar and these are recent additions. Legend has it that Netai Dhubuni was also a sorcerer who was much feared for her black magic and I am a little surprised why the Assam government's tourism department decided to install her statue.

A few people are sitting on concrete benches under trees. Some have stretched out and gone to sleep. I go and stand near the railing and watch the massive Brahmaputra which stretches to the horizon and puts the opposite bank out of sight. The river has shrunk in the winter and a large sandbar has emerged beyond the middle of it. A short distance from the bank, fishermen in three boats wait after casting their nets between two large rocks protruding from the water. A large bamboo raft flows inland and a man standing at one end of it uses an oar to steer it near the bank where traders are waiting to buy the bamboo.

Far away, a motor launch with a full complement of passengers passes by. I crane my neck to my right and see that many large boats are lined up about a hundred yards away. I come out of the park and walk a few metres and take a flight of narrow stairs that goes to the river bank. On either side of the stairs is a small market with shops selling clothes, utensils, vegetables, cereals, and spices. Customers haggling loudly with shopkeepers, music blaring from some shops and the fog horn of boats combine to make the atmosphere a noisy one. I cross the market and reach the bank where a boat waits for a few more passengers to start the journey. A tea stall owner is frying jalebis and asks if I would like to eat some but I ask for tea.

He looks at my riding jacket and boots and asks if I am a tourist.

'No. I am just retracing my roots,' I tell him.

I ask him if all the boats ferry passengers.

'Not all. Some belong to traders who come to this market with their goods.'

The river is a formidable one and its monstrous width has so far entailed a lengthy detour for road travel between Assam and Meghalaya. But that is about to change with the Dhubri-Phulbari bridge which would connect the two states. The surveys have been completed and construction is about to start. By the time it is completed in 2027, it will be India's longest bridge over water spanning more than 19 km. It will connect Dhubri with Phulbari in Meghalaya's Garo Hills. The bridge will cut the distance from 205 km to only 19 km between Dhubri and Phulbari and the travelling time from five hours to less than 30 minutes.

'This place won't be the same after a few years. Have you heard of the bridge which is coming up over the river?' the tea stall owner asks me.

'Yes, I did. I wonder if these boats will remain in service once the bridge is built.' I tell him.

'I am sure they will be there, at least the ones that ply shorter distances because the bridge in unlikely to have exit points mid-river. But it will surely increase vehicular traffic to and from Dhubri and maybe it will be good for our business. Of course, that will happen only if this end of the bridge is near here.'

A small group of passengers climb on the boat that had been waiting and sit on a long bench along one side. The boatman starts the outboard motor and another man takes a headcount of passengers before the boat sails away.

On this November day, the river seems almost benign and far removed from the devastating torrent that it becomes in the monsoon. I take a few photographs of the boats, passengers, and the fishermen and head back to my motorcycle. The road is getting crowded as more people head for the park. Less than half a kilometre from the river is Dhubri's only gurudwara and the oldest in Assam. Named after Tegh Bahadur, the ninth Sikh guru, it was founded in the second half of the 17th century. I decide to visit Guru Tegh Bahadur Sahib to learn how history, mythology, and legend have blended into the gurudwara.

I enter the gurudwara and walk through a shallow trough of water meant to cleanse the feet of visitors. It is evident that the gurudwara has been extended over the years and is now a sprawling building. I climb the steps to the main hall and find that it is almost empty but I am not surprised. A man in a blue salwar-kameez and white turban is cleaning up part of the hall and I go up to him and ask what time is *gurbani*. 'That's at six o'clock in the morning.'

'How many people show up for it?'

'Not many. In any case there are just a few Sikh families in Dhubri. But for three days next month this place will be full of visitors who come here to observe the martyrdom of Guru Tegh Bahadur. Sikhs from many parts of the country come here,' he says as he walks to a table at a corner of the room.

There is a large aluminium saucepan and some paper plates on the table. He removes the lid and scoops out two spoons of halwa on a plate and gives it to me.

'This is from the *langar*. You can go around and see this place for yourself.'

I eat the halwa and look around the gurudwara. One room is a memorial of sorts dedicated to Sikh heroes who laid down their lives fighting against oppression or protecting their faith. Most stories of these heroes are in pictorial form and large pictures and paintings are framed on the wall. I climb up another flight of stairs and get to see a different view of the Brahmaputra.

It is said that the Guru ended the black magic and sorcery of Netai Dhubuni when she wanted to harm Mughal general Raja Ram Singh, who had been ordered by Emperor Aurangzeb to subdue a revolt by King Chakradhwaj Singh of Kamrup (Assam). According to one account, Ram Singh had called on Guru Tegh Bahadur at Dhaka and requested that he accompany him on his expedition to Assam and protect him from sorcery. The Guru had agreed.

Guru Tegh Bahadur had camped at the site where the gurudwara now stands. From the nearby riverbank, Netai Dhuboni is said to have hurled a 26-foot long stone which flew like a missile and struck the ground, near the guru's camp embedding nearly half its length in the ground. It can still be seen in the same position it is said to have landed.

When the stone failed to harm the Guru, Netai Dhubuni flung a tree which fell very close to the Guru's camp. Guru Tegh Bahadur then took his bow and shot an arrow at the altar of magic and all sorcery came to a sudden end. Disarmed and powerless, Netai Dhubuni and others of her ilk approached the Guru and begged forgiveness. A few later years later, Guru Tegh Bahadur was executed on Aurangzeb's order in Delhi in 1675.

The gurudwara is quiet and almost empty. A couple of visitors walk through the gate as I exit. On the way back I stop opposite Netai Dhubuni Park and walk into the Panch Peer dargah, a shrine dedicated to five Sufi saints who had accompanied Mughal general Raja Ram Singh to Dhubri. There is a small mosque at the dargah where a lone man is offering namaz. A few tourists stand at one corner and peek into it. The complex also contains the graves of some of the Sufi saints. I stand and offer prayers for their souls and wonder what could have inspired them to move from North India to this part of the country more than 350 years ago.

By 4 pm I leave Dhubri and head back to Gauripur. I park my motorcycle and walk up the Matiabag hillock to meet Prabir Barua. His ancestral house on top of the hillock overlooks the Gadadhar river. On one side of it there used to be a large mango orchard but over the years the family has sold parts of it and many houses have come up in what used to be an idyllic place. Much of the foliage on the hill that gave it the look of a mini forest has also disappeared. At its base, a women's college has come up, painted in shocking pink and bright yellow and it sticks out like a sore thumb.

At the top of the hillock, the large, two-storeyed building was originally built as a guest house for visitors but Prakritish Barua later started staying there. For some reason, people used to call the building Rajbari or palace. The sun is setting and its reflection on the winding Gadadhar looks like a picture postcard. A heron sits on a log embedded in the river, its gaze fixed on the water as it waits patiently for a fish. Three young men pose for photographs outside the building where a small signboard still says 'Beware of dogs'. The dogs had disappeared years ago, but for some strange reason the signboard is still there.

Two of the three men are from Upper Assam and the third is their friend from Gauripur. They had also gotten in touch with Prabir Barua because they wanted to see the trophy room. We wait for five more minutes before he comes down from the first floor. We introduce ourselves and Barua, who is in his sixties, leads us along the wide verandah to the trophy room. I ask him about the signboard about dogs which I had seen as a child.

'That has become so much part of the house that no one has ever thought of removing it even though we don't have dogs anymore,' he tells me.

He opens the door of a room along the verandah and switches on the light and the sight breaks my heart. It is a large room full of exhibits worth a fortune but now decaying fast. In the middle of the room is a low bed covered with newspapers over which firearms including an ancient muzzleloader are laid out. The muzzleloader looks like it is withering away but a flintlock rifle that seems to weigh a ton, looks in better shape. Two other guns lie in pieces, their butts and barrels separated. There is also a miniature cannon that used to be fired on ceremonial occasions. A couple of blunt and rusting machetes also form part of the armoury.

Barua's father, Lalji, was a wildlife expert and a legend when it came to capturing wild elephants which were later sent to various national parks in the Northeast for use by forest officials. He also shot a couple of man-eating tigers. His elder brother, Pramathesh Chandra Barua, was also into game hunting before he moved to the world of films in Kolkata and is best known as the actor and director for the movie *Devdas* in 1935.

The walls in the trophy rooms are filled with heads of tigers, deer, wild buffaloes and even a rhino with the horn missing. I ask Barua about the missing horn and I am astonished by his reply.

'There was a theft in this room once and thieves made off with a few elephant tusks that were kept in a corner. My father then ordered to saw off the rhino's horn fearing that thieves might target the trophy room once again given the high price that a horn fetches in the black market.'

It must have been ages since these trophies were properly cleaned and serviced. The tiger heads look shabby probably because of the dust that has settled over them. The rhino's head already looks strange without a horn and now its ears are perforating. Dust and the elements have also robbed the deer trophies of their sheen and a couple of them have completely decayed. Even the paintings seem to be in a state of ruin. Lalji had some photographs of hunting expeditions but he also loved paintings and on many occasions he would take artists with him who would witness a hunt and then paint pictures.

One such painting that shows Lalji firing from an elephant's back at a leaping tiger, has dislodged from the frame. The colours have faded probably because the insulation is no longer enough to keep out moisture and dust and I doubt if this dramatic painting can be restored to its original glory. I begin to wonder if this family of zamindars has fallen on such hard times that it can't take care of its heritage anymore.

On one side of the room there are large brass and copper utensils which Barua says were used to cook food for the entire retinue during expeditions to catch elephants.

Half an hour later, we come out of the room and the three men leave. Barua takes me upstairs to his section of the building. We sit in his spacious drawing room and I notice that the floor is wooden. I ask him how old the house is.

'My grandfather started building it in 1904 and it was completed in 1914. So that makes it more than a hundred years. Chinese masons worked on it.'

I mention the trophy room and ask him why he doesn't do anything to restore its glory.

'The trouble is there is no consensus in the family. You see, my father had married thrice and we were nine siblings but a consensus on how to run the estate has remained elusive. I had even approached the state government and suggested that the culture or tourism department take responsibility of the trophy room. But nothing came of it. The government is useless. And, on my own, I can't do much,' Barua, who retired as a manager of the Jute Corporation of India, tells me.

I ask him if he ever was part of any of his father's hunting expeditions.

His eyes light up. 'Yes, and quite a few times when we were kids. But my father wouldn't just pick us up as if we were headed for a picnic. He trained us for life in the jungle. He would make us stand in the open in the sun, rain, and at night for about 15 minutes every day over a certain period of days to toughen us. He also taught us swimming to ensure that we would survive in the forest.'

Prabir Barua becomes nostalgic as he speaks.

'A hunting expedition used to involve the movement of a large number of people. The expedition used to head to a predetermined place usually on the outskirts of a forest and near a river where camps were pitched. Small bamboo and thatch structures used to become living quarters. We had to have food before dusk because we were forbidden to use light at night. We were told not to use soap or oil to prevent elephants from detecting our presence.'

The hunt itself was the biggest event that Prabir Barua and his siblings used to look forward to although they were not always taken inside the forest to see the exercise of rounding up wild elephants.

'There were different methods my father used to capture elephants. Sometimes wild elephants used to be driven into a stockade and sometimes they used to be driven to shallow pits. When it came to the stockade, females with calves and adults were freed and the required number of adolescent elephants was rounded up.'

'If he had to use pits to capture them, the targeted elephants were separated from the herd and directed towards the pits where they would be trapped once they fell into them. The expedition elephants would then be used to pull them out. There was another method of capturing them by using a lasso. But that was rarely used because it needed an expert to do so and there was a risk of a young elephant choking.'

'So, what was it like after the elephants were captured?' I ask him.

'They were tied up for a day or two near the campsite. Then the mahouts on the expedition's elephants would lead them to the river to give them a bath. Their hair would be burnt off with a torch. This exercise would go on for a few days until they started following commands.'

I tell Barua that as a child I had seen a part of this exercise behind the hillock on the banks of the Gadadhar—an elephant chained to a tree and the mahout using a torch to singe its prickly hair and then using a hard brush to rub its body for the hair to fall off. I remember the mahout singing a song that seemed to enchant the elephant into virtual submission.

'Yes, that song was a kind of signature instrument to tame wild elephants,' Barua tells me.

Barua's half-sister and Lalji's eldest child, Pratima Barua Pandey, would go on to immortalize that Goalpariya folk song 'O mor mahout bandhu re' (O my mahout friend) and another one 'Hastir kanya' (Elephant princess) and would go on to win the Padma Shri and Sangeet Natak Akademi Award. Irreverent, flamboyant, and down-to-earth, she charmed a few generations before she died in December 2002.

'I must tell you that elephants were not just elephants. They were given identities. For example, a tusker was called *dantal*, an elephant with one tusk was called *Ganesh*; *chakma* was one with small tusks. *Makna* was for an elephant without tusks and *dhui* meant an elephant which has recently given birth,' Barua tells me.

For a large part of Prabir Barua's life, elephants were a dominant feature in the family. Lalji owned many elephants. Two most famous of them were Jung Bahadur, which was then India's tallest elephant at 10 ft 5 inches, and later Pratap Singh, which was his favourite mount during hunting expeditions.

'But Pratap Singh was temperamental. And if my father had to go out of Gauripur for a few days he would leave behind a shirt that the mahout would sometime use to fan Pratap Singh and the familiar smell would cool him down if he showed signs of disobedience.'

Barua gets up from the sofa and picks up a thick, narrow logbook and flips the pages.

'My father was very meticulous. This is a diary of sorts and has the record of every elephant he captured and includes the date and place of capture.' He shows me the entries in blue ink. I see that Lalji had neat handwriting.

I learn that the expeditions were spread across Kokrajhar in Assam, North Bengal, Nongpoh, and the Garo Hills which were once part of Assam before Meghalaya was carved out. Lalji flirted briefly with politics and was an independent member of the Assam Legislative Assembly for a single term from 1957.

I thank Barua for telling me his stories. He leads me downstairs and out of the house. A light outside the house illuminates a small area while the area near the river is in darkness. The incessant sound of crickets attracts bats which swoop into the slope towards the river looking for dinner. I walk back to my motorcycle wondering how the fortunes of Lalji's family plunged so badly that there is no money now for the upkeep of the 'palace'.

I have to head for Guwahati the next day, so I take an early dinner and go to sleep. After a quick breakfast, I start my journey. Guwahati is about 250 km from Gauripur through the shortest route but I have to make a detour to visit Kokrajhar and I would end up travelling over 350 km through the day.

I cross the BSF camp and the Panbari mosque once more and after sometime turn left from the highway for Kokrajhar. The road is newly laid and my ride suddenly turns thrilling. I watch the speedometer needle climb beyond 100 kmph and slow down after some time after I see a few cows on the road. My main purpose of riding through Kokrajhar is to meet a man named Monir whose brother, Islam, had died of cancer two months earlier. Both Monir and Islam had stayed with our family for some years in the 1980s. Before my father retired from the Public Works Department, he had helped Islam get a government job. Monir also went on to find a job in the same department. But I hadn't met the brothers after they got married. Both stayed in the same house in Kokrajhar.

In the spring of 2018 I had learnt that Islam was suffering from stomach cancer and started a fundraising campaign for him. I was fortunate that I could raise enough money for him to travel to Mumbai twice for treatment at the Tata Memorial Hospital. But it wasn't enough to save his life because the cancer had spread fast. He died a few months later in September. He was a jovial, loyal, and honest man and too young to die at

45. His death had left me heartbroken and I wanted to meet his wife, two young sons, and Monir.

About ten kilometres later the blacktop disappears and the road is just full of rocks and gravel. There is very little traffic and most of them are two wheelers. I cross security pickets at a few places which are reminders that Kokrajhar is still susceptible to violence. The town and the places around it have suffered from sporadic violence between the dominant Bodo tribe and non-tribals, particularly Muslims. In the late 1980s, a demand for a separate state of Bodoland had turned violent with an extremist group launching an insurgency. Since then, security in and around Kokrajhar has remained fragile despite deployment of paramilitary forces.

By 11 am, I am on the edge of the town and stop near a police picket to call Monir. He tells me to wait and arrives in five minutes in an electric rickshaw and asks me to follow him. A few hundred metres later, he gets off the rickshaw and directs me to stop in front of a house. I walk into a small, Assam type house with a few rooms and a kitchen built separately. There is enough open space outside the house and Monir has grown a kitchen garden. He ushers me into a room and asks me to sit and runs to get a glass of water. He also introduces me to Islam's wife Anwara, who breaks down while speaking to me. Between sobs, she thanks me for making a detour to visit them.

'My husband used to speak highly of you and your family. I wish he was around to see you today. He would have been so happy,' she tells me as she wipes her tears. She excuses herself saying she will get tea for me.

A little later, Monir gets Islam's two sons and his own son into the room. Islam's eldest son is preparing to appear in the tenth standard finals and Monir asks me to tell him that he should study hard because he hasn't fared well in the last test in school. I suspect Islam's illness had much to do with his son's falling grades but I tell the teenager that since his father had worked so hard to put him and his brother in school, he should make the most of his good fortune of getting access to education. He nods and tells me that he would try his best. His younger brother, who is eight, struggles to contain his restlessness. Monir had told me that his father's death had affected him badly and he had developed a violent streak towards everybody. It is only recently that he had become sober. Monir's son is the youngest of the three boys who go to the same school.

Anwara serves tea and snacks which I share with the boys. The eldest one tells me he loves playing cricket while the other two are fond of football and cartoons. I finish my tea and get up to go. But Monir, his wife, and Anwara insist that I have lunch.

'It is the first time you have come to see us in Kokrajhar. You can't go without having lunch and Guwahati is still far away,' Monir tells me. I protest, but they are not willing to budge. I give in and wait for lunch and talk to Monir about the need to complete formalities quickly to ensure that Anwara gets Islam's pension payments. The lunch arrives after some time and the chicken curry is delicious. I eat quickly and get ready to leave. I put one of my bags on the pillion seat and tie it securely with a bungee cord. Anwara tells me to get my wife along the next time I visit them.

'Insha allah,' I tell her as I start the bike.

Monir tells me to take the same road back and then get on the national highway to Guwahati. I hit the rocky stretch of the road once again and stop a couple of times to check if my bag is securely tied. A little later I reach the blacktop and speed up before a herd of cattle crossing the road stops me. I turn my head once to check my bag and see that it is not there and it is obvious that it has fallen off somewhere on the rocky road. I fight down a brief panic attack and take stock. The bag contained my diary, a selfie stick, copies of the motorcycle's registration papers, and a pair of spare gloves. I call Monir and tell him of the loss and ask him to check out the road while I will do the same from my end.

I can't see the bag anywhere on the road. Sometime later I see Monir cycling from the opposite side and he tells me that hasn't spotted it either. I have another copy of the motorcycle's registration papers so that is not a major worry. But the diary could be a headache because I noted down events during the expedition and I suspect I may not be able to recall everything. I tell Monir that I don't want to take the rocky road yet again and he gives me the direction to another road but he is not very happy.

'That road is better but it passes through a jungle,' he tells me.

'Are there wild animals there?' I ask.

'Yes, but they won't attack during daylight. I am worried that you might run into militants.'

'Don't worry, they won't rob a solo traveller,' I try to reassure him.

I exit the town which has an outward appearance of being normal. But the security pickets are constant reminders of tension. Traffic is sparse and I ride at a comfortable speed under a balmy winter sun. The forest that Monir had told me about soon appears, its silence broken only by the sound of the motorcycle's exhaust and the odd vehicle coming from the opposite direction. I take a curve on the road and see two foxes scoot inside the forest. At some places there are tracks that cut through the red soil of the forest and are probably used by trucks to carry earth from excavation sites. I cross the forest area in about 20 minutes and come across tea gardens spread over hillocks. A few villages appear after the tea gardens and there is a weekly market off the road near one of the villages. I ride slowly as I pass the market because many villagers on bicycles climb on the road and head home.

I finally reach the highway to Guwahati and reach Jogighopa to take the bridge across the Brahmaputra. I stop briefly a few kilometres ahead of the bridge to buy cigarettes and see that there are two missed calls on my phone from a number that I can't recognize. I call back and the man on the on the other side asks me my location.

'I found your bag and I called to tell you that you can collect it from me in Kokrajhar,' he tells me and introduces himself as Drupad Das.

It's a huge relief to hear that news and I thank him. I also tell him that I can't return to collect my bag and will ask Monir to get in touch with him. He agrees. I call up Monir and tell him about Drupad and give his number.

'I will speak to him and collect it and I will take the train tomorrow to Guwahati,' Monir tells me. That sounds fine because I would be spending a couple of days in Guwahati.

The sun is setting, a huge red ball dipping into the horizon in the countryside. I watch it plunge into oblivion before I start the motorcycle. I am not happy because dropping my bag meant that I have lost two hours and now I would have to ride at night which I don't like. I am still 160 km away from Guwahati. I cross the 3-km long, double-decker bridge called Naranarayan Setu and a little later dusk falls.

I cut down on speed as vehicles drive in from the opposite directions with headlights on high beam. There is no divider on the highway and vehicles from the opposite direction sometimes come dangerously close to me. The temperature begins to fall as dusk gives way to the night.

I make brief pit stops at small towns for tea to warm myself up and for some relief to my aching back. At one such stop I walk into a small restaurant and ask for tea and snacks. Four Assamese Muslim men in skull caps, kurtas, and lungis with shawls wrapped over them are at the next table talking animatedly about the Assam government's exercise to update the National Register of Citizens or NRC. The exercise had been a controversial one with allegations that many genuine Indians were among more than 40 lakh of the state's population who were left out of the draft list published in July 2018. Many of those were Bengali speaking Hindus and Muslims. The exercise which was meant to weed out foreigners and illegal immigrants ended up causing a lot of heartburn after many genuine Indian citizens found their names missing from the list.[1]

The four men were discussing some of their neighbours whose names had been left out. 'I told them to file their claims as soon as possible so that the names will reflect when the final list is prepared,' one of them tells the other three.

I butt in and ask them about the situation regarding the NRC.

'Most people in our village have been included in the list. But some of them have been left out and if their claims are rejected once again they will be labelled foreigners despite being Indians. I hope things don't come to such a pass that somebody does something dangerous if he doesn't find his name in the final list when it is published.'

'Dangerous like what?' I ask.

'You never know. There have been so many instances in Assam of people becoming armed rebels over various issues and I am wary some of the people who would be left out of the list may follow the same path of rebellion. And that would only mean bloodshed.'

'That sounds far-fetched to me.'

'I know. But it is not impossible because a backlash against those whose names don't figure in the list could push those people to adopt some extreme measures. The NRC exercise has

---

[1] The final list of the NRC published on 31 August 2019 excluded 19 lakh people and set off a lengthy process of correcting or reversing any wrongful exclusions.

simply not been done properly and the government doesn't seem to pay heed to ground realities. And that's not the only thing. The government is also trying to change the citizenship law to favour non-Muslim refugees from Bangladesh and that is inherently a dangerous idea.'

That complaint about the NRC had been constant during the entire exercise. I resume my ride and run into lengthy stretches of road building where the surface is yet to be tarred. I reach the outskirts of Guwahati around 8 pm and cross the university where I never completed my Master's degree and then I am bewildered by the new road alignments and diversions before I find my bearings and head home.

My mother, sister Nazneen, and youngest brother Sadiq welcome me home. I unload my luggage, freshen up for dinner, and talk with my mother for some time before going to sleep. I get up late in the morning and spend a couple of hours with my mother before I head for the office of the Arunachal Pradesh Resident Commissioner for an Inner Line Permit to visit Bomdila and Tawang. My plan is to leave Guwahati after two days. There is a queue of people including tour operators and ordinary citizens applying for the permits. My turn to submit the form comes at noon and then the woman at the counter tells me to collect the pass between 2–4 pm.

I return home to find that Monir has come with my bag. Everything in the bag is intact. Monir leaves after lunch to take the train back to Kokrajhar. At 3:30 pm, I go once again to the Resident Commissioner's office to collect my permit which is valid for ten days and then head to the office of one of my sponsors'—Star Cement—to collect the company's stickers that I have to put on the motorcycle's tank. The traffic is very heavy and it moves agonizingly slowly. I find it torturous to ride partly because the Himalayan isn't meant to be used in stop-go traffic. I wonder what it must be like to ride in the heat and humidity of summer on this road. I begin to feel the engine heat on my legs but I reach my destination before it gets any worse.

I park the motorcycle near the pavement on an arterial road and quickly collect the stickers and return. I am about to wear my helmet when a young man standing on the pavement waves at me. I wave back and he comes down and asks if I am from Tamil Nadu.

'No. I am from Guwahati,' I tell him.

'I saw your bike's number plate and I thought you are from Tamil Nadu,' he tells me and introduces himself as Jitu Sharma.

I tell him that I am on a solo motorcycle expedition of the Northeast and he becomes even more interested in me. I learn that he works with an insurance company and is also an avid biker. He asks me about my itinerary in Arunachal Pradesh and I tell him the dates.

'I also have the same motorcycle and I have been to a few places where you would be going. I usually travel with my wife as my pillion rider. I have friends near the Arunachal Pradesh border and if you need help, I can tell them. You can take my phone number,' Jitu tells me.

I am completely floored by the kindness of a total stranger. I take his number and tell him that I will keep in touch. He gives me a few tips about the motorcycle and tells me to be careful on the way to Tawang.

I return home after lunch and stay put for the rest of the day.

The next morning I go out to buy a pump because I wasn't carrying one. I would be riding through some desolate places in Arunachal Pradesh and other states and I want to insure myself against being stranded due to a flat tyre. The shop is about two km away and I notice that the locality has changed drastically. An unending row of shops has filled up much of the vacant plots along the road. Eateries have mushroomed and they reflect the changing demographic pattern. Until a few years ago there were a few meat shops and restaurants selling chicken, mutton, and beef which serviced a substantial Muslim population. Now, almost every new roadside eatery sells all these and pork dishes as well to cater to a large clientele of students from other Northeastern states living in that area.

I return home and spend a few hours with my mother. She has been battling asthma for many years but her health seems a little better now. She mourns Islam's death and wonders if cancer has a hereditary link given that his mother had also died of it. She eats lunch and then takes a nap.

I go out to meet my colleague Sadiq Naqvi. Over lunch at a restaurant, we exchange notes and he asks me about my itinerary and the time I would take for my journey.

He also tells me about another young motorcyclist who was on his way to a few Southeast Asian countries and whom he had met a couple of weeks ago.

'Have you made any reservations for your stay in Bomdila?' Sadiq asks.

'Not yet. But I will try to find a place when I get there.'

'I will forward you the Bomdila police chief's number. If you can't find any accommodation you can request him for a room at the circuit house.'

After I return home I pack my bags for the next day's ride. Rubaiyat calls in the late afternoon and we decide to get together in the evening with four other friends. Six of us meet after many years. Other than Rubaiyat, there are Ranjan Sharma, a bureaucrat, Maluf Ahmed, a computer whiz kid, and two doctors—Dhrubojyoti Kalita and Bhaskar Borkotoky. I tell them the highs and lows of my trip so far and my plans for the rest of the expedition.

Bhaskar and I exchange notes about Ladakh and the Pangong Lake and Rubaiyat recalls his visit to Tawang almost 20 years ago when he drove an old Premier Padmini with his wife and two kids. Ranjan asks me where I would be staying when I leave Guwahati the next day.

'Somewhere in Nameri but I am not sure of which place to stay,' I tell him and ask if he knows anybody in the government's tourism department whom I could talk to for an accommodation.

'Yes, I know someone and I will speak to him and forward you his number.'

A couple of hours pass quickly before we head home.

I leave next morning at around eight and quickly hit the highway for Nameri, 220 km away. It is cold but a bright sun makes it an exhilarating morning to ride. Along the highway, villagers wait for motorists at their small stalls selling fruits and handicraft items made of bamboo. Most of the stalls are stacked with oranges, bananas, and tender coconuts.

The phone rings and I pull up on the edge of the road and answer the call. The caller introduces himself as Basab Bora, an officer of Assam Tourism Development Corporation and tells me that Ranjan had spoken to him about me. He also tells me that he has spoken to the manager, Joy, at a resort in Nameri and would forward his number to me so that I can get in touch with him. Assured that I won't have to hunt for a place to stay the night, I resume my ride.

I cross the small town of Jagiroad where Nazneen and I first went to school. I remember my father's quarter was just off the highway but almost 50 years since we moved out of Jagiroad, the town's landscape has changed drastically and I can't locate the house where we used to stay. It is the same with the school. The only thing I remember is that it was across a rail track which is still there but I can't see any sign of the school. I wonder if it still exists. The hills around Jagiroad, which were once thick with forest cover, have denuded and I suspect that the wildlife too has suffered the same fate. The small town is bustling and I slow down as I cross it. A paper mill, which was set up a few decades ago and was hailed as an economic game changer for Jagiroad, has been shut down and I notice banners put up by the employees' union protesting the closure.

Two hours after I started my ride, I make a brief stop at a fork on the outskirts of Nagaon to break the monotony of the ride. I ask a local man who is cycling down the road if I should ride through the town or remain on the highway to find a place to eat.

'Don't get into the town. You will get stuck in traffic. Stay on the highway and you will find restaurants a few kilometres ahead,' he tells me.

A group of bikers on Harley Davidson motorcycles zoom past as I am about to start. None of them have any luggage and I guess that an SUV which is following them is carrying their cargo. I find a restaurant and stop for brunch. The parathas and the omelette are filling and I tell myself that I won't have to stop for food again until I reach Nameri. After a refreshing cup of tea, I straddle the motorcycle again. As I switch on the ignition, I see a service reminder sign flashing on the instrument console. I switch off the ignition and switch it on again but the sign keeps flashing. I suspect it is some kind of malfunction but I have no idea how to fix it. I call up Shahwar in Delhi for some advice and he tells me a few troubleshooting tricks but it still doesn't work. He suggests that I take it to a Royal Enfield service centre in Nagaon.

The road inside Nagaon is chaotic with traffic. Near the Royal Enfield service centre, a drain has overflown and half the road has gone under water. At the service centre, the helpful manager introduces himself as Banty Das and when I tell him that the motorcycle is the company's and not mine, he assures me that the problem will be fixed. I wait in the customer's lounge while Banty takes the motorcycle to a service bay and returns in 15 minutes.

'The problem has been solved. It won't happen again. But if it does when you are out of Nagaon, give me a call and I will try to arrange a service engineer to look into it,' he tells me as he gives me his visiting card.

I thank him and ride back the same way to the highway. I am tempted to check out Loyola School inside the town where my sister and I studied after we moved from Jagiroad but the traffic deters me and besides the dashboard panel malfunction has already cost me an hour. I climb on the highway again but on this side of Nagaon the road has narrowed down and there is no divider. Many stretches of the highway are being rebuilt and there are traffic diversions which cut down my speed.

At Koliabor I turn left for Tezpur and see that the road has turned into a patchwork after an exercise to fill up potholes. A little later I cross the three-km long Kolia Bhomora road bridge over the Brahmaputra and reach the outskirts of Tezpur. I stop to call Joy and tell him that I have reached Tezpur.

'Okay. You will cross a place called Balipara and after that there is a hamlet called Chariduar. I have come to the weekly market at Chariduar so when you reach here please call me again. The market is on the highway,' Joy tells me.

I notice that my fuel has halved and stop at a petrol pump to top up the tank. I ask the fuel station attendant about Nameri National Park and he tells me to ride carefully because wild elephants are known to suddenly appear on the road that runs through the forest.

Out of Tezpur, tea gardens begin to appear on either side of the road. About 45 minutes later, I ride into Chariduar and see that the weekly market is on one side of the road. Two wheelers and a few cars are parked on both sides of the road and I ride slowly looking for a place to stop. I finally find a place at the edge of the market and stop and call Joy to tell him my location.

I dismount and stand near my motorcycle and watch the shoppers come out of the market with bags full of vegetables. Some are going back home with freshwater fish. A quack sitting in an autorickshaw starts playing a recorded advertisement of his medicines for a range of ailments from toothache to liver damage to hairfall. The voiceover is in Hindi and I am a little surprised at the sales pitch because the population around this place is largely Assamese.

A young man on a battered, small motorcycle with a sack of vegetables on the pillion seat secured with bungee cords comes and stops near me and asks, 'Mr. Hussain?'

'Yes. You must be Joy.'

'Please follow me. The resort is about ten km from here.'

This is the first time in my life that I have had a hotel manager meeting me ten km away from the accommodation. I start riding behind Joy before we stop parallel to each other at a railway crossing. There is a signboard on the side of the road at the level crossing that says Nameri Kanya Resort. Joy points to the signboard and says, 'That's our place.'

A passenger train passes and the gateman lifts the barrier and we are on our way again. We are soon riding through a dense forest. A couple of signboards warn motorists that animals have the right of way around this place. It is also an elephant corridor and now the fuel station attendant's warning makes sense to me. A troop of monkeys sit on the edge of road and eye every car and two wheeler hoping for some food.

Nameri Kanya, just off the highway, is a lovely place with a wire fence around the perimeter. Behind an iron gate, two bullock cart wheels on either side of a driveway lend an ethnic touch to the sprawling setting. I count four structures in the massive compound. The first one is an exclusive accommodation—a bamboo structure on stilts. Then there is the manager's office and living quarter and the dining hall. There is also a machan restaurant. There are two other Assam type structures a little further away and one of them has a grille across the balcony to keep away monkeys.

Joy shows me both the places and I choose a room in the structure which doesn't have a grille. The room is very large and the bed is made of bamboo. There are two plastic chairs and a table and a wooden clothesline. I carry my bags inside, freshen up, and go to the reception and ask Joy for a cup of tea. I also ask him about the machan restaurant and he tells me that he is still working on it.

'Is there any other guest?' I ask.

'No. You are the only one today. Five other tourists from Maharashtra left for Tezpur this morning.'

He serves me tea and biscuits. It is 3 pm and there just about 90 minutes of daylight left. I tell Joy I want to check out the nearby areas and he suggests that I ride ahead towards Bhalukpong on the Arunachal Pradesh border about 20 km away. I head out but stop much before Bhalukpong to watch a football match outside a village. I spend about 15 minutes watching the match that takes me back to my own childhood when I played both football and cricket with equal passion. I start the ride again and stop a couple of kilometres away at another village to buy some emergency rations like biscuits.

I ask the shopkeeper if they have trouble with wild elephants.

'Not really,' he tells me. 'There's enough food for them in the forest. Of course, sometimes a rogue elephant strays into paddy fields but we chase it away.'

'Are elephants the only threat?'

'Sometimes wild boars also raid paddy fields. We either chase them away or catch a couple of them for food. And that's not hunting because hunting is banned. We have also had a couple of instances of leopards killing our goats and dogs. But I haven't seen a tiger yet because they live deep inside the forest.'

The sun begins to wane and I drop the idea of riding to Bhalukpong, partly because I would be riding in the same direction the next day and partly because I did not want to ride back after dark lest I run into elephants.

I ride a little ahead and then go off the road and stop by the Jia Bharali river which is also called Kameng river which flows in from Arunachal Pradesh and goes on to join the Brahmaputra. The setting is picturesque and the silence is broken only by the sound of the river and the birds returning home at the end of a day.

The sun is beginning to set when I get back on the motorcycle and start riding back to Nameri Kanya. The sun plays hide and seek with me among the sal trees as I ride. A little later I notice a pick-up truck on my rear view mirror. I slow down and let it pass and then I stop at a place where I get a relatively clear sight of the setting sun. I resume my ride in fading light and as I near Nameri Kanya, I hear a loud, screeching sound. I am on an upward climb and my line of vision is limited. It is only when I clear the slope that I notice that the pick-up truck which had overtaken me a few minutes ago is in trouble. The vehicle's left rear wheel has come off and by the time the driver has stopped, the hub has made a deep gash on the tarmac, at least 20 metres long. The driver and the handyman are inspecting the mess when I stop near them on the approach to Nameri Kanya. I ask them if they need any help.

'No, we can't do anything until this hub is replaced. It is damaged and we can't fix the spare wheel on it. I will call a mechanic in Tezpur and he should be here in about 90 minutes,' the driver tells me.

I am appalled that he had no idea that the screws of the wheel hub had been coming loose.

'When did you last service your vehicle?' I ask him.

'I don't remember. I don't service it until it gives me trouble,' he tells me.

I sigh at his happy-go-lucky attitude. It is something I have scrupulously avoided adopting when it came to my car or motorcycle simply because I don't like being caught on the wrong foot. I tell myself that driver has probably never heard of the saying: A stitch in time saves nine.

I suggest that he and his handyman go and talk to Joy and rest there until the mechanic arrives, but he refuses.

I return to my accommodation and ask Joy for another cup of tea.

There are bamboo chairs in the balcony of Joy's accommodation and I sit on one of them. A young man serves me tea and a little later Joy joins me.

'Who makes this stuff?' I ask pointing to the bamboo chairs.

'A few villagers are involved in it. Some time ago the government launched a scheme to train villagers to make bamboo furniture and some people were enterprising enough to launch their own bamboo furniture business and make a decent living. The scheme taught them how to treat bamboo with chemicals to make it pest-proof. And once it is treated, bamboo furniture last a lifetime. Do you want to buy some?'

'I would love to. I like that bed in my room.'

'It won't cost you more than Rs 15,000.'

'That's a steal but it would cost me almost double to truck it to Delhi.'

'Maybe you can dismantle the bed and drive in your own car or hire a van for Delhi. Then it won't cost so much.'

Joy gives me food for thought.

I change the topic and ask him how long has he been at Nameri Kanya.

'It has been two years since my brother and I took it on lease from the government.'

'I thought it was being run by the government.'

'The government can't run it. Government officials are just too lazy to work because they have guaranteed salaries. In our case it is different. We have to make this place profitable to survive after paying the government. We have gone online and the traffic has increased. We have to pay the government a particular amount and to make sure that we stay afloat we haven't employed formal staff. We do the work ourselves. A couple of youngsters from my village who are unemployed are helping me out. I pay them for their efforts.'

Night falls quickly and the forest's nocturnal residents announce their presence. The sound of crickets, the occasional hoots of owls and the howls of jackals break the silence of the night under a starry sky and a moon which is almost full.

The young man who served me tea returns to pick up the cup. His name is Shyam Chetri. I ask him how long he has been at Nameri Kanya.

'I come on and off to help Joy. I was a cook at a small hotel in Mumbai but I left the job to return home. I want to join the army and I am waiting for the next round of recruitment.'

'Where does the recruitment take place?'

'It is in Shillong. And it costs money for the journey and staying in Shillong for at least three days. I hope I make it.'

'Do you want to join the army as a cook?'

'No. I want to be a regular soldier. But I won't mind joining as a cook. At least, I won't be unemployed,' he tells me as he takes the cup and goes inside. I wonder if it is hunger or patriotism that makes young men like Shyam join the army.

I ask Joy about the wire fence.

'It is electrified to keep away wild elephants. But the power has been calibrated so that it doesn't kill them. There are big herds around here and they cross this place regularly.'

He takes out his phone and shows me a video he shot a few days ago of a herd of elephants walking through the outskirts of a nearby village.

'I had gone to meet a friend in the afternoon when the elephants came and there were quite a few of them. If you are lucky you might see them tonight because they normally cross around this time.'

Joy tells me he has bookings for Christmas and he needs to decorate the place. He gets up and walks to his desk and takes cut-outs of stars made of paper and starts arranging them to be hanged from the ceiling and the trees. Suddenly, he stops and asks me, 'Did you hear that?'

'What?'

'The sound of a trumpet.'

'I thought it was the horn of a truck.'

The trumpet sounds again, this time a little louder.

'That's the herd on its way. Let's go,' Joy tells me and runs to his room and comes out with a large flashlight.

Joy, Shyam, and I run towards the part of the resort which has the widest span of the fencing and hide behind trees and wait. For some time there is just some rumbling noise and the sound of trumpets. And then they appear like silhouettes under the scattered moonlight among the giant trees. The elephants take a dirt track, about ten yards away along the fence. There are a few calves among them and older elephants nudge and guide them to stay in a line as they go past us. My heart thumps with excitement.

'This is the first batch with the females and the calves. More will come now,' Joy tells me in a low voice. A little later the rest of the herd arrives. A couple of them stop midway and look around as to make sure that the coast is clear before they head for the forest. Joy gets up and shines his torch on the last of the elephants and I try to shoot a few pictures with my phone. We watch them disappear into the night and then head back to the reception, my heart still racing after witnessing the spectacle. It is the first time that I have seen wild elephants from such close quarters.

'You are lucky,' says Joy. 'The tourists who left this morning stayed two nights here but they could not see the elephants because they must have taken a different path.'

It is cold in the balcony so I go inside the dining hall and decide to check the kitchen which is quite large. Shyam and another young man are cooking dinner. I learn that there's cauliflower and potatoes, dal, mixed vegetables for dinner.

Shyam appears a little worried. 'I had to go home because we have to harvest paddy tomorrow morning. But I am not sure I should leave because I might run into the elephants. My village is down the road the elephants took and if they have stopped midway then I might run into trouble.'

'Stay the night here,' I suggest.

'Yes, I think I will do that and leave in the morning after you go. What time do you want to start?'

'I am aiming to get out by 7:30 am.'

I return to the reception and see that Joy has hung two large stars and is preparing to hang a third one. There is a road map under the glass top of his table and I check the road for Bomdila. Joy tells me that Bomdila is about 120 km away.

Shyam announces that dinner has been served. The dining tables and chairs are also made of bamboo. Shyam is a good cook and the food is tasty. I eat well and make small talk. He tells me to wear my thermals in the morning because Bomdila would be much colder than Nameri. I finish my meal and tell Joy that I would like to have breakfast before leaving.

I head for my room and go to sleep. The resident rooster's call wakes me up at the crack of dawn. I laze in bed and wait for sunrise before I get up. The jungle's ambience of the night changes and the resort begins to resonate with calls of different birds—doves, parrots and hornbills. Water birds fly over the resort to the river nearby. I take a bath and get ready for my ride. Shyam has already made breakfast of puri, potato curry, and omelette and I eat to my heart's content.

Joy gives me the bill and I make the payment. I return to my room and take out my luggage and load the motorcycle, wishing that I could have stayed a day more.

'Next time, stay for a couple of days more. There is a jungle trek you will love,' Joy tells me. I tell him that I will return sometime later and will definitely go on the trek. I ride out of the dirt track of Nameri Kanya and climb on to the highway.

5

Bomdila and Tawang

21 November 2018

Like the previous day, the early winter sun is a joy. In half an hour, I reach Bhalukpong, a small town spread across Assam and Arunachal Pradesh. I stop and call Sudha to give her a brief update about my progress and then call Bomdila's police chief Raja Banthia and request him to facilitate my stay at the circuit house. He asks me to wait for a few minutes and then sends me a message that a room has been booked.

I ride on and make another stop a few minutes later to shoot a few pictures of the Kameng river. I am about to start when Shahwar calls from Delhi and asks my location.

'One of my friends just called and mentioned that the road to Bomdila is quite bad. It starts from about 20 km from where you are right now. There have been landslides and long stretches have been dug up for road building.'

I am worried because when Shahwar says the road is quite bad, it is an understatement. He makes a living mostly from the seat of a motorcycle and knows the roads of the Northeast like the back of his hand.

'I can't turn back now. I will ride carefully,' I tell him.

Twenty kilometres later I run into the remains of a landslide. Earthmovers have removed much of the debris but it is still a long rocky and slushy stretch. Parts of the road seem to have been scooped up by the landslide. I ride carefully through it and get onto broken tarmac. The mountains with evergreen forests begin to soar and suddenly there is an eerie feeling because there is no traffic either behind me or from the opposite direction.

A little later I run into another long, slushy stretch where road builders have scrapped off the mountainside and dug up the road to lay it once again. Trucks which have passed on the road have created two depressions on the soft surface while the middle of the road is substantially raised. I slow down to a crawl and try my best to avoid the watery stretches but mud splatters my boots. The motorcycle's tyres are new and I manage to clear the stretch without much difficulty.

I finally reach a hamlet called Sessa and stop for lunch at a small eatery. I order noodles and egg and a cold drink and notice that most of the shops and eateries are selling kiwifruit of which Arunachal Pradesh is a major producer. I ask the woman at the eatery about the cost of kiwifruit.

'We sell them between Rs 100 to Rs 120 a kilo depending on their size. Do you want some?'

'Not now. Maybe I will buy some on the way back.' I tell her.

I come out after finishing my food and stand in the sun. An SUV heading for Tezpur had stopped while I was eating and a few passengers are also standing in the sun. One of them asks me how far I am travelling.

'Bomdila and Tawang,' I tell him.

'Is there someone else with you?'

I shake my head and he tells me to be careful because the road is in bad condition for much of the way to Bomdila.

The road remains awful. Sometime later, I reach another stretch where a mountain side has been blown off and an earth mover is clearing the debris about 150 metres away. The earthmover driver sees me approaching and raises his hand signalling me to stop and then he shouts, 'Wait until I signal you to start.'

I switch off the engine and wait. The earthmover moves back and forth several metres to push the debris off the road and down a slope. But rocks and earth continue to fall on the road from the part of the mountain that has been blown off. I wait for almost half an hour but there is still no traffic and I ask myself why I am the only one on the road. The earthmover driver finally signals me to start. The fresh earth is soft and the wheels sink into them. Loose soil from the mountain slope continues to fall on the road. I struggle to maintain balance and manage to clear much of the distance to the earthmover when the front tyre hits a large rock hidden under the earth. I lose balance and the motorcycle topples to the right as if in slow motion. The earthmover driver's assistant rushes to help me lift the bike. I clear the rest of the stretch without much trouble.

The road begins to improve but remains narrow for some more kilometres with hairpin curves and deep vertical drops to oblivion. It is difficult to speed on this road. There is virtually no habitation for miles and fleetingly, I worry about getting stranded in case of any trouble but I push that thought out of my mind. The road eventually becomes more pleasurable to ride about 35 km before Bomdila. Signs of Buddhism begin to appear in the form of small gompas and monasteries. The road continues to climb. Soon, I am in Tenga Valley in West Kameng district at 6,500 feet.

Tenga Valley is a strategic military base and it stretches for miles and army personnel seem to outnumber locals. I finally run into traffic including army trucks and SUVs going up and down. Most of the land of the army camp had been acquired after the 1962 Sino-India conflict which saw fierce fighting in several theatres in Arunachal Pradesh. Many of those whose land had been acquired have been paid compensation only recently by the central government. I want to meet some of those who have been paid compensation.

The scenery is heavenly and I stop briefly in the middle of nowhere simply to admire the view. A cold wind lashes my face as I take off my helmet. I adjust my balaclava and scarf and put on the helmet once again. Along the way I see a road sign showing the direction towards Guwahati via Rupa. Many people who have received compensation for their land from the Central Government live in Rupa. I tell myself that I could take this road on the way back to Guwahati.

I ride into the circuit house in Bomdila at 2 pm and tell the man at the reception that I have a reservation. He checks the reservation register and then gets up and takes me to the first floor and opens a room for me. I put down the luggage and the man who introduces himself as Tenzing, tells me that he would get me some tea and snacks while I freshen up. The room is a huge one with two beds, a sofa, a dressing table, and a desk. The building itself is new and the balcony offers a great view of the mountains.

The cold has increased and I tell myself that it is only to be expected given Bomdila's altitude of 8,500 feet.

Tenzing comes back with tea and snacks and tells me that they are expecting a VIP guest and must hurry downstairs to supervise some work. I am fatigued after the punishing ride and I drink the tea slowly and doze off on the sofa. The noise of a few vehicles in the parking wakes me up. I go to the balcony and see a row of SUVs parked in a line and a few policemen standing near them.

I decide to go for a walk and check out the town. A few police officers are standing near the reception and I recognize Superintendent of Police Raja Banthia when I see his name tag above his shirt pocket. I introduce myself and ask him if I can meet him after he is done with the circuit house duty.

'Yes, you can come to my office at 4:30 pm. It is just down this road, about 100 metres,' Banthia tells me.

On the way out I ask another policeman why they are at the circuit house. He tells me that they are busy with the security arrangement for a judge of the Central Administrative Tribunal or CAT who is visiting Bomdila. I walk down a steep slope and reach the main road and take the road downhill. A little later I cross Banthia's office. A man overtakes me and looks at my riding jacket and asks, 'Motorcycle tourist?'

I nod and he slows down to walk with me. 'I am Dorjee Phuntso,' he says extending his hand. He is well built and looks like he is in his 40s. I ask him if he knows any senior citizen who was in Bomdila when the Chinese occupied the town in 1962.

'Most of them have died. A few others live out of the town but there is one man here named Rinchin who runs a shop. I am going that way and you can come with me if you want.'

'I would love to meet him.'

'Let's take a shortcut,' Dorjee tells me as he heads towards a flight of stairs going down. It is a long winding way down to another road in a market. He asks me about my travel plans and warns me that some parts of the road between Bomdila and Tawang are atrocious.

The market is a bustling one with different kinds of shops. Dorjee goes inside a shop stuffed with winter wear and I follow him. There is a woman at the counter and Dorjee speaks to her in the local language and then turns to me.

'She says her father has gone to Tezpur for treatment and will be back day after tomorrow.'

That puts paid to my hope of meeting him but I tell myself there will be other veterans of 1962 whom I can meet.

I thank Dorjee for his efforts and he goes away. I check out the market and notice that women not only run regular shops but wine shops as well, something unthinkable in North India. I check out a shop selling winter wear but the prices are too steep for my liking.

Bomdila is a quaint, little town and spick and span. I head back to the staircase and huff and puff my way up. I stop to catch my breath after I reach the road and then walk to

Banthia's office. It is 4:30 pm and the sun has already set. The officer is not there but one of the policemen who had seen me at the circuit house asks me wait and tells me that his boss would soon be there.

I wait for about ten minutes before Banthia walks in and a little later an aide ushers me into his room which is a large one with wooden walls. A board at the centre of the wall behind Banthia's chair displays the names of Bomdila's previous police chiefs. He orders two cups of tea and turns to me, 'I was expecting a much younger man. What brings you here?'

'I had always wanted to ride across Arunachal Pradesh and the rest of the Northeast on a motorcycle but wasn't able to do so earlier. It is only now that things have fallen in place, so here I am.'

'I am from Rajasthan but I have settled in Delhi although I never tell anyone I am a Delhiwalla now,' he tells me. Banthia, who is probably in his late 30s or early 40s, is also a closet biker. He had served in Delhi Police before being transferred to Bomdila.

'I love reading road travel books and I dream of riding from Bikaner to Jaisalmer. It is on my bucket list. I don't want to undertake the extreme type of motorcycling that you are doing.'

I tell him that I have written a travel book after a solo ride to Kashmir and Ladakh and he says he would love to read it.

'I am carrying a copy of it and I will give it to you tomorrow morning before I leave for Tawang.'

I ask him about his job and whether it is taxing.

'No. It is mainly about security arrangements for VIPs who keep visiting Bomdila. Law and order is not much of a problem here. It is a largely a peaceful place. We had a scrap with the army last month but that's now history.'

He is not willing to talk about the incident but three weeks earlier I had handled the news reports about the incident so

I knew about it. The 'scrap' with the army had threatened to snowball into a major crisis after the police arrested two soldiers for allegedly misbehaving with police personnel and civilians including women at the Buddha Mahotsav celebrations. The soldiers were said to have been drunk.

The soldiers' unit claimed they were beaten up in police custody and were severely injured before they were released. The police had maintained that the soldiers had suffered minor injuries. An army contingent allegedly vandalized the Bomdila Police station the next day and assaulted police personnel before authorities brokered peace. The police had claimed that the two soldiers who were arrested were in the forefront of the attack which proved that they were not seriously injured.

'Where will you be staying in Tawang?' Banthia asks.

'I was thinking about the circuit house,' I answer.

'Don't go there. The Tawang Circuit House is costly. I will arrange a place for you but you will get the confirmation only tomorrow when you will be on your way.'

'That's good enough.'

An aide comes in with a bunch of files which Banthia has to sign. I get up to go. We shake hands and he tells me, 'Remember to give me your book tomorrow.'

'I will leave it here with someone who is on duty.'

Outside the office, it is freezing. I pull my balaclava tightly over my ears and shove my fists deep into my trouser pockets and walk uphill to the circuit house. I meet Tenzing at the reception to fill up my details in the guest register. It is almost 6 pm and he tells me that I can have dinner at 8 o'clock.

I go to my room and review the photographs I have taken in the day and fill up my diary. The large room feels cold and I call up Tenzing and ask for a heater. A few minutes later he arrives with a heater and switches it on. At 8 pm I go downstairs to the dining hall and take a seat. A couple of other guests are also present and a little later Tenzing serves us.

There is rice, fish curry, egg curry, dal, mixed vegetables, and salad. I settle for rice, fish curry, and salad. After dinner, Tenzing asks me when I would be leaving for Tawang.

'I am planning to leave around 8 am.'

'In that case you can have breakfast. We serve breakfast between 7 and 8 am.'

I go to my room and sleep. I get up at the crack of dawn, take bath, offer my prayers, and start packing. A spectacular sunrise in the mountains adds to the feel-good factor. I run a double check on my belongings and go down at 7 am to load the motorcycle and then head for the dining hall for breakfast. The puri-sabzi is substantial and I fill myself up to make sure that I won't have to stop for food soon. I pay Tenzing and tell him that I will be back after two days and would like to stay for one more night.

'I can't promise you a room in this building because some ministers are scheduled to be here. You can stay in the old building just in case there is no vacancy in this one.'

'That's fair enough.'

I ride out and stop briefly in front of Banthia's office and leave a copy of my book *Battlefields & Paradise* with a policeman at the reception before I head for Tawang which is little over 200 km northwest.

The road is very good and I maintain a good speed. Shortly out of Bomdila I see the first snow clad peaks in the distance. About half an hour later a huge red and golden gate announces that I am in Dirang but the town is still a few kilometres away. The road narrows inside the small town and I soon find myself behind a clutch of taxis—all SUVs—headed for

Tawang. I notice that the fuel gauge is showing that the tank is only half full and I stop at the first fuel station I see. There are many small cars and motorcycles at the petrol pump and it takes time. I ask a local man on a motorcycle if there are any more petrol pumps on the way and he tells me that the next pump is at Jang, 100 km away. So I wait for my turn to fill up the tank. I also want to check the tyre pressure but the fuel station doesn't have air filling facility.

I finally find a tyre repair shop on the edge of the town. A young man in his 20s is busy fitting a battery into a motorcycle. I stop and tell him that I need to check the tyre pressure.

'We are closed today. The Chief Minister has come to the village so it is a holiday,' he says without batting an eyelid.

That's a strange explanation but I don't waste time and ride on and find another shop a few kilometres away and fill up air. The road improves but Sela Pass, the gateway to Tawang, seems elusive. Somewhere along the way I see a signboard announcing the proposed site of the Sela tunnel. When completed, it would make the drive between Bomdila and Tawang more pleasurable, much like the Zoji La tunnel would do to a drive from Kashmir to Ladakh.

The road continues uphill and soon I am beyond the tree line and the mountains are brown with only barren rocks and craggy cliffs and peaks with snow at the top. Five kilometres ahead of Sela Pass, the road disappears into sand and stones that have been laid to build it again. The sand and stones have made the surface tricky for a two-wheeler, particularly at the turns. I am forced to reduce my speed and SUVs which rumble past dump coats of dust on me. The air becomes thinner and I notice that I am breathing harder. I eventually reach the top of Sela Pass at 13,700 feet and stop. Another huge gate welcomes motorists to Tawang district. I take a few photographs and head for the army cafeteria. There is no power to run the hot plate so I can't order tea that I badly want.

'Have a samosa. It is still hot,' the trooper at the counter tells me. I buy it and a pack of fruit juice. The trooper tells me that the next seven kilometres to Jaswantgarh is in terrible condition and that I should ride carefully.

'Is there snow melt or slush?' I ask.

'No. There are just rocks. They are laying the road again.'

At least I won't get wet, I tell myself as I start the motorcycle again.

The cold increases on this side of Sela Pass and the mountains are covered with a thin layer of snow. The Sela lake is beginning to freeze near the banks. For the next seven kilometres I bump over rocks, sand, and gravel but the motorcycle's suspension soaks up much of the bumps with aplomb. The blacktop finally returns and the ride improves. But the five kilometres of bad road before Sela and the seven kilometres after it have cost me much time and I am now running late and won't be able to reach Tawang, which is also the district headquarter, before sundown. I skip a visit to a memorial to fallen soldiers at Jaswantgarh and tell myself that I will see it on the way back.

I cross a bridge and get onto a blacktop road which has just been laid. I speed up as I exit the bridge but fail to notice black gravel on the surface. The motorcycle suddenly skids and I slide with it for quite a distance diagonally from the left to the right of the road. There is no way I can stop the slide towards the edge of the road beyond which is a vertical drop to the next loop of the highway. There are no guard rails to stop my slide but the nightmare ends a few feet from the edge as the momentum runs out. I pick myself up and discover that my riding jacket and shin guards have prevented any major injury but I have a minor sprain on my right ankle and I can't put my weight on that foot to lift the motorcycle.

But I am lucky. Two army trucks coming from the opposite direction stop and a captain disembarks from the first vehicle and runs towards me and helps me lift the motorcycle. He asks me if I am hurt and I reply in the negative. I thank him and move on. The road goes downhill and I stop at a small restaurant for tea and calm my frayed nerves after the fall. A local man tells me that I am still 50 km from Tawang and it will take me about two hours. I calculate that it would be 5:30 pm by the time I reach Tawang, more than an hour after sunset. We drink tea standing on the road and he points the way to Tawang, a few mountains away. Much below in one of the mountains, the roof of a monastery painted in golden colour glints in the late afternoon sun.

I ride on and reach the small town of Jang. The road inside the town is narrow and quite a bit of it is muddy and slushy. Domestic cows amble along the road and climb on to the mountain slopes to graze. The ride through Jang becomes torturous because it is difficult to overtake any vehicle and it gets worse when trucks drive in from the opposite direction.

Out of Jang, the road gets relatively better but fatigue is setting in. Close to sunset, I make the last stop at a small hamlet 15 km short of Tawang for tea and snacks. I check my phone and see that there is a missed call from Banthia. I call him up and he tells me to get in touch with Sagar Singh Kalsi, the Superintendent of Police in Tawang.

'He has booked a place for you. I will forward you his number so you can speak to him,' Banthia tells me.

I call Kalsi and introduce myself but the line is crackling badly. I manage to tell him that I am 15 km away and he instructs me to head for the guest house of the Sashastra Seema Bal (SSB), one of India's Central Armed Police Forces. He tells me that he will show up at the guest house around 6 pm.

Dusk falls and envelops the mountains in darkness. I reach Tawang and ask a few locals for the way to the SSB guest house. The sentry at the gate stops me to ask my details before letting me ride inside.

Two troopers come out of a sprawling building and one of them confirms my booking. He tells me the building houses a conference room, officers' mess and dining hall and that the guest house is just beyond the building.

'You can park in front of the guest house. I will show you your room,' he tells me.

I park and dismount and take off my bags and a trooper arrives with a jug of water and a glass. He takes one of my bags and we go inside the double storey guest house. There's a drawing room and two other rooms on the ground floor and I am assigned the one at the rear.

'Would you like to have tea or coffee?' he asks.

'Tea and some snacks, please.'

'We start cooking dinner at 7 pm. Should I serve dinner in the room or will you come to the dining hall?'

'I will eat at the dining hall,' I tell him.

He switches on the room heater and tells me that there is no other guest in the facility and that they rarely get to see a civilian staying in the guest house. I go to freshen up and discover that the water is freezing. I switch on the geyser and wait for a few minutes before I wash my hands and face. The trooper returns with a tea pot, a cup and some hot, fried snacks, which I polish off.

I go for a stroll along the perimeter of the guest house. The moon is almost full and I can see the outlines of mountains all around Tawang. The wind is cold and after ten minutes I head back for my room. It is 6 pm but there is no sign of Kalsi. I tell myself that he must be caught up in work and then I start writing my diary.

Kalsi arrives at 7 pm. A strapping Sikh, he is in civilian clothes. He shakes my hand, looks at my four-day-old grey stubble and says, 'I thought you would be younger than me. Raja Banthia also didn't tell me that you are older than both of us.'

He apologizes for the delay but it wasn't police work that held him up. It was more of humanitarian effort that took up his time.

'There is a large delegation of the Rashtriya Swayamsevak Sangh (RSS) in town and one of its senior members suffered a heart attack. I was busy arranging for his transport to the district hospital and sounded the air force for an evacuation by helicopter. I don't know if that will be possible now.'

Kalsi had served in the Delhi Police before he was transferred to Arunachal Pradesh. Like Banthia, Kalsi also tells me that there is no law and order problem in his town and district. He asks if I would like to visit Bum La (pronounced Boomla) which was the scene of some heavy fighting in 1962. I tell him I would love to see the place.

'But you will need a pass. I will speak to the army chaps right now.'

He calls up someone and gives my name and other details. After he finishes speaking, he tells me to collect the pass from a particular gate of an army unit in the morning. He leaves after sometime and I go for my dinner in the officers' mess and return to my room to sleep.

I wake up to a glorious sunrise and quickly get ready for breakfast. I hear helicopters buzzing and there seems to be regular flights in and out of Tawang. The trooper at the dining hall tells me the ride to Bum La and back would take at least three hours. I head for the army camp and pick up my permit. Another helicopter is landing nearby and the sound is deafening.

At the first check point shortly after a gigantic statue of Buddha, a soldier scrutinizes my pass and tells me that Bum La is 31 km away.

'The first 21 km is blacktop. The last 10 km are quite bad and rocky,' he tells me as he hands back the pass after stamping it.

The road goes uphill in a sharp gradient and Tawang is soon much below me. The Buddha statue painted in golden colour sparkles in the bright sun. A few kilometres later I run into another army check point and stop. I notice that the soldiers are from the Maratha Light Infantry. As I dismount, one of them tells me something that I don't understand. I suspect that he is speaking to me in Tamil and I tell him in Hindi that I don't speak or understand that language.

'Your motorcycle has a Tamil Nadu number plate and so I thought you are from that state.'

Another soldier notes down my pass details and lets me go. The road is narrow but it remains a blacktop which makes riding a pleasure. As the elevation increases, I run into yaks grazing in the sloping grassland. There are some abandoned bunkers, now overgrown with grass and a few yaks stand on top of them and graze. I stop and dismount and get close to a yak to take pictures. The shiny black animal with pointed horns looks up briefly and then concentrates on eating the grass.

I take a curve uphill and see that an entire slope is filled up with Buddhist prayer flags. A little later I come across a small lake. As far as Himalayan lakes go, this one is pretty small. But the P Tso lake is simply spectacular to look at from any angle. Under an azure sky the lake looks a stunning shade of blue. A few water birds frolic at one end of it. I resist the temptation of taking a dirt road to the lake because my focus is on Bum La.

I reach a part of the road which has just been finished. But the ride on the spanking new road ends abruptly and it suddenly looks like it has been sliced off. The bad road that the soldier at the first check point warned me about, stares at me. It is simply too rocky. I ride slowly to control the motorcycle which wobbles on the uneven surface. I must have travelled about two km when three SUVs filled with tourists overtake me in quick succession. And the last one cuts short my trip to Bum La.

As the last SUV rumbles past me, a small stone flies from of one of its left tyres and hits the calf of my right leg. The impact triggers an excruciating pain. I stop the bike and dismount and massage the calf. The right ankle is still sore from the fall of the previous day but the latest hit is much more painful. I stop the bike and take out an analgesic gel from my bag and apply it on the affected part which has swollen and turned bluish. I hobble around for a while just to make sure that I will be able to walk. Given the condition of my leg and the road, I decide against proceeding further. It is a pain to turn the motorcycle back on that road but I manage to do it and start riding back to the guest house. I stop midway to rest my leg for some more time and reach the guest house at 11.30 am.

The trooper who had served me breakfast is surprised to see me. 'You are back early. I was expecting you about two hours later,' he tells me.

I tell him of my misfortune which forced an early return and ask him to serve me lunch at noon. I limp to my room and pop a painkiller and sit in front of the blower. The pain lessens a lot after about half an hour but I still can't walk without a limp. After lunch, I go out to look for senior citizens who could tell me about their life under Chinese occupation in 1962. I have no idea where to begin my search so I stop at Tawang's Old Market and ask a few shopkeepers if they know anybody who was in the town in 1962. Five shopkeepers say they have no idea about such people.

I get lucky at the sixth shop. Jambey Tenzing runs a small shop selling a range of goods from sunglasses to wallets and nail clippers and gift items and small electronic stuff.

'Oh, you should have come in the morning. A few of the veterans show up in the square and spend a couple of hours together,' Jambey tells me.

His mother, who is 87, also has a lot of memories of the events of 1962, but his house is some distance away and he can't take me there. Besides, his mother is not in the best of health.

'Why don't you come back tomorrow morning and catch them here?'

'I am leaving in the morning for Bomdila so that won't be possible.'

'Well, there is someone you can still meet. His name is Theckchin and he lives near the Tawang monastery which is about five kilometres away from here.'

Jambey gives me the directions and then to make sure that I don't get lost, he also draws a map. He can't remember the name of a hotel where I have to stop and take a staircase down to Theckchin's house.

'Let's go to this shop nearby. I will find out the name of the hotel.'

He locks his shop and we walk to a large shop selling electronic goods and household appliances. He addresses the elderly shop owner as Guruji and asks the name of the hotel. Unfortunately, Guruji also cannot remember it. I tell Jambey not to worry and that his map would help me find Theckchin.

I return to the guest house to get on the motorcycle and ride away. But despite Jambey's detailed map, I overshoot slightly and park outside the monastery. I start walking downhill and stop a young man coming from the opposite direction and ask him if he knows Theckchin.

'Yes. But you have crossed his place.'

He points to a multi-storey building and tells me that it is a hotel and I should take the stairs down on the opposite side of that building. 'Ask anyone there and they will show you the way.'

I retrace my steps and start panting. I sit on a small pillar to catch my breath and then ride back to the hotel and park in front of it. I walk down a steep flight of stairs and see a man breaking stones on the roof of a house that is under construction. I ask aloud if he knows Theckchin's place but he doesn't hear me and continues to hammer the stones. But someone else hears my query.

A man in his early 40s waves at me. 'I know his place. Come this way,' he says and starts going down the stairs. I despair at climbing down because I will have to climb up as well on the way back. He tells me his name is Lobsang Sonam and Theckchin is his maternal uncle.

Soon, we reach Theckchin's house. A beautiful porch with flowers and a small kitchen garden that overlooks the lower part of Tawang complete a lovely picture. Theckchin is inside the house wearing an Army woollen shirt and track pants and sneakers. He comes out to the porch and shakes my hand. His grip is firm and that of a man who exudes confidence. The hand is hard and rough, suggesting that he is still involved in manual labour. He asks me to sit and I pull a plastic chair in the shade while he prefers to sit in the sun.

The sun is on his weather beaten face and he squints as he asks, 'So what it is that you wanted to see me about?'

'I want to know what it was like when the Chinese moved into Tawang in 1962,' I tell him.

He raises his eyebrows and shakes his head.

'That was so many years ago. I was 15 when the Chinese overran Tawang. There wasn't much fighting in Tawang. Our soldiers had been killed in Bum La and along the road to Tawang. We had yaks and horses which we used as pack animals. When the Chinese settled here they hired our animals for their use. They paid us the hire charges.'

'But they were an occupation army. And how did they behave with the locals?'

'They did not really bother the locals because they wanted to be seen as one of us. They wanted us to believe that they were same as us. They helped farmers with the winter harvest and organized cultural functions in different villages to win over the local population. But it simply didn't happen. Much of Tawang's population had already left in the initial stages of the war and after the Chinese occupation almost the whole population had moved away. It was a ghost town.'

'And, you stayed put through the length of the occupation?'

'No. I don't remember how long we stayed. But we later moved to Udalguri in Assam. We returned three months later after the Chinese had left.'

Theckchin went on to join the Special Frontier Force which was set up towards the end the Sino-India conflict. Its main goal was to conduct covert operations behind Chinese lines in the event of another war but it saw action elsewhere.

'I fought in the Bangladesh war and I am so proud of it. It was such a different terrain. Paddy fields, marshes, rivers, and small hills. It was nothing like the landscape here. '

But he is sore at the army.

'I got nothing when I retired in 1985. No pension.'

Perhaps he doesn't know that the Special Frontier Force works under the Indian intelligence agency, Research and Analysis Wing, and not the Defence Ministry.

He lives off his land. His son is a policeman who stays separately. Two of his married daughters also live in Tawang.

We finish our chat and I head back. Lobsang tells me to accompany him to the monastery where I could meet other veterans. I trudge along and gasp my way up the stairs. 'Stop smoking,' I tell myself as I make a pit stop on the stairs. Lobsang stands near me and tells me that he too was a soldier before he left the army to set up his tailoring shop. We finally reach the road and walk to the monastery.

On a huge ground outside the monastery, a group of young monks are dancing—a slow rhythmic dance to the sound of cymbals. A handful of locals are sitting on the edge of the ground watching the dance. Suddenly, the tranquil atmosphere is shattered by the sound of trumpets. I turn around and see that three senior monks sitting on chairs are blowing the trumpets that are so long that their ends rest on the ground. Lobsang tells me that the monks are practising for an upcoming festival in February.

We walk towards a small group of senior citizens sitting under a tree. Lobsang introduces me to Dorjee Urup who is almost 80. He is sitting silently counting prayer beads. Lobsang tells him that I want to talk to him. I sit beside him on the ground and learn that Urup retired from the Subsidiary Intelligence Bureau (SIB), which he joined shortly after the Sino-India War.

'It was such a long time ago. The Chinese stayed in Tawang for 49 days. They helped local villagers harvest the crops. Some locals carried out barter trade with them, mostly salt and butter. They had taken a lot of POWs, who were released about two months after the end of hostilities,' he tells me and falls silent and resumes counting his beads.

The man sitting next to him is Phuge. He is 78 and a little hard of hearing. He was a porter in 1962 and worked for some time for the Chinese before his entire family left for Udalguri in Assam.

'They tried to win us over. But our hearts did not agree. I guess we were lucky that they did not kill civilians although they showed no mercy to our soldiers in the battles. We left for Udalguri and returned three months later on foot. Can you imagine the conditions we had to endure crossing the Sela in those days?'

After they returned, Phuge started working with the SIB. Despite the hardship of moving out of Tawang during the conflict, these senior citizens are glad that they could return home and not live as refugees in another state. We finish talking and I get up and say goodbye to the old men. Lobsang accompanies me back to my motorcycle and says, 'Have a cup of ginger tea before you go. It will keep you warm. The evening is setting in.' I oblige.

We go to a small restaurant and Lobsang orders tea. 'You don't look like you belong to Delhi,' he says. I can't make out if that is a comment or a question.

'I am from Assam. I moved to Delhi in 1990 and never really had an opportunity to return to Assam to work,' I tell him as a waiter serves us the tea.

'You know, I just can't understand something about Delhiwallas and North Indians. I mean when I was in the army, I had lots of friends from North India who were very warm and we gelled so well. But I can't make out why civilians in North India make fun of people from the Northeast. They call our kids Chinkies because of our Mongoloid features and they think we eat anything that moves, crawls or flies. That's just racism,' Lobsang gives vent to some angst.

'You are right. I think it is plain ignorance about the Northeast and superiority complex based on an erroneous and supposedly higher civilization,' I try to explain it to him.

He nods and then shakes his head. 'It has nothing to do with civilization. We are more civil in the way we behave with women. You won't hear of dowry death and rapes in Arunachal Pradesh or for that matter in most parts of the Northeast. I wish I could know what fuels their derision about us. Most of them won't be able to name the capitals of the seven Northeastern states and they think they are superior to us in every way.'

He orders two more cups of tea. I notice that the menu has a lot a of chicken items. I ask Lobsang if restaurants also sell food made of mithun's meat (Mithun is a large domestic bovine widely found in Arunachal Pradesh and a few other Northeastern states).

'No, we don't eat mithun. It is like a cow and we treat it like a mother. People in the eastern part of state eat mithun.

They eat anything,' Lobsang replies with barely concealed contempt for the population in the state's east.

He had seemed such a gentle soul until I asked the question of mithun's meat and I am at a loss to understand his disdain for those who eat the animal's meat.

I return to the guest house and park my motorcycle and walk back to the market. I take a shortcut from Tawang's stadium through a flight of stairs that leads straight to the market. Tawang is largely a garrison town and the army is visible everywhere including the Old Market. I want to thank Jambey for suggesting that I meet Theckchin. But his shop is closed. I wonder if he has gone to Guruji's shop and go there to check. He is not there either and Guruji tells me that he has gone home. I learn that the elderly shop owner's name is actually Kumar Guru but the locals call him Guruji.

'That's an unusual name in Arunachal Pradesh,' I tell him.

'I know. I wonder why my parents named me that,' he laughs.

I mention the standoff between India and China in 2017 over troop deployment in Doklam near the Bhutanese border and close to Arunachal Pradesh.

Guruji is adamant that there is no tension with China.

'Sino-India tension is only a media creation. I haven't heard of a single shot fired since 1962.'

'Well, it is not really a media creation. The army says there is tension but that things are under control,' I tell him.

He laughs. 'The army needs a reason to exist. Without the Chinese threat, more perceived than real, they won't be here.'

Guruji sounds so simplistic that he seems to have no notion of geopolitics and the deep suspicion that New Delhi harbours about Beijing's expansionist plans. I ask him about the relations between the locals and the army.

'Oh, locals have a great relationship with the army. It is a very peaceful place. Sometimes I laugh when I see a senior army officer walk around with armed bodyguards.'

I tell him it is probably protocol. But he is not convinced.

'Well, protocol can be given the go by in a place as peaceful as this. Tawang is certainly not like Kashmir or a Maoist stronghold.'

We talk of connectivity and I tell him about the signboard I saw that mentioned the proposed site of the Sela tunnel. He shakes his head.

'It is like a fairy tale. I am convinced I will not see it. Maybe, I will see it in my next birth. I have heard a lot about it but not even a rat has dug a burrow at the proposed site,' he tells me as if to emphasize how difficult it would be to build that tunnel.

A customer walks in and I leave Guruji's shop and walk back to the guest house. I start writing my notes and wonder how Theckchin and thousands of others endured those days of 1962 when it would have been colder that what it is tonight. I can't even imagine the adversities that under equipped Indian soldiers faced while fighting. Much of the Chinese attacks were launched early morning or late afternoon across different fronts in Arunachal Pradesh.

Kalsi shows up at 7:45 pm. 'I was held up with some work. That RSS man I told you about last night was finally evacuated mid-morning. The helicopter had attempted a landing past midnight but there was too much fog so it came back later in the morning. That man is stable now.'

I tell him about my meeting with Theckchin and the other veterans.

'The locals are very patriotic. You should see Tawang on Independence Day. There are so many cultural functions including dances depicting different cultures. Very few people leave the function midway.'

I also tell him about the veterans' assertions that the Chinese could never win them over.

'I understand that very well. It comes down to kinship, like I felt with the Pakistani boys in school in Dubai instead of boys from South India. I could relate to the Pakistani boys because they were all Punjabis and the language and culture was common. The Chinese miscalculated. They were simply not the same as Arunachalis.'

I mention Guruji and his claim of absolute peace in Arunachal Pradesh and that there is no military threat from China.

'Who knows? He may be right. China already has such a huge leverage over India as far as balance of trade is concerned that it doesn't really need to start a war and spend money on it. But 1962 will always be a major reason why we will continue to have a huge army deployment in this area,' Kalsi reasons.

A trooper comes to announce that dinner has been served in the dining hall. Kalsi gets up and I walk him to his vehicle and then go and eat my dinner. I fall asleep quickly and get ready in the morning and leave after breakfast. I refuel at Jang and reach Jaswantgarh almost two hours after leaving Tawang and stop at the memorial to fallen soldiers.

At this memorial, the greatest hero is Jaswant Singh Rawat who killed several Chinese soldiers in close quarter combat before he was shot and beheaded. But the Chinese later returned his head. He was posthumously awarded the Mahavir Chakra, India's second highest military decoration. Jaswant Singh Rawat was only 22.

Many Chinese soldiers were also killed in the battle of Nuranang which was later renamed Jaswantgarh in honour of Jaswant Singh Rawat. They are buried in a small graveyard but there are no markings or headstones. A few abandoned bunkers still dot the mountain slope. A few soldiers are preparing for a ceremony to unveil a plaque and a red carpet has been laid leading up to the concrete block where the plaque is embedded near a bunker. Some of the troopers lay a camouflage net over the bunker which gives an impression that it is an active one. I ask one of the soldiers about the time of the function.

'It's at 11 o'clock. The Brigadier is coming to unveil it. If you stay for a while you can see the function.'

I check the time. It is 10:45 am and I decide to wait and check out the cemetery. I climb up a flight of stairs that leads to a hall. There are statues of two dragons on either side of the staircase at its base and statues of four carnivores on pillars on either side of the stairs. I can't make out what big cat the white and green statues represent. The hall's roof is like that of a pagoda. Inside, there is a headstone of white marble in honour of Jaswant Singh and a small bust of the soldier on top of it.

On the walls hang the photographs of other soldiers killed in the battle of Nuranang. There is also a tree inside the hall which goes through the roof. The reason why it wasn't chopped when making the hall is that the Chinese left Jaswant Singh's head on it.

I walk out and head for one of the bunkers made of stone blocks. I walk down a short flight of stairs and discover that it is replica of a command post of 1962. There are a few rooms including one with a telephone of that era and a radio set. Other rooms seem to be for resting and storing ammunition. And, of course, there are the openings for mounting machine guns.

I come out of it and go to the next bunker which is different. It is smaller and has a different layout. There is a large table and benches on two sides along its length. There are dozen cups and plates and glasses neatly arranged on the table as if soldiers are ready to be served. Another room seems to be the living quarters for soldiers on rest. There are two mandatory gun posts also in the bunker. The feeling inside the bunker is eerie. I wonder what it would have been like during the thick of battle in 1962.

The foliage has claimed most of the other bunkers in Jaswantgarh. Grass and moss grow on the walls and roofs of many of them. I head for a third bunker but when I reach it I realize that I won't be able to go inside. There is a huge yak sitting at the entrance, chewing its cud. Two other yaks standing nearby look menacingly and I can't make out if they are wild or domesticated. I retreat and take their photographs from a safe distance. Jaswantgarh seems such a peaceful, desolate place that it is hard to imagine it was the scene of a ferocious battle.

It is already 11:15 am and the Brigadier hasn't yet arrived. I walk out of the memorial and cross the road to an army cafeteria where a few mini buses carrying tourists have stopped. I buy a snack and the trooper at the counter tells me the tea is free. Many tourists stand in a circle around a huge flask to pour themselves cups of tea.

A Military Police personnel comes and stands on the road near the entrance of the memorial. I walk up to him and ask him if the Brigadier is about to arrive.

'No. I was told he is arriving at noon,' he says.

I can't afford to wait any longer and resume my ride. Road builders have dumped more stones on the stretch between Jaswantgarh and Sela in the last two days. A few loops ahead of Sela, a group of soldiers flag down vehicles going up. I stop behind three buses and dismount and walk to the soldiers to ask the reason for the stoppage.

'There are two big trucks headed downhill. It will be over in ten minutes.'

I wait. A little later an army SUV acting as a pilot vehicle heads towards our way. Shortly after it passes, the flatbed trucks come into view. Lumbering behemoths, the trucks are carrying a few missiles. I guess the drivers of these trucks are the best in the business given that there are so many hairpin bends along the way. A smaller truck brings up the tail of the short convoy. We start on our way as soon as the last truck crosses us.

By the time I reach the base of Sela Pass, I find that much of the Sela Lake has frozen. But the ice is not yet hard and is still transparent. I park by the road and walk through a dirt track to the lake to take photographs. Buddhist prayer flags tied at different angles across the lake flutter in the cold wind. One end of the shore has pillars and railings and there are two other motorcyclists taking photographs. One of them is from Uttar Pradesh and the other from Odisha. They are headed for Tawang. We exchange notes, take selfies, and then head in opposite directions.

I roll downhill for half an hour before stopping for lunch at another army canteen. Two mini buses are parked by the roadside and I see a group of tourists coming out of the canteen and heading for the buses. One of the tourists, who is in his 50s, comes straight to me and starts speaking in Tamil. I take off my helmet and tell him with a smile that I don't speak the language. I know he has been foxed by the motorcycle's number plate.

'The motorcycle is from Tamil Nadu. I am from Assam but I have settled in Delhi,' I tell him.

'I guess it must be very challenging to be on an expedition like this through such roads.' I am not sure if that is a statement or a question.

'Yes, it does get tiring sometimes on bad roads but since I love long distance motorcycling, I am not particularly worried. I know these roads aren't the best in the country.'

'But still, it is quite a job to be riding for so long,' the tourist tells me.

'You can do it too if you set your heart on it.'

But he doesn't buy it. 'Not for me. I am not cut out for that.'

The driver honks and the man signals him to wait. He gives me his visiting card and then heads for the bus. The name on the card says S Natarajan, a Chartered Accountant from Salem.

The canteen has run out of rice, chapatis, and dal so I settle for idlis. It is not my favourite dish but I am not fussy about food when I am travelling. The road snakes endlessly as I ride towards Dirang. Dusk falls shortly after I cross Dirang. But since much of the road between Dirang and Bomdila is good, I ride without worrying. I finally reach Bomdila at 5:30 pm and ride straight to the circuit house.

Tenzing is in the kitchen. He tells me that the new building is completely booked and I will have to stay in the old building. The room is even larger than the one in the new building where I had stayed earlier. There is a sofa set and even an adjoining dressing room. The sofa has seen better days and so has the bathroom where the fittings seem to be antique. I rest for some time and then go to the dining hall in the new building for dinner.

I wake up early to a bright sunny morning and get ready to move. I walk into the kitchen and ask Tenzing for breakfast and tea. A man standing next to Tenzing comes forward, smiles and extends his hand and introduces himself.

'I am Kesang Wangda. I am a Circle Officer in the Deputy Commissioner's office. I saw you the other day and wanted to speak to you.'

'Have you come to meet a guest?' I ask.

'No. We had to report to office early and I came over here for breakfast.'

Kesang is in his late 30s. Tenzing serves breakfast and Kesang sits next to me. He tells me that I should visit a nearby war memorial. I ask him about people whose descendants have been given compensation for land that the army had acquired in 1962.

'You can meet Tsewang Norbu in Pedung village just out of the town. He can tell you a lot of stories about 1962 and possibly knows some of those who have been paid compensation. I personally don't know anyone who has received compensation.'

We finish our breakfast and go out to the parking and drink tea standing in the sun. Kesang gives me the directions to the war memorial and Pedung village. I head for the war memorial first which is nearer. But it is closed for the day because some senior army officer is visiting it. I ride back to the circuit house, load my luggage and start for Pedung. The road becomes narrow as soon as I exit Bomdila's main market. Pedung is four kilometres away and I discover that Norbu is quite well known in the village which is a sprawling one in a valley. I am still on a higher elevation.

A woman points out Norbu's house and tells me that I can either ride or trek down. I choose to ride but the last kilometre to Norbu's house is a nightmare through a narrow dirt track with rocks, slush, and sand. I finally reach his place but his wife tells me that he has gone out of town and will be back only in the evening. I get stuck on the way back to Bomdila because a pick-up truck has broken down on the dirt track and is blocking the way. A few villagers push it to a side and I manage to get out but the exercise to find Norbu's house has already cost me an hour.

I don't want to spend more time in Bomdila and I head out for Guwahati, stopping briefly only to fill fuel in the only petrol station of the town. It is almost 10 am when I exit Bomdila. I decide to take the road via Rupa instead of returning through Nameri simply to avoid the dangerous road up to Bhalukpong. Traffic is sparse and it is a joy to ride along the twisting road.

I cross a bridge and reach Rupa and stop in the market to ask a shopkeeper if he knew anybody who has received compensation for land. He shakes his head. My luck improves soon when I ask a restaurant owner the same question. The woman tells me to head for the monastery.

'You will find a few such families there.'

The road to the monastery goes gently uphill for about a kilometre and I park outside the monastery. As I dismount I see a small procession with some people dressed in ceremonial dresses and headgear heading the opposite way. They are chanting as they walk. By the time I take off my helmet, the group has disappeared into various lanes. I walk towards a wooden house on stilts where a group of young people are sitting on the balcony. Three young girls dressed in tribal attire are sitting on a bench and a stocky man is eating rice and curry sitting on the stairs. I tell him who I am looking for.

'Wait here,' he says and goes inside. He comes out after some time and tells me to go inside but doesn't say anything if any of the landowners is present inside. I walk through a low door into a large, oblong room filled with the aroma of food. There are a dozen people inside. A young man is sitting in front of a stove fired by wood. There is a large wok on the stove and he is stirring some meat in it. In one corner of the room, there is another firewood stove with a large saucepan on it. Two other women are standing by a gas stove with two burners cooking something else. An elderly man is pounding dried red chilies in a wooden grinder made of a log.

The room is smoky and the sunlight streaming in through numerous holes on the wooden roof and one of the walls creates an eerie scene at midday. At one end of the room the skull of a yak is nailed to the wall. The skull must have been put up ages ago because it has been completely blackened by smoke. A young man sitting under skull is making some kind of a headgear.

The man cooking the meat sees me and gets up and comes towards me. I introduce myself and tell him what I am looking for. He asks me to sit on a sofa alongside a wall. His name is Rinchin Khandu Mosidi.

'Let me see if I can help. Today is the third day of a festival and everyone is out. I will try to contact one of the men you are looking for,' Rinchin tells me.

I learn that Khik Saba is a winter harvest festival of the local Buddhist community. Rinchin makes a call but there is no response. 'I will try again after some time,' he says and goes back to cooking. He stirs the meat, adds some onions and chilies before he comes back to sit with me.

He tells me that they belong to the Sherdukpen tribe and according to clan hierarchy, only the upper clans get to host Khik Saba feasts.

'This is a clan house and this year our family is hosting today's feast. Villagers will come here and eat and in the evening we take the food to the monastery for a community meal after the festivities. Why don't you stay the night? You can see the functions.'

I tell him I am hard pressed for time and can't stay. His sister, a government officer in Tezu, serves me tea. Rinchin tells me that his brother-in-law is the district police chief in Tezu. Rinchin had been to college in Delhi and had recently found a government job in Rupa.

'When I was in college I couldn't take part in all these functions. This time I want to be completely involved. We need to preserve these cultural festivals for future generations.'

He doesn't remember when the clan house was built but it was generations ago. 'Not a single nail has been used in this house, only wooden pegs.'

The floor is fine but the roof and one of the walls, like I mentioned earlier, has sprung quite a few holes. The man pounding the dried red chilies is Rinchin's uncle. Rinchin makes the call again and this time he connects.

'The man will come. He is from the village council and he can tell you about the land compensation. A former Member of Parliament, Rinchin Khandu Khirme, is also coming. Would you like some rice beer? It is not as strong as the bottled stuff.'

'I will be riding for the whole day today. But I can have a sip for its novelty,' I tell him.

His sister gives me a cup of the brew. The colour is light grey and it smells like normal beer and tastes almost similar.

'How much do the locals drink?' I ask.

'Quite a lot. Some of them can drink seven or eight large glasses in one sitting.'

I guess the cold weather slows down the intoxication.

The former MP arrives with two other men and sit cross-legged on a carpet near the wall opposite to the sofa where I am sitting. Rinchin offers the beer in ceremonial cups to all three. Khirme chats with Rinchin and his uncle before Rinchin introduces me to him.

The former lawmaker takes a good look at me as if he is sizing me up and then says, 'You should have undertaken this journey at least 25 years ago.'

I wonder if my grey stubble and receding hairline prompted that remark but I tell him that I believe in the saying 'better late than never'.

'Yes, I can't fault you for that,' he agrees and wishes me luck. He has to visit a few other people and leaves. A little later, the man I want to talk to, Netan Dorjee Thongdok, walks in. He is dressed in casual wear with a traditional scarf draped over his jacket. He is the secretary of the Tukpen village council and a recipient of the compensation for the land the army had taken from his father. Netan is in his 40s.

I ask him about the people who have been paid monstrous sums of money, in some cases over five crore rupees in compensation.

'It is not exactly like that. The money is actually to be shared among various land owners. The cheque was made out in the name of the largest land owner. It has to be deposited with the village council which decides how much each of the land owners will get.'

It sounds a little complicated to me. 'Doesn't it create resentment? Particularly for the man in whose name the cheque has been issued?'

'No, it doesn't. There are minor differences sometimes. In any case it is no longer possible to determine the exact size of land someone owned in 1962. And, most of the original owners have died. The descendants are the ones who have got the compensation.'

Rupa also has a heavy military presence across a river that separates the village from the cantonment area.

'The money took such a long time to come. And, it will take some more time before it is actually disbursed,' Netan tells me.

'Is there any danger of the recipients being defrauded by conmen or by outsiders?' I ask.

'No chance of it,' Netan answers. 'The council keeps a strict vigil and in any case this is a close knit society so no fraudster can hope to lure even one individual.'

As we talk, more locals walk in for lunch. Rinchin and his sister serve the guests from large utensils containing rice, vegetables, dal, chicken, and pork.

'Why don't you take lunch as well?' Rinchin asks me. I tell him that I am not hungry. Rinchin tells me that in earlier times, the harvest festival feasts were made mostly of the crop harvested like rice and vegetables. But over the years, meat has become an integral part of Khik Saba.

Netan and I exchange phone numbers and I get up to leave. Rinchin sees me off at the door and Netan walks with me towards the motorcycle. He insists that I visit the monastery before I leave. We go to the first floor of the monastery which is a museum of sorts with artifacts and weapons. It also is a storeroom with a row of masks that are used in plays during festivals.

I leave Rupa at 12:30 pm. The road is certainly much better than the Bomdila-Bhalukpong road. Much of the road is downhill and after about ten minutes there is virtually no sign of civilization. I ride through a thick forest with the mountains one side and a deep drop on the other and sometimes through flat stretches with a river on my left.

An hour into the ride I begin to feel hungry but there is no place to stop. A few settlements that I cross have no shops. The loneliness of long distance motorcycling begins to set in and I make random stops to eat from my emergency ration of chocolates and biscuits. By 2 pm, I am in another hamlet with three small eateries and a fuel station. I stop and head for the nearest eatery and ask for a plate of noodles. The young woman at the shop puts the noodles on the stove and makes baby talk with her toddler in a pram.

By the time she serves me, her husband returns. He asks me where I am headed.

'You should have crossed this stretch much earlier. You still have such a long way to go and there is no way you can ride fast on this mountain road,' he tells me. And then almost as an afterthought he adds, 'Don't stop in the middle of the jungle.'

'Because of wild animals?' I ask.

'Not as much because of wild animals as because of dacoits. A few months ago dacoits waylaid two pickup trucks carrying tomatoes, robbed the drivers, and killed them. That happened on the road on Assam's side of the border. You won't find robbers in Arunachal.'

His name is also Netan.

'I will be careful,' I tell him. I am still a long way from home and the lunch break has cost me 30 minutes. Netan must have meant well when he cautioned me so I make less stops but the road still seems endless. There is virtually no traffic and as I move through the mountains, the muffled sound of my motorcycle's exhaust is the only noise I can hear.

Somewhere along the way the road begins to climb again. From the highest point I can see the plains of Assam and a winding road going downhill that leads to them. The lonely road begins to get disconcerting. There is still an hour left for sunset but the mountains cast deep shadows which usher in dusk much earlier.

There are no milestones and I can't make how far I am from Orang in Assam. I run into a family of road builders standing outside their bamboo and thatch house in the middle of nowhere and stop to ask them. The head of the family tells me I am still 70 km away. I groan inside my helmet. Seventy kilometres in the mountains would mean more than two hours and then another four hours to Guwahati. I calculate that I won't be home before 9 pm.

Just before sunset I see a restaurant in the middle of the jungle and stop for tea. A young man sitting on a bench is darning a sock. He asks me where I am going.

'I am Neema Tamang from Bhalukpong,' he introduces himself. 'We run this hotel and we have taken it on lease.'

He also tells me that I am running a risk by riding late in the day. 'How far is Orang?' I ask him.

'You don't have to go to Orang to reach Guwahati. Just before you reach the police checkpost in Balamu, take the right cut and head for Bhairav Kund and then to Mangoldoi and Guwahati is only 70 km away. It will save you a lot of time.'

I am glad I stopped at this hotel. The evening gives way to the night and it gets pitch dark. The moon is hidden behind a cloud cover. The forests come alive with the sounds of nocturnal creatures, crickets, owls, and foxes. Fortunately, the road remains good. I take a curve and catch a fox in my headlight and brake hard. The fox is momentarily nonplussed before it scoots away into the forest.

Balamu seems elusive despite being only 15 km from Neema's hotel. There are still no milestones and no signage either. I overshoot the cut that Neema had mentioned and ride into the police checkpost. A policeman tells me to backtrack and turn left. Three kilometres through a very narrow road takes me to small town called Bhairav Kund which is already shutting down at 6 pm. A new road is being laid and although a road roller has flattened the stones, it is yet to be tarred. I cross Rowta and then reach Mangoldoi and take the highway to Guwahati. By 10 pm, I am home and see that Shahwar has arrived from Delhi. The day's ride had worn me out completely. I eat dinner almost mechanically and go off to sleep.

6

Through the Length of Assam

29 November 2018

The next morning I take the motorcycle for some minor repair to a Royal Enfield service centre near our home. When I return I see that my mother is coughing and has caught a cold. It worries me, my sister, and two brothers because her immunity level has dropped drastically after years of acute asthma. She has already taken some medicine and is lying in bed and soon drifts off to sleep. Later in the day, I go to the Arunachal Pradesh Deputy Commissioner's office again for another permit to visit Tezu and Walong in the eastern part of the state.

I am a little worried about my mother's health. I won't be returning to Guwahati for a long time because after Tezu and Walong I would be travelling to Jairampur which is also in eastern Arunachal Pradesh and then cross to Nagaland, Manipur, Silchar, and Meghalaya before returning home. Shahwar has brought a new pair of saddle bags for me and I pack my clothes and supplies in them.

I plan to spend the next night in Jorhat and call up my classmate from school, Ajanto Hazarika, whom I last met in 1982. Ajanto, who is a scientist at the Tocklai Tea Research Institute in Jorhat, is delighted to hear from me. I ask him if he could book a room for me at this company's guest house. But he insists that I stay in one of the two houses he owns and part of which is vacant.

I head out for Jorhat in the morning and ride through the same road till Koliabor from where I had turned left for Tezpur when I was heading for Bomdila. This time I head straight on the highway that is now without a divider and after some time I enter the Kaziranga National Park. Signage warns motorists that it is an animal corridor and that there is a heavy fine for over speeding. I ease the throttle to get under the speed limit but local drivers do not seem bothered about the warning and they thunder past me. Deeper into Kaziranga I see that park's flagship animal, the one-horned rhino in a catchment area eating water hyacinth about 500 yards off the highway. A little later I see an off-duty park elephant ambling along the highway and I stop to ask the mahout its name.

'Urvashi,' he says.

Urvashi isn't shy. She suddenly changes direction from the edge of the road to the middle of the highway and forces a mini truck to stop. She forces her trunk though the window of the driver's cabin and then withdraws after the driver satisfies her with a few oranges.

Barely two kilometres later, there is an even more interesting sight. Three other elephants are coming out of the park area and climb on the road and I stop to take their photographs. On the other side of the road, three army trucks are parked and the soldiers who are headed for Guwahati have just finished their lunch. There is a large saucepan with a lot of rice left in it. The first elephant ignores the truck and moves past them but the other two stop between two of the three trucks and start taking out the rice from the saucepan with their trunks. Some of the soldiers decide to help and make large balls of the rice and hold them in their hands. A few other soldiers take out their phone and start clicking selfies.

'Ganesh has come. Ganesh has come,' says one soldier in deference to the elephant-headed Hindu god by that name. I take a few photographs of the soldiers feeding the elephants. The mahouts finally prod the jumbos and they move on and the soldiers start loading the utensils into one of the trucks.

I move on and cross a few small towns. The road begins to wear off and in some places there are large potholes which can be dangerous for two-wheeler riders. At 2 pm I stop at a sprawling restaurant at Numaligarh where Assam's fourth refinery went into production in 1999. The dining area is expansive and the tables seem larger than normal four-seaters. I ask for rice and fish curry. A waiter arrives after some time with the food and I notice that the piece of *rohu* fish is a very large one.

'Where do you get the fish from?' I ask the waiter.

'From our fisheries. We don't buy fish,' he tells me as he points to two large rectangular ponds at the rear of the restaurant.

He also serves dal and mixed vegetables and tells me that they come with the dish. And the cook has done a good job. Ajanto calls and wants to know my location.

'I am eating lunch at Numaligarh,' I tell him.

'You will take a little more than an hour to reach Jorhat. Give me a call when you are inside the town and I will guide you in.'

I overeat and feel lethargic after I finish my meal and don't feel like riding immediately. I spend some time strolling in the parking lot before I get on the motorcycle at 2:30 pm. A little over half an hour later I cross the town of Dergaon and shortly after 4 pm I am on the outskirts of Jorhat. I stop to call Ajanto and on the rear view mirrors I watch the sun set. That stretch of the highway is being built again and I ride slowly before the traffic in the city slows me down further. Jorhat is largely a tea town and it still seems as laidback as I last saw it in the 1980s.

Ajanto is waiting on the road outside his house and we meet for the first time after 36 years. Ajanto had been shorter than me in school. Now he seems to be an inch taller. And, unlike me, he hasn't lost any hair. It is still black and I suspect he dyes them. We shake hands and hug before he leads me to the first floor of the house which is vacant. The ground floor is occupied by a couple of tenants and a caretaker. Ajanto and his family live in a new flat a short distance away.

'You must be tired after a long ride. You can freshen up and rest for some time after you have your tea. I will return at 8:30 pm and take you home for dinner.'

I doze off and wake up a little before Ajanto calls to tell me that he will be showing up in ten minutes. As a matter of routine he drops his father, a retired doctor, in the old house in the evening where he plays cards with his friends before he picks him up at 8:30 pm and heads back home for dinner.

Ajanto drives us to his new flat which is a penthouse on the sixth floor in a quieter locality. We sit in the drawing room and talk of school days, classmates, and the fun we had. His wife Edna comes to meet me before she goes back to cooking. His daughter goes to college and his son is about to finish high school.

'How do you manage to ride so long? I mean we aren't 25-year-olds anymore, and isn't it scary sometimes?' Ajanto asks.

'I had set my heart on this expedition and I didn't want to regret in my last days of not having done it. And so, here I am. It does get scary sometimes but I have taught myself not to panic. The trip has gone fine so far,' I reply.

I also tell him that I am headed for Tezu and then to Walong.

'Do you know the exact route?'

'No. But I have a fair idea and I will ask people on the way.'

'Wait. I will ask a friend of mine who has been there.'

Ajanto calls up his friend and tells him to explain to me the route and hands over the phone to me. The man on the other side asks me to write down the route which I do. It would certainly make things easier for me.

Edna serves dinner and there is both fish and chicken on the menu but I prefer the fish. Edna is an excellent cook and I eat to my heart's content. I learn that Edna will be heading for Kohima the next morning with her sister and a few friends to attend the Hornbill Festival. That festival is also on my itinerary but it is beginning to look unlikely that I will make it.

We finish dinner and Ajanto drops me back to the old house. We agree to leave at 8:15 am for the Tocklai Tea Research Institute that I want to see. I sleep well in the night. The caretaker serves me tea in the morning after which I take a bath and load the motorcycle. I eat breakfast and wait for Ajanto. He finally calls around 8:30 am to tell me that he got delayed because he had to drop his son at school and sign some papers for his exams. He finally shows up at 9:15 am and I follow him to the Tocklai Tea Research Centre, a few kilometres out of the town.

It is a sprawling complex, completely cut off from the din and bustle of the town. Ajanto introduces me to two of his colleagues and then takes me on a tour of the facility.

More than a hundred years old now, Tocklai is a fascinating place. The mother tree from which saplings were used to grow tea bushes in Tocklai for research is still alive—a substantially large version of a normal tea bush. I ask Ajanto why tea bushes are trimmed at a certain height.

'It's called plucking table. That height makes it easier for the workers to pluck the leaves and buds,' Ajanto explains.

'But if you don't trim a tea bush, it can reach up to a height of ten feet, like that one,' he says pointing to one.

This particular specimen looks like a tree with flowers which I have never seen on a tea bush. We walk towards a small factory where Ajanto gives me the lowdown of how tea is produced once the leaves reach the conveyor belt.

'This is a small factory because we are not into commercial production. Factories at major tea gardens are much larger than this.'

We exit the factory and head for the laboratory at the facility. In one of the labs, a young researcher tells me about the rows of saplings under controlled light, heat, and moisture that would be used in a few weeks in experimental plantings in the institute's own tea garden. In the middle of my conversation with the young woman, Ajanto decides to introduce me formally to her in an utterly funny way.

'Which year were you born?' he asks her.

She is taken aback and blushes a little before answering, '1986, sir.'

'We are meeting for the first time since we passed out of school in 1982. He is a journalist and is now on a motorcycle expedition of the Northeast all by himself with no backup,' Ajanto finishes his flattering introduction leaving me a little embarrassed.

A little later, we are done with the tour. Before I leave, Ajanto hands me a large packet of factory fresh tea and we take a photograph as I get on the motorcycle. It is close to noon and I know I won't make it to Tezu which is just over 300 km. I will have to stay the night at Tinsukia. On the way I have to meet Ron Duarah, a senior journalist with *The Assam Tribune* in Dibrugarh.

The road alternates between good and bad and for those who travel daily on this stretch, it must be an unpleasant experience. The rural elections are a few days away and much of the countryside is awash with flags of different political parties, posters, and buntings. More than an hour and about 50 km later, I stop at the small town of Gaurisagar for lunch. I order noodles at a restaurant and pick up a conversation with the owner. I ask him which party he thinks will win the rural elections.

'I have no idea, but the BJP might win although I wish it wouldn't.'

'Bad governance?' I ask.

'I don't know about that but only on the condition of the awful roads people shouldn't vote for the BJP. All they do is blame the Congress. Can they not just do some real work and let it do the talking? They have been polarizing voters but that's their standard practice.'

A waiter serves the noodles and I start eating.

'My brother also has a Himalayan, but I have never been on it. Do you like it?' the owner asks when I go to pay the bill.

'Yes, it rides very well and it hasn't given me any trouble so far,' I tell him.

I am still almost 100 km away from Dibrugarh. I ride fast trying to make up for the late start from Jorhat. But outside Dibrugarh, the abominable road condition slows me down once again. On a long stretch of the road along the Dibrugarh University there are gigantic potholes than can break a car's axle. By 3:30 pm, I roll into the town and head for *The Assam Tribune* office.

I wait for some time before an office assistant ushers me into Ron Duarah's room which is a large one. Ron, who is probably a little older than me, is a warm and affable person.

'So when were you in *The Sentinel*?' he asks after I tell him that I started my career with that newspaper.

'I joined in the first quarter of 1988. It was then quite a nice place to work.'

Ron had worked in several major newspapers before he joined *The Assam Tribune*.

'So what's this trip of yours all about?'

I tell him that it is my second solo trip after having done Ladakh in 2013.

'In 2013 I went on my own. This one is backed by Royal Enfield who gave me the motorcycle and Star Cement who have funded me partly and I raised the rest of the money through crowdfunding from well-wishers. I am looking for some publicity for my sponsors.'

'Okay, I will see if any of our reporters are around. Most of them have gone out to the outskirts to cover the rural elections,' he says and calls up one of his own reporters and a few others from different organizations and asks them to come to the office so that they can talk to me.

As we wait for the reporters, Ron mourns the decline of fearless journalism.

'Are we really doing our jobs? Sometimes you feel as if your hands are tied. And now we have this new fad of giving all sorts of awards to journalists. None of them are for ground-breaking journalism.'

I ask him about the Assam government. 'Is Chief Minister Sarbananda Sonowal running the government or is Himanta Biswa Sarma the de facto CM?'[1]

Sarma, who is the Finance Minister of Assam, had been with the Congress before he jumped ship to join the BJP ahead of the state elections in 2016. Since then he has helped the BJP increase its footprints in Northeast India and is widely believed to be even more powerful than the Chief Minister.

'It doesn't matter if there is a Chief Minister or Deputy Chief Minister. The RSS calls the shots. There is an RSS guy at the CM's office and only if he approves of any initiative can the government announce it.'

---

[1] Himanta Biswa Sarma would go on to become the Chief Minister of Assam in 2021.

I don't really have an idea of how powerful the RSS is but I have heard from other government servants that the presence of this outfit is all pervasive across departments.

A large map of Assam and the other Northeastern states hangs from one wall. I walk to the map and to see the route that I have to take. Ron suggests that I go to Tezu through Parshuram Kund and return to Dibrugarh through Roing.

'That way you will also be able to see India's longest road bridge over the Brahmaputra at Dhola-Sadiya. And the entire road is in very good condition.'

About half an hour later a few local reporters enter the room. We get talking and they seem genuinely interested in my trip. One asks how I managed to get leave for two months to go on an expedition.

'I was prepared to resign for this trip but luckily my office agreed. Of course, it is without pay. But it meant that I was able to chase my dream.'

Another one asks how my wife agreed to let me undertake this trip.

'I took her on a car trip to Ladakh retracing the route of my solo motorcycle expedition of 2013. So she has a fair idea of how roads are in remote places and did not panic when I told her that I was planning a ride across the Northeast.'

'Don't you get fatigued?' a younger one among them asks. 'I rode a Bullet once to Tezu on a three-day trip and my body ached badly for days.'

'I do get fatigued, particularly when the roads are bad. I also get body aches but they get over after a good night's sleep,' I tell him.

The conversation with the journalists lasts about an hour. By sunset, I leave Ron's office and head for Tinsukia, 50 km away. I exit Dibrugarh quickly. A rail track runs parallel to the road for almost the entire length of the road to Tinsukia. It is a single lane road without any streetlights. Oncoming traffic speeding down with headlights on high beam is a pain in the neck and a potential danger to a two-wheeler rider.

Shortly out of Dibrugarh the road becomes uneven with miles of patchwork repairs and I ride at a modest speed to spare myself the bumps. The road begins to deteriorate near Chabua and becomes dreadful with large craters that trigger traffic jams. Chabua is also an Air Force station and it beats me why a town with such a vital facility where some of India's latest war planes are based should put up with such abominable roads.

I rock and roll through Chabua, crawl between trucks, buses, and cars and finally leave it behind. I begin to feel hungry and start scanning the roadside for eateries. I see a signboard that says 'Family Restaurant cum Dhaba'. What on earth does that mean, I wonder and tell myself that I will stop either at a restaurant or a dhaba. But on this road that turns out to be a mirage. Every eatery is a 'Family Restaurant cum Dhaba'. I give up and stop at one such place. It is 6:30 pm and the eatery only has dinner to serve. It is too early for me to take dinner so I opt for a cup of tea.

Before leaving I ask the manager about the condition of the road ahead. 'It is fine from here. The worst got over at Chabua.' He is right.

By the time I ride into Tinsukia, I am fatigued. I check out the first hotel I see near the railway station but the price is not what I am willing to pay. I move on. Further down the road in the heart of the town, I find another hotel more pocket-friendly, haggle a little and check in. I keep my luggage in the room, freshen up, and go out for a walk. The next building is a large restaurant which calls itself 'Lions of Punjab'. I find the name quite funny and wonder if it is a literal translation of 'Sher-e-Punjab'. Restaurants by this name are quite common in North India.

Tinsukia is also a commercial hub and an industrial district and boasts of India's oldest oil refinery at Digboi while places like Margherita and Ledo are famous for open cast coal mining. It also produces a sizeable quantity of tea, oranges, and paddy.

I walk into a restaurant and order rice and fish after the waiter insists that it is local fish and not something imported from Andhra Pradesh. From the number of diners present in the restaurant it is easy to guess that it does good business.

The manager and the staff are Bengalis but they speak Assamese fluently. Tinsukia has a large Bengali speaking population. As I go to pay my bill, the middle-aged manager is talking to a younger man in Assamese.

'Tell Dilip to get me a large bottle of Old Monk rum from Arunachal Pradesh when he comes here this week. But don't tell him I have asked for it.'

'Relax, dada. I will tell him that I need it,' the young man assures the manager.

Alcohol is much cheaper in Arunachal Pradesh than in Assam so it is understandable why the manager wants a bottle from that state.

I can't help but ask the manager. 'You still drink Old Monk? People of your age normally drink whisky.'

'Old Monk doesn't give me a hangover. If I drink whisky I feel a hundred goblins dancing on my head the next morning. It's unbearable,' he tells me.

I return to my hotel and quickly drift off to sleep despite the cacophony of vehicular traffic in the front of the hotel and a rail track behind it with a couple of trains thundering through it.

7

India's East End

30 November 2018

I had set the alarm on my phone for 6 am but the horn of a locomotive wakes me up earlier. I take a bath, pack my bags again, and take the elevator down. It is just past 7 am and the hotel's restaurant hasn't yet opened.

'If you wait half an hour, you can have breakfast and go,' the man at the front desk tells me as I make the payment. I am wary of this kind of assurances so I tell him that I would stop on the way to eat. I have to travel 202 km to Tezu and after my experience between Nameri and Bomdila, I am not willing to waste time not knowing what the condition of the road is.

Traffic is sparse and I quickly exit Tinsukia only to run into a convoy of army trucks. The road is narrow and it is difficult to overtake more than one truck at a time because of inbound vehicles. I cross Makum, a small town that once had many Chinese families and tell myself to check out if any Chinese family still lives there. But that would not be on this leg of the ride. Separated by a steel barrier, the rail track remains parallel to the road. I ride patiently behind the army trucks and kill the boredom by admiring the picturesque tea gardens that dot one side of the road and sometimes both sides after the rail track changes direction. By the time I overtake the last of the trucks I am already in the next town, Doomdooma, 26 km away from Tinsukia.

At Doomdooma, the rail track again runs parallel to the road. Along the barrier of the track, small kiosks sell chicken, lamb, and pork. I cross the track at a level crossing and head for Kakopathar close to the Arunachal Pradesh border. The population thins out and the road is virtually empty. The winter harvest is on and men and women are at work in the fields where golden paddy sway in the breeze. On the horizon, the mountains of Arunachal Pradesh begin to appear. One of the peaks is snow-clad and the others appear dark blue from a distance. It is a sunny day and there are few clouds in the sky. I cross small villages through which the highway runs. Small houses with neat porches and mango and jamun trees or betel nut trees seem common.

A little later I am in Kakopathar and stop for breakfast. It is 8:30 am and I have taken a little over an hour to ride about 50 km from Tinsukia.

I order an omelette, rotis, and tea. An elderly man serves me the breakfast. I finish my food, pay the bill. 'Where have you been riding from?' he asks.

'Siliguri,' I tell him.

'That's already quite a distance. Is this your last leg?' he asks.

'No. I still have to visit a few more states,' I reply.

'Some nerve you have. But good luck,' he wishes me as I get on the motorcycle.

Less than 20 km later I stop at the Assam-Arunachal Pradesh border to show my pass to the policemen at the post called Dirak Gate. There are many Assamese people on the Arunachal side of the border but that is not surprising because much of the state which was earlier called the North East Frontier Agency (NEFA) was once a part of Assam. I ride on and cross the Arunachal University in Namsai which is the headquarters of the district by the same name. Outside the main gate of the university is a parking for two wheelers. A signage warns riders and drivers against speeding. The warning on a yellow slab of concrete reads 'Fast Want Last'. Clearly, the painter was speeding with his job.

I cross a small tea garden and then ride through a long stretch of thick forest on either side of the highway. At some places there are signs of habitation with a few huts near which little girls sit in shacks by the highway selling oranges and honey. None of them seem apprehensive of sitting near a forest. Half an hour and 15 km later I stop at Tengapani to ask for directions for the Golden Pagoda. I turn left from the highway and ride up a gentle slope and reach the parking lot of the pagoda. Even the main gate has gold paint on it.

The Golden Pagoda is built on a hillock that resembles a plateau overlooking the plains at the foothill of the Patkai mountain range. The name itself suggests that it is built in Burmese architectural design and style complete with spires. Spread over an area of 20 hectares, the Golden Pagoda complex consists of 12 sub domes with the largest dome on the main shrine. The circumambulation path is laid in concrete. Inside the shrine hall, is a bronze Buddha statue in a meditating pose.

The serenity inside the complex seems to be reinforced by huge trees. To get inside any of the shrines visitors must take off their shoes. I decide against going inside and take photographs from the circumambulation path or beyond. A few tourists are busy taking selfies inside the shrine, sitting on the steps and in front of statues outside the shrines.

I see a local man walking towards me. 'Will you be going inside the shrine?' he asks.

'No,' I reply.

'Then it is okay. I just wanted to tell you that photography inside the shrine is not allowed.'

I wonder if he came to ask me because he saw a camera in my hand. He didn't seem bothered that others were using their phones to shoot inside the shrine, but I let it pass.

Strangely, there is no monk to be seen. As I exit the complex I ask a man at a souvenir shop if there are any monks in the pagoda. 'Oh yes. But there are all out today. There are also little boys who are trainee monks who come from nearby villages to learn the scriptures.'

It is 11 am when I walk out of the Golden Pagoda and resume my ride. Traffic is very thin. An occasional SUV or two wheeler is all that can be seen. I was told to turn right at a place called Chongkham but I forget and keep riding straight. The road is good, the sky is clear, and the spectacular scenery fuels an adrenalin rush. I rev the engine harder, ride faster and wish the road never ends. I eventually slow down when I reach a crossroad and ask a dhabawala for directions for Parshuram Kund.

'You have overshot. Go back to Chongkham and take the forest road. You can go through this road also but this will be through a mountain and will slow you down. Take the mountain road to Tezu from Parshuram Kund,' the man tells me.

I turn back and race towards Chongkham, about 20 km away, to make up for lost time. Chongkham is just an outpost with a few shops and thankfully a fuel station. It is just past noon and I stop at a small eatery for tea and some snacks. The shopkeeper is an Assamese. I ask him how many of the other shopkeepers are Assamese. 'Most of them are. There are very few families of the Tai Khamti tribe. But you will find more of them along the way to Parshuram Kund. They are the dominant tribe in Namsai district,' he informs me. Parshuram Kund is still 50 km away and possibly more than a 90-minute ride.

I stop at a fuel station and tank up. The road narrows down substantially but it remains a blacktop through a plain topography. For much of the way it runs through deep forests and isolated clearings with a few wooden houses with tin roofs. An hour later, the road beings to climb and I am soon on a mountain. I see a signage announcing that the area is the Wakro Tiger Reserve—a name that I haven't heard before.

A small settlement appears after a few kilometres. I stop at a restaurant for lunch and order instant noodles. I put my camera on a table and head for the balcony to walk around to relieve a minor cramp in my right leg. In a corner of the balcony, dry fish wrapped in banana leaves and packed in slightly conical bamboo baskets about 18 inches long are on sale at Rs 600 a basket.

'What fish are these?' I ask the man who runs the restaurant. 'Local fish from the river below. Assorted varieties,' he replies. I want to know how much a packet weighs. 'They are sold by the basket not by weight. We pack a specific number of fish into each basket.'

The noodle arrives and I sit for lunch. I finish the noodles quickly and take a cup of tea to the balcony. The restaurant owner looks at the motorcycle and says he hasn't seen the model before. I tell him it is a relatively new model and will take time before it becomes more visible. I ask him about what kind of animals are there in the Wakro Tiger Reserve.

'You will get leopards, bears, foxes, deer and a large variety of birds. The tigers are deeper in the forests. You wouldn't want to get lost in this forest,' he tells me.

I had seen people walking with a machete (*dao* in local language) along the way and I ask if the locals carry the weapon to protect themselves against wild animals. 'Sometimes you can run into a leopard or a bear. So it helps to have a weapon. But it is also used to hack one's way through a forest if he or she has to go through it or chop small branches for firewood. More of a tool than a weapon,' the restaurant owner enlightens me.

That chat lasted longer than I thought. It is already 2 pm and by now I know I would reach Tezu well after sunset. Parshuram Kund is still 15 km away. The road is still in good shape but in the mountain speed remains elusive. Thirty minutes later I see an armed trooper of the Indo Tibetan Border Police (ITBP) standing on the road not far from the force's office slightly uphill. I ask him how far away Parshuram Kund is.

'You are almost there. It is just a couple of hundred metres downhill from here. If you want to go to the temple, that's uphill on your right,' he tells me.

I decide to skip the temple because I want to spend more time at Parshuram Kund which soon appears as a truly stunning sight on the Lohit river which joins the Siang downstream in Arunachal Pradesh to form the Brahmaputra near Sadiya in Assam. I stop on a bridge over the river and walk to the railing and look down. The Lohit is in its lower stretches in this part of Arunachal Pradesh but it still flows furiously with its blue water crashing against rocks and raising foam in its wake. Ron Duarah was so right in suggesting that I take this route to Tezu.

Set against towering mountains on a raging river, the kund (which means a small reservoir, but in this case it is a huge piece of rock that rises from the riverbed in the middle of the river) is truly one of nature's jaw-dropping sights. There is also a long stretch of rocky island of sorts or more likely an elevated part of an uneven riverbed that almost joins the main rock face. I wonder if the rocky island is submerged when the river swells in the monsoon.

Parshuram Kund is also the site of a minor Hindu pilgrimage. Every year at Makar Sankranti, which is observed in the middle of January across India to mark the beginning of longer days, pilgrims visit Parshuram Kund for a dip to wash away their sins. Legend has it that Parshuram, an incarnation of Hindu god Vishnu, had come to the site to wash away his sins after he had killed his mother with an axe in a test of obedience to his father. According to one version of the legend, the axe got attached to his hand even after his mother was restored back to life on a boon he had asked his father. He eventually reached the Lohit river and as soon as he dipped his hands into the water, the axe detached from his hand, and that became symbolic of washing away sins. For the pilgrims who take that dip in January, it must be an act of bravery given how cold the water is at that time.

The river flows west under the bridge. The sun has begun to wane and on this side of the bridge the water appears orange in the sun's reflection. I spend about 45 minutes at Parshuram Kund taking photographs and simply admiring its grandeur and I wish I had reached earlier. It is now 3:30 pm and the sun would be setting soon. Tezu is still 50 km away which means at least another two hours' ride because most of it will be through a mountain.

I start the ride again for Tezu. As I exit the bridge, the road takes a sharp right turn uphill. I hear the horn of a vehicle heading downhill and slow down on the narrow road. A dumper truck soon appears at a curve kicking up a huge cloud of dust as it passes me. For about a couple of kilometres the road is terrible and the ride becomes worse when I have to make way for the trucks which barrel down from uphill and leave me with another coat of dust. The tarmac finally appears and it seems to have been newly laid. But the road remains narrow, just enough for two small cars to pass each other. I can't understand why the government can't make a wider road at the first attempt and save money. It is quite likely that this stretch of the road will have to be widened in the not-so-distant future which will entail another huge investment.

But I soon put my grouse against the government on the backburner after a bend in the road reveals a heavenly sunset over the Lohit river basin. I take a few photographs before the sun sinks into the horizon leaving a reddish sky with an orange tinge in its wake.

It gets dark soon and I begin to feel that familiar discomfort of riding in the mountains in the evening mainly because it slows me down further, particularly if I am riding uphill like now. The road stays good for much of the way till a fork at a hamlet called Tohangam with signage showing directions to Tezu and Hayuliang. There are three dhabas at the junction and I stop in front of one and head inside. It is 5:30 pm but feels like 8 pm. I ask for a cup of tea and rest for half an hour. Two other young men are eating rice with chicken curry. It feels a little strange to see somebody eating dinner at 5.30 pm but I remind myself that in a place where daybreak is around 4 am, dinner after 90 minutes of sunset is probably normal. One of the two men also orders a peg of whisky. I had no idea that dhabas in this part of Arunachal Pradesh sell alcohol so openly.

The road to Tezu is now mostly downhill and I take some comfort in it. But that feeling of comfort is soon wiped out after I run into a stretch where the road had caved in and road builders had been trying to patch it up. Part of that stretch is rocky and waterlogged. The night is pitch dark and I send up a silent prayer that nothing should go wrong with the motorcycle now. The road curves frequently and I am unable to shift beyond the third gear. The mountain stretch ends in about 45 excruciating minutes and I hit the plains again.

A road sign tells me that Tezu is 15 km away but suddenly, even that distance seems too far. I am simply too tired and stop under a dim street light on the highway just to get off the motorcycle and stretch my legs. My thighs ache and my back hurts badly. I walk around a bit while suspecting that I must be looking like a ghost on a highway with no traffic. The silence of the night is broken only by the sound of crickets and the hoots of owls. I long for a bed to lie down and tell myself that unless I reach the circuit house in Tezu I might as well forget a bed. I force myself to ride on. For some time there is no traffic from the opposite side before I see two uneven specks of light moving towards me. Only when we get nearer each other I see two cyclists using their mobile phone flashlights to illuminate the road as they pedal along.

I eventually reach Tezu at 7:30 pm and ride into the circuit house where Rinchin Khandu Mosibi's sister, SW Mosibi, had booked a room for me. I walk into the old-fashioned building with sloping tin roofs and find two men sitting in the lounge.

'Where can I find the caretaker?' I ask them.

'He is in the kitchen,' one of them tells me pointing towards a door.

The caretaker, Subhash Debnath, a man in his mid-40s, is chopping vegetables on a large table in the kitchen. 'I have a booking,' I tell him. He stops chopping the vegetables and looks up the register.

'Sabir Hussain? Your room is this way. Please come,' he tells me.

Subhash opens the door and we step into a large room with two beds, a large almirah, a dressing table, and a wooden clothesline. The bathroom is a huge one, a size you won't find in a hotel. The setting takes me back to my childhood when we sometimes stayed in these kind of sprawling circuit houses during our travels. I am so glad this particular circuit house still exists.

I go out into the porch to get my luggage and discover that I can't take off the saddle bags because a strap of the left bag has gotten into the hub of the rear wheel. I return to the kitchen and borrow a knife from Subhash and cut the strap and carry the luggage to the room. I lie down on the bed and drift off to sleep with my shoes on before a knock on the door wakes me up. Subhash wants to know if he can serve dinner in half an hour and I nod in approval. I head for the bathroom and discover that the geyser connection is not quite all right. There is no water when I open the only tap for hot water. I use the cold water to wash my face and decide to tell the caretaker about the hot water tap at dinner.

Another guest is already at the dining table when I go for dinner. There is rice, ḍal, mixed vegetable, and fish laid out.

Subhash is a good cook and I eat well. The other man at the table asks me where I have come from and so I tell him about my journey. He tells me he is from the government's health department and has come from the capital Itanagar for an inspection of some state-run health facilities in Tezu.

'You can surely do with some more hospitals in the state. So many people have to travel to different places in Assam for treatment even now,' I tell him.

'We are trying. We are setting up medical colleges and hopefully in a few years our people won't have to travel out of the state for treatment,' he assures me.

Arunachal Pradesh's first medical college, the Tomo Riba Institute of Health and Medical Sciences, began its academic session a few months earlier in July and it will be some years before the state produces its own doctors.

He asks me about the trip, the places I have been to and where I would be going from Tezu. 'I am heading for Walong day after tomorrow,' I tell him.

He raises his eyebrows and says, 'Careful about what you wish for.'

'Why?'

'Bad roads and no roads.'

I think of Royal Enfield's tagline for the Himalayan motorcycle—Built For All Roads. Built For No Roads. Strangely, I am thankful that he warned me about the road conditions. It was better than being caught without notice. I focus on the excellent dinner and tell Subhash that the fish is very tasty. 'One of the joys of living in Arunachal Pradesh is that fresh fish is always available,' he says.

We finish dinner and head to our rooms. I have to cross the lounge to reach mine and I see four men walk in and sit on the sofas. A couple of them are moaning about the bumpy ride they have had. I learn they are carrying out a survey for a rail track that would link Parshuram Kund to Tezu and Pasighat.

I want to talk more but the men are too tired and I tell myself that I will try to catch one of them the next day.

I sleep like a log and wake up at 7 am. Subhash is already in the kitchen and gives me a cup of tea. I ask him how long he has been in Tezu. 'Two years now. I was earlier working in Hawai and Walong for 14 years.'

I learn that he is from Nagaon district in Assam. He is a Bengali but speaks fluent Assamese. He is glad that he has been posted to Tezu which is nearer to Nagaon than either Hawai or Walong. His family stays in Nagaon.

'At least there is some life here,' he tells me as he kneads the dough. 'Guests are more frequent here than they were either in Hawai or Walong. You will know what it is like when you reach Walong.'

I leave the kitchen and head outside to sit on the bike in the sun. It is cold but the sun is shining brightly and the sky is azure. The lawn is huge and flower beds are neatly arranged but it needs more landscaping.

I soak in the sun before I suddenly remember that the saddle bag strap had got entangled into the rear wheel's hub the previous night. I get down to check and see that the torn portion of the strap is still inside the hub and has to removed. I head back to my room and get the tools to extract the strap and free the wheel completely.

One of the four men carrying out the survey for the rail track comes out and stands beside the bike. I ask him his name.

'Insarul Haque.'

'What is the engine capacity of this one?' he asks. '400 cc, 24.5 bhp,' I tell him.

The motorcycle needs to be tilted to allow me better access to take out the strap stuck inside the hub. Insarul helps by holding the motorcycle at an angle while I use a long screwdriver and a pair of pliers to pull out the offending piece that could have given me a lot of trouble if it had gotten into the chain drive.

I tell him that I would like to talk about the survey of the rail track.

'We are going to Parshuram Kund now and will be back in the evening. We can talk then,' he tells me and goes off to join his colleagues in an SUV. I check the motorcycle's brakes and tighten the chain and head for a bath. I had switched on the geyser shortly after waking up but when I open the tap there is only a faint hissing sound and no water. I remember that the previous night too there was no water in that tap.

I go to the kitchen and tell Subhash about it. He comes with me to take a look, closes the tap and opens it again and repeats the exercise a few times before whacking the pipe and the water starts flowing. Why didn't I think of that?

I take a leisurely bath and then head for breakfast. Subhash has made aloo, puri, and omelette for me. I ask him of places I could see around Tezu. 'Not much here. You can go to Digaru to see the river and the forests. Don't bother about the botanical garden because it has become a jungle. You can also go for a ride towards the airport.'

I decide first to check out nearby parts of the town on foot. I walk out of the circuit house and turn right. Next door is an indoor stadium named after a former chief minister, Kalikho Pul. I see a few children walk in with badminton racquets and I follow them inside. There are two courts inside the stadium and in both of them players are training for doubles matches. The halogen lights are switched off but there is enough natural light for good visibility.

Along the sidelines a few boys and girls wait for their turns to play. A little boy tells me that he has just joined the coaching camp and can't wait to get on the court. On a wall on one side of the first court a sign has the timings written. The first court becomes out of bounds for students and younger people after 6 pm when it is reserved for government officials.

I find the coach, Apali Mega, a young woman who is also a doubles champion. She tells me that the coaching camp is to select players to represent the state in various badminton championships in the country.

'There is so much enthusiasm among the kids. I wish we had more courts to train them. But we have made a beginning and we can only improve from here,' she says.

She points to a teenaged boy in the far court and says, 'This boy can go places is he sticks to the game.' Two little girls come to Apali and tell her something in the local language. She pats them on their heads and points towards a bench along the wall where they go and sit. 'They have been waiting for some time and are getting restless.'

The trial match gets over and Apali calls for the next contestants to come to the court. I wish her luck and leave the stadium thinking of Kalikho Pul.

Once a carpenter before he joined politics, Pul had broken away from the Congress Party in late 2015 and become the Chief Minister of Arunachal Pradesh in February 2016. His government was supported by the opposition, Bharatiya Janata Party. A month later, Pul and 30 dissident Congress MLAs, joined the People's Party of Arunachal. But his chief ministership was shortlived with the Supreme Court of India dismissing his government in July that year. Pul died by suicide on 9 August 2016. He was just 47. By most accounts he remains a popular figure which perhaps explains why the stadium was named after him.

As I walk out of the stadium I come across the Deputy Commissioner's sprawling residence. The perks of the Indian Administrative Service (IAS), I tell myself. There are guards at the gate and all I can see is a long driveway and a glimpse of the bungalow obscured by trees in the garden. The next house is the district police chief's. I want to meet Rinchin Mosibi's sister to thank her for booking the room at the circuit house for me but learn that she hasn't yet arrived from Rupa.

I am still on the edge of the town and decide to head for the market. I discover that the Buddhist influence is much less in this part of Arunachal Pradesh unlike the Bomdila-Tawang sector. There is an Assamese naamghar (prayer hall for Assamese followers of the 15th century saint-scholar Srimanta Sankardev), a temple dedicated to Krishna and another to Shiva, and only two Buddhist monasteries.

The market is the heart of the town and several service roads run parallel from the highway into the market. There are many counters for bus services to different places in Assam. There are subtle differences between Tezu and Bomdila/Tawang. I see men at wine shops instead of women. But like Bomdila and Tawang, many shops are run by outsiders, in this case from Assam and Rajasthan. Restaurants are largely owned by locals and advertise a range of meat dishes.

Christmas is still three weeks away but many shopkeepers have already put the decor on display. No one seems to be in any hurry as shoppers take their time to examine the goods and often leave without buying anything.

By 11 am, I decide to return to the circuit house which takes me another 20 minutes. I wear my riding gear and head out for Digaru. On the edge of the town, I see a large banner advertising a lottery, but there are no cash prizes to be won. Instead, the first prize is a 'Big Mithun'. The second prize is a 'Medium Mithun', the third prize a 'Small Mithun'. There are three more prizes. The fourth prize is a Big Pig, the fifth is a Big Goat, and the sixth comprises three roosters and a large bottle of Teacher's whisky. Seven consolation prizes include a rooster and a bottle of another brand of whisky. Photographs of all the animals are in the banner so that anyone buying a coupon knows what he or she might win. Each coupon costs Rs 500.

I exit Tezu quickly and then slow down simply to enjoy the sights. A little out of the town I see mustard cultivation with the bright yellow crop standing like a picture postcard against a range of blue mountains. The mustard fields soon give away to a stretch of forest before the Digaru river which is a tributary of the Lohit, appears.

It is a Sunday and I see cars and SUVs go off the road and take the dirt track to the river bank which, I quickly figure out, is a favourite picnic spot. I stop in the middle of a bridge over the Digaru to take pictures. As I take off my helmet I hear people singing somewhere under the bridge. I cross to the other side of the bridge and see a large group of men frolicking in the river that is now less than hip deep. The river has split into two streams with a rocky sandbar between them. Almost everyone in the picnic party has a bottle or can in their hands and they are wading across the river from the sandbar to one of the banks. One man slips on the rocks and loses his can of cold drink as he flays his arms. Another man who had already reached the bank tries to retrieve the can but fails. The rest of the group sits on rocks in the river as the water flows over them. I guess the river acts as a terrific balm and simultaneously fuels an adrenaline rush in the lap of nature.

A few of the cars that had gone off-road stop at different places along the bank and the occupants begin taking out their food and utensils. Soon, music fills the air. Someone plays Bhupen Hazarika's soulful songs dedicated to the Brahmaputra and the setting seems just perfect. But I begin to feel that I am sticking out like a sore thumb, virtually staring down at the picnickers from the bridge and decide to ride on.

A couple of kilometres from the bridge is a tri-junction with a few dhabas and I stop at one for tea and snacks. 'No snacks, only lunch. But you can have tea,' Hiralal Manjhi, the owner of the dhaba tells me. I settle for tea and we talk. Manjhi's ancestral home is in Ballia, Uttar Pradesh. His father had settled down in Tezu in the mid-1980s and he followed him a decade later.

'How's business?' I ask him.

'It's good. But these days we close a little early because it is winter,' he replies.

'How often do you go home?'

'There is nothing fixed. It is more like a need-to-go basis.'

'Why did you come so far? Couldn't you find any work in Ballia?'

'I don't think you have been to Ballia. Life is difficult there. It is much more peaceful here, people are nice and there is decent income.'

On the way back to the circuit house I notice that the picnics at Digaru are in full swing and the music is louder. I ride slowly once again and take 30 minutes to reach the circuit house. Subhash has cooked rice, dal, and some fried potatoes for lunch. The food lulls me to sleep and I wake up only in the late afternoon.

I ask Subhash for a cup of tea and start writing my diary. It begins to get cold after sunset. After an hour of writing I head out for a walk. I see a family trying to hang a large star with light bulbs inside from a tree on the driveway while their neighbour has already put up his star on a pole. I keep walking for some time before turning back.

Insarul and his colleagues are back and he soon comes to my room carrying two oranges for me. 'I picked these from a tree near the site where we had gone,' he tells me.

He also tells me that the initial survey of the railway track was carried out in 2015. 'This is the full and final survey for the line from Doomdooma through Parshuram Kund to Pasighat. There was a problem with the alignment going through a village.'

Somehow, the survey has excited me as if it was an expedition through some uncharted territory. Or maybe in a way it was.

'What exactly do you do during the survey?'

'Well, the actual survey is carried out by the other two men who are from a private company from Mumbai. My colleague and I record the coordinates and send them to our boss who checks whether it is right or whether it needs any adjustment.'

'How long does it take for a survey like this?'

'It depends on various factors such as access, weather conditions, and the locations. If there is human habitation along the trajectory of the rail line, we need to find another alignment and that takes time,' Insarul explains. 'We are heading for another site tomorrow and we will be here for four more days before we return to Guwahati. Our boss who is a senior engineer has caught a fever and is going back tomorrow.'

I want to talk more but Insarul's colleague comes looking for him because their boss wants to speak to him. A little after Insarul leaves, I go for dinner and tell Subhash that I would be leaving for Walong in the morning.

'Try to leave by 6 am so you can reach Walong before sunset,' he advises.

'I doubt if I can get out by 6.'

I pack my bags before going to sleep. Walong is 200 km away but I have a feeling that it is going to take the whole day to reach. It is already 6:30 am when I wake up so I rush through a bath and get ready. I skip breakfast and head for Walong after telling Subhash that I would be back after two days and would like to stay one more night. 'I can't promise you a room. But if there is a vacant room you can surely stay,' he tells me. That's a standard reply at circuit houses if you don't have a prior booking and I did not have one.

The first 15 km out of Tezu is a breeze. And then the road suddenly narrows as it winds towards Tohangam. Two nights earlier when I was riding down this road from Parshuram Kund, I hadn't realized that the broken stretches were really that bad. Another 15 km uphill and I reach Tohangam and stop for breakfast at a dhaba. After I finish eating I ask the dhaba owner about the condition of the road. 'I have been only up to Hayuliang and it is mostly bad,' he says. In any case, I had already been warned the night before about the road condition.

An SUV stops and the passengers in the two rear seats rush out. Three head for the dhaba, three others head for a tap to wash their faces. A teenager on the passenger seat in the front just leans out of the window and vomits, soiling the SUV's door and footboard. The second passenger in the front exits through the driver's door. The teenager sits motionless for some time before he gets down and fetches a bucket of water and washes away the mess. Then he comes inside the dhaba, takes a seat and puts his head down on a table.

'God! I shouldn't have eaten so much at breakfast,' he mutters to himself. I learn that the SUV is also heading for Walong and feel sorry for the teenager because there is still more than 150 km to go.

I resume my journey and stop after two kilometres uphill at a much-hyped viewpoint called Lohit View. But the view from there is worth its weight in gold. Much of the sprawling Lohit river basin, complete with different streams of the river against a mountainous background is visible. The setting is also a photographer's delight. I spend about 20 minutes at Lohit viewpoint and then start again.

The uphill section ends and the road begins to deteriorate quickly as a downhill stretch starts. The only thing that remains constant is the thick vegetation. On a sharp downhill stretch I notice large rocks that seem to have been laid for rebuilding the road but slush has made it worse. As if that wasn't enough, a mithun is ambling leisurely down the slope. I have no idea about a mithun's temperament and wait for some time before the animal clears the slope and disappears into the mountain on the right. I crawl slowly through the broken stretch of the road and reach a relatively clear part of the road.

Sometime later, I cross into Anjaw district. The road is broken for most part till Hayulinag which I reach around noon. A policeman at a checkpost flags me down to check my permit and then waves me on. I want to stop for lunch but make the mistake of not asking a local about the location of eateries. I had thought I would find a restaurant or a dhaba along the road but it turns out to be a mirage and I am still about 100 km away from Walong.

On the outskirts of Hayuliang, road builders have scraped off the mountains for miles to widen the road. But the road hasn't been laid yet. Road rollers have ensured that the surface is at least even but they can't do anything about the inherent slipperiness of red soil. The motorcycle stays true to its pedigree but I don't push it to the limit that Royal Enfield says I can.

Along the way I see a hospital named Kalikho Pul Memorial District Hospital. Pul was from Hayuliang. I sincerely hope the hospital will address the health issue of the people in such a remote place where illness can often be fatal for lack of treatment.

The road of red soil continues for some kilometres interspersed with broken tarmac and water crossings at a few places. I cross a few nondescript villages desperately hoping to find an eatery. There is none for a long time. I eventually stop and take out my emergency ration of biscuits, chocolates, and oranges for lunch.

By 3 pm I finally find a restaurant right on the road. I eat noodles and scrambled eggs before heading off. There is more road building work along the way and road rollers, earthmovers, and trucks carrying either rocks or soil slow me down. The sun begins to set and I start feeling uncomfortable that I have to ride in the dark on such an atrocious road. Twilight gives way to darkness and a cold wind magnifies my discomfort. I make a few more pit stops in the middle of nowhere simply to fight off fatigue.

I keep a track of the distance on the motorcycle's odometer. The road finally improves about 40 km ahead of Walong. But I discover even that has a catch. For some reason, the approach and exit to every bridge is simply terrible as if the blacktop road has suddenly disappeared leaving jagged rocks behind.

I am thrilled when the lights of Walong come into view. There is only one place to stay—the Inspection Bungalow or IB—and I don't have a booking. I ask a local man the way to the IB and ride uphill a couple of kilometres to find it. I park the bike and walk into the wooden structure with a tin roof. The caretaker is eating his dinner at 7 pm. I tell him that I need a room.

'Do you have a booking?'

'No.'

He is not pleased but tells me I can stay because there is no other guest at the facility. I carry my luggage to a large room that has two beds, a couple of chairs, and a table with a candle and a matchbox. The room is completely wooden—walls, floor, and ceiling.

'I have made rice, dal, and mixed vegetables. Would you like something else?' the caretaker asks.

'Only an omelette.'

His name is Krishna. 'I am from Tinsukia district,' he tells me.

'Are you Assamese?'

'No. I am Nepali.'

I take my phone out of my pocket and keep in on the table as I sit for dinner and I see that there is no signal.

'Phones don't work here; 4G and Digital India do not exist here. And there is no bank, no ATM, and no fuel station either,' Krishna informs me.

The dead phone bugs me. I had read there is an STD booth in Walong so I tell Krishna that I would use it the next morning to call my wife.

'It is not there anymore. BSNL removed it after they introduced mobile phone service here some time ago and now even mobile phones don't work.'

I shrug it off but find it hard to believe that in such a strategic place as Walong communication could be so difficult. I finish dinner and go to my room. There are two thick blankets on the bed. I get into the bed and tuck myself tightly under the blankets and fall asleep. A few hours later I wake up feeling cold. I take another blanket from the other bed but I still feel cold. I get up once again and check the windows. They are shut properly. And then I discover that there are gaps between the wooden planks that make up the wall and cold wind easily gets into the room. There is nothing I can do at that hour so I take the fourth blanket which improves the insulation.

It is 5 am when I wake up. There is a gap between the curtains in one of the windows and I see the sun rise between the mountains. This is the closest that I have come to see the sun rise in India's easternmost sector.

I laze around in bed for half an hour and then head for the kitchen and ask Krishna for a cup of tea. I also tell him to give me another room. He tells me that I can take one of the three rooms on another block of the Assam type building just above a flight of stairs.

'This wooden thing is the original IB. It was built in 1965. This Assam type block was built in 2000 and the RCC block down was built in 2007,' he tells me. I suspect the original structure hasn't been renovated for a long time and no wonder the wooden planks have either shrunk or bent to make those gaps.

I take the tea and go back to my room and open the door to the balcony and promptly get floored by a sight I couldn't have imagined. Orange trees on the slope in front of the balcony and then a stretch of the town, a raging Lohit and an airstrip surrounded by towering mountains combine to create a surreal effect. The airstrip is small and I figure out that it is for helicopters.

I have to leave for two of India's easternmost villages—Kibithu and Kaho, 30 km away on either side of the Lohit. There is no hot water so I skip a bath, dress up, and go to the kitchen where Krishna is making breakfast. He is kneading dough to make puris and has already cooked the vegetables. He puts a wok on a stove fired by wood and pours oil in it. I stand near the stove and warm my hands. A gas stove lies on a table on one side of the kitchen and a cylinder stands at a corner.

'Why don't you use the gas?'

'It's empty and I can't get a replacement here. It has to come from Tezu for which I have to pay a taxi driver Rs 1,000 to get it. And that pushes the cost of a cylinder to more than Rs 2,100. And to think that Prime Minister Modi said he would bring down prices!'

He is certainly no fan of Narendra Modi.

After breakfast I take my luggage to a room in the Assam-type block and ride out. The fuel gauge is showing half a tank of petrol and there is no way I can reach Hayuliang the next day to top up. As I come down from the IB to the town, I see a shop with a motorcycle in front of it. I stop and ask the shopkeeper where do bikers buy their petrol from.

'Most of us sell petrol at Rs 110 a litre,' he says, nonchalantly.

It is almost double the normal price of petrol in Arunachal Pradesh but I am not surprised that a flourishing black market exists in Walong.

My next stop is the Walong War Memorial down the road. I climb up a flight of stairs and find an officer and a trooper standing there. I introduce myself to the two men. The officer is Captain Bishnoi, a doctor in the Army's Medical Corps. The two of them are waiting for a senior officer to arrive.

Captain Bishnoi asks me about my trip. I tell him that the road from Tezu to Walong was probably the worst I have seen in Arunachal Pradesh. He seems surprised. 'I thought it has improved quite a lot. I wonder what you would have said if you had seen it three years ago when I came here.'

Set against the airstrip, a statue of a Gorkha soldier with his rifle reversed serves as a reminder of the Battle of Walong of 1962. On the statue's pedestal are those immortal words of an ancient Roman army officer Publius Horatius: 'And how can a man die better than facing fearful odds, for the ashes of his fathers and the temples of his gods.' On the left of the statue are black marble slabs with names of fallen soldiers inscribed on them.

The citation at the memorial chronicles the battle of Walong that stopped the Chinese advance towards Tezu and quotes *Time* magazine that 'At Walong Indian troops lacked everything. The only thing they did not lack was guts.'

By all accounts it was a bloody battle in November 1962. A third of Indians out of the garrison strength of 2,191 were either killed or wounded and over 300 were taken prisoners of war. Many Indian soldiers were killed fighting to their last bullet. The Chinese paid a higher price with 752 casualties. Inside a small room at the memorial are photographs of some of the officers and soldiers who displayed exemplary bravery in the face of heavy odds. But almost 60 years after the Sino-India war, Walong still remains essentially a military outpost that only has a road and an airstrip to show for any sort of development.

Captain Bishnoi leaves while I am inside the room but the trooper is still there. 'You know, sir, I am so proud to serve in the Army. I only wish every Indian would just be honest. Our country can then progress by leaps and bounds,' he tells me.

'You are probably right. But don't call me sir.'

'You are so much senior to me I have to call you sir.'

It's an argument I can't win so I let it be and he continues. 'I am ready to die if the Chinese invade once again. But I want an honourable life. And I tell you, sir, if every Indian is true to himself or herself, we can leave China far behind.'

I can't figure out why he is fixated with China and wonder if it is the Army pep talk that has primed him up.

'I am sure you will live an honourable life. And by now you must have already inspired many people in your village to follow you in the Army. And that itself must count as an honour.'

We shake hands and I leave. For much of the ride, the Lohit keeps me company but now its currents are even stronger and in many stretches it is all foam and fury. A few kilometres down the road, I see smoke on the mountains and then as I descend, the smoke seems to be hanging over the river for hundreds of metres. I have never seen a sight like that before. I stop briefly to take a look but can't see where the smoke has originated.

I continue to ride and see a milestone that says Kibithu is five kilometres away. Four of those five kilometres are uphill with sand and gravel which a road roller is trying to stabilize. The last kilometre is a blacktop and I soon find myself at a gate manned by troopers of the Assam Rifles. I stop and ask a trooper about the village and he asks me to go straight and a little left off the road.

I ride into the village and park the motorcycle by the side of the road and walk. A few villagers are putting up a new gate of a school. Further down the road is a small shop selling grocery and small household items. I ask the woman in the shop if I could get a cup tea.

'People here don't drink tea. They drink something else,' she responds, brusquely. Her voice has a Bihari accent.

I wonder if something is bugging her and ask her where she is from.

'Muzaffarpur.' I was right. She is from Bihar.

'Where is your husband?'

'He is gone for work. He is with the Border Roads Organization.'

I buy a small bottle of water from her shop and walk through the village. Kibithu is a small village and the difference between the wealthy villagers and the less fortunate ones is quite visible. Some of the houses are large, double-storeyed with a porch and kitchen garden and a cowshed. The poorer ones only have small houses and kitchen gardens.

Two young men carrying firewood in bamboo baskets with the strap set against their forehead walk down a slope and disappear into an alley.

I see an old couple tending their kitchen garden and walk in. I tell the senior citizen that I want to speak a villager.

'I am actually from Nepal but I have settled here. I am going for a walk and I can take you to meet some local villagers.'

He is wearing a woollen shirt, Bermuda shorts, a hat, and boots.

He points to a house. 'This is a lama's place. Let's see if he is there. No. The door is locked.'

We walk back towards the shop run by the woman from Muzaffarpur and stop at the next house. The man is not there, he tells me after speaking to the lady of the house.

'He will be back soon. He has gone to the Army medical camp.'

We barely walk about a hundred yards when the senior citizen points to a man walking from the opposite direction. 'That's him.'

I stop the man to introduce myself and tell him that I want to talk to him.

'Sure. Let's go to my house.'

My guide leaves me and goes back to his house.

Prem Kumar Gorkha takes me to his house which is built on a wooden platform with a cowshed in a basement of sorts. He owns a dozen heads of cattle. The shop that the woman from Muzaffarpur runs is also his property which he has rented out. He is certainly a prosperous villager.

'Your name suggests you are from Nepal,' I tell him as he brings two chairs for us to sit in the sun.

'Yes. I belong to Lumbini in Nepal. I settled here 35 years ago and married a local woman. My wife is from the Meyor tribe and since I never went back to Nepal, I guess I am as good as a local,' he reasons.

Prem Kumar was a trooper in the Assam Rifles and had served in various places in the Northeast including Kibithu before he retired in 2008. It made sense for him to settle down in Kibithu because his wife owns land there.

'So, why did you go to the Army medical camp?' I ask him.

'I have high blood pressure so I went for a regular check-up. You must have noticed that there are no civil hospitals here.'

I ask him about the village and he tells me that there are about 50 households. The Meyor tribe is the dominant group in that area. There are a few outsiders who run business like the shopkeeper from Bihar, he tells me.

'And what have you been doing after retirement?' I ask.

'Not much. There is not much scope for a regular source of income unless you have a job. And jobs under the government's rural employment guarantee scheme are just too sporadic. I am lucky I have a farm and the cows.'

He has an ironic sense of humour. 'You can say people in Kibithu survive because of fresh air, clean water, and rice beer.'

Not far from Kibithu, the Lohit flows into India from China. Kibithu is just a dot on the map and despite its strategic location it remains an impoverished frontier village.

'There is so much economic potential here but bad road connectivity and the lack of basic infrastructure mean very few people want to come here either for a visit or for business. And politicians talk about India's growth rate being higher than China. Does it mean anything for the people of Walong, Kibithu or Kaho whose lives haven't changed in decades?

A couple of military helipads don't really paint a nice overall picture,' Prem Kumar reveals his angst.

He tells me he has two sons. The elder one has just married and moved out and the younger one studies in the fifth standard. As if on cue, the younger one shows up, humming a song as he returns from school. The little boy's name is Tenzing. He quickly changes his clothes and runs out to play with his friends.

Prem Kumar says Tenzing can study in the school in Kibithu only up to the eighth standard. 'After that he will have to go to Hawai. There is a hostel facility for tribal students in Hawai.'

His wife comes out after some time with two cups of tea and biscuits. I see corn hung over the kitchen door and ask the reason for it. 'That's for drying the corn before they are crushed to make flour,' she tells me.

I tell him I also have to visit Kaho.

'Do you have a pass from the Army?'

'No.'

'Then don't go ahead on this road because they won't let you cross the bridge to Kaho. Go back towards Walong until you find the iron bridge you crossed on your way here. Head straight after crossing the bridge instead of turning right and the road will take you to Kaho. And you can meet Kheti Meyor, the *gaon bura* (village headman) in Kaho. He is my brother-in-law and can tell you a lot about local traditions.'

It is 2 pm. That atrocious stretch of road with sand and gravel slows me down again. The smoke over the Lohit has disappeared but I can smell it in the air. It smells like burnt vegetation. I cross the iron bridge over a large mountain stream and head straight like Prem Kumar told me. Another bridge takes me across the Lohit and suddenly the road disappears. It's a complete dirt track for a few kilometres before a narrow broken tarmac reappears. A little later I come across a minor waterfall whose flow has created a fairly large depression in the road and which is full of water and rocks. The motorcycle wobbles in the middle of the depression and I put my legs down to stabilize the bike. The water immediately fills my shoes. As soon as I clear the depression I stop and take off my shoes and socks and put them on a rock to dry in the strong sun and sit on another rock. Thirty minutes later they are still not dry but no more uncomfortable to wear.

I resume my ride and come across a stretch of a mountain slope from which the embers of a burnt out forest are still smoking. So this was the smoke I saw over the Lohit in the morning. It is part of the slash and burn agriculture or jhum cultivation that I knew about but had never seen villagers actually work on a patch after the vegetation had been burnt. A few men with faces covered by mufflers are inspecting the patch.

The road condition alternates between average and bad. Somewhere near Kaho a suspension bridge links the opposite bank. Soon, I am in Kaho. The first house in the village is also a shop with a faded sign in white paint saying 'Welcome To Kaho'. On the other side of the road is a small monastery—the first I had seen beyond Walong. I cross the first house and stop at a small kiosk and ask two young women about Kheti Meyor's house. It is very near from where I have stopped. I walk down a gentle slope to a small wooden house with a wooden railing and see a woman sifting through some documents and stapling passport size photographs on them. The house is painted brown and the tin roof is red.

'I am looking for Kheti Meyor,' I tell her.

'He has gone to the forest to collect firewood and will be back by sundown. I am his wife,' she tells me.

Her name is Chachi Meyor.

'Is there anything in particular you wanted to talk about with my husband?'

'Not really. Kheti Meyor's brother-in-law Prem Kumar whom I met in Kibithu today suggested that I meet him when I told him that I was going to Kaho.'

'Well, I can tell you a few things about this village. Let's have tea.'

She leads me to another similar house adjacent to the one where I found her. We sit in the balcony and her grand-daughter who is not yet three, comes and climbs on her lap and starts fiddling with her phone.

'What were you doing with those papers and photographs?'

'Oh, some government officials are coming tomorrow so I was just keeping our ID papers, documents, and others papers ready. There is a lot of pressure these days to keep our documents updated because it is a border area.'

Her daughter brings the tea and I ask her about cooking fuel.

'There is only firewood. And collecting it is a daily chore. In the winter we collect as much as we can and store them because in the monsoon you can't find dry wood.'

'And if it snows in the winter?'

'Then it gets difficult although it is still better than rain. And it hasn't snowed here for the last four years.'

I tell her that her house looks beautiful. She smiles.

'We built it ourselves because you can't find labour here to build a house. For that matter, every villager builds his own house.'

'How much time did it take to build your house?'

'Six months.'

I learn that there are 12 houses in Kaho.

'The villagers not only build their houses, they have also laid the water pipeline that you see in this village.'

I ask her about the monastery and tell her that I haven't seen any monk.

'There is no lama. Villagers take turns to conduct prayers and rituals.'

Her granddaughter finds her favourite song on the phone and gets down. She put the phone on the floor and tries to match the dance moves in the video. The little girl ends her dance with a flourish and climbs back on her grandma's lap.

'What's the phone for since you can't make a call or accept one?'

'To listen to music,' she laughs. 'I don't know why my daughter bought it for me. It's better to listen to music on the radio.'

She seems to have read my mind. 'You must be wondering how we survive without phones, shops, banks, hospitals, schools and a lot of other things. We are almost self-contained. We grow our rice and vegetables, raise cattle and poultry and catch fish from the river. The kids go to Kibithu to attend school and if we fall sick we visit the Army medical camp which is also in Kibithu.'

I want to know how important the post of a *gaon bura* is in a village of 12 households.

'I don't know. There was no *gaon bura* in this village for almost 12 years until my husband was elected a couple of years ago. Like I told you, the government wants to formalize a lot of things in border areas and part of it means that every village must have its *gaon bura*.'

Kaho is India's easternmost village where the sun rises first in the country. I ask Chachi Meyor if any tourist visits Kaho to watch the sunrise.

'Very few come here. Some had come a few years ago to watch the sunrise in the new year. I don't know where they had stayed in the night but they showed up around sunrise and left soon after. There is no place nearby for visitors to stay.'

As I get up to leave, she asks how long would I be in the state.

'I will be Walong tonight. I will leave for Dibrugarh day after tomorrow and enter Arunachal Pradesh again to visit Jairampur.'

'You are lucky you could see so many places. We just can't afford it. It costs Rs 800 one way to Tezu from here.'

I almost feel guilty that I have a sponsorship to ride.

As I step down from her balcony, a raft of ducks and a brood of chicken troop into the porch and head for their enclosure. It is 4 pm and they clearly know their timings. I start the ride back to Walong. I make sure my shoes don't take another dip at the water crossing that had cost me half an hour.

Dusk is about to fall and road builders, mostly from Jharkhand and Odisha, head back to labour camps. Kaho and Kibithu are in Anjaw district, one of the least populated with a population density of three persons per square km and that perhaps explains why all road builders are outsiders. By the time I reach Walong, it is dark at just past 5 pm. I am hungry and I stop at a shop that sells vegetables and grocery and doubles up as a bar and restaurant. I order two egg cutlets and tea.

A man in his 30s and an old woman of indeterminate age also walk in and ask for two glasses. The young man takes out a bottle of rum from his bag and pours two large pegs. The woman tells him something in the local language which I don't understand. Then she dips her middle finger in her glass and sprinkles the area around her thrice before finishing the drink in one gulp. She puts down the glass and leaves.

The man searches for something in his bag before he too dips a finger in the glass and sprinkles the area thrice. I wonder if this is some kind of a ritual before drinking. He takes longer to finish his drink than the old woman and then buys some biscuits and leaves.

The vegetables look fresh. I ask a young woman at the cash counter if these are local vegetables.

'No. They are mostly from Assam. People here don't grow enough vegetables to sell in the market. They grow them mostly for their own use.'

'Does it mean there is no commercial farming of any kind here?'

'There is. It is mostly for cash crop like large cardamom that Marwari traders from Assam buy.'

I guess commercial farming of vegetables hasn't taken off despite such vast swathes of land because of lack of manpower.

I return to the IB and take off my shoes and socks and put them out in the balcony hoping that by the morning they would be dry. I sit on the chair and put my feet on the bed and cover them with a blanket and review the photographs I have taken. Sometime later, without realizing, I doze off before Krishna wakes me up to tell me that he would serve dinner in 10 minutes. It is 7:30 pm but feels like 10 pm.

I reach the dining hall as Krishna lays the table. There are two more plates for other guests. I start eating when two young women walk in and take their seats. They are wearing thick jackets and caps. We introduce each other and get talking. They are from Pune. Trishna Mohanty is a writer and photographer and her friend Harsha, a software professional. Both are also keen travellers and take out time to go to places together.

They are scheduled to visit Kibithu the next morning and I tell them as much I had learnt of that village.

'How will you go there?'

'We happened to meet a government official who is visiting Kibithu tomorrow and we will be going in his vehicle.'

Trishna, the more extroverted of the two, tells me she has ghost written books but she is also passionate about photography. 'There isn't much money in travel photography, though.'

We talk some more and exchange notes on our travels, experiences, and anecdotes. Among other places, they would also be going to Cherrapunji which is in my itinerary, too. We exchange phone numbers before heading back to our rooms.

I wake up early and start loading the motorcycle. Trishna and Harsha come down after sometime and head for their designated place to catch the vehicle for Kibithu. I eat breakfast, make the payment, and leave for Tezu. At the shop where I had asked about petrol the previous day, I stop and buy three litres that would take me safely to Hayuliang where I can fill up the tank at the normal rate.

It is a sunny day and I make the most of the good stretches of the road. An hour later, the pain in my neck tells me to take a break. I stop on the edge of the road above the Lohit river and dismount. There is also a car and two motorcycles parked along the road. I am surprised because there is no habitation until I see a suspension bridge that leads to a village across the river. The car and the bike possibly belong to some of the villagers.

The bridge is a short distance away and I can't resist the temptation of taking a walk on it. As I climb on it and start walking, it begins to sway. It is a long bridge and I walk till the middle of it. There is no one else on the bridge. I stop and look over the railing into the roaring river below. A strong wind suddenly whips up and buffets the bridge and I wonder how the villagers cross it while carrying goods. It probably takes very strong nerves not to panic when the bridges sways uncomfortably over a turbulent river.

The walk on the bridge rejuvenates me as I resume my ride. Three hours later I reach the outskirts of Hayuliang but road building activity has sparked a jam. A long stretch has been watered and road rollers have gone over it but the surface is still soft and many cars get stuck as the wheels sink into the soft earth and lose traction. Many of them have to be pushed out.

I am finally in Hayuliang at 1 pm and stop for lunch. A plate of momos later I leave to refuel my motorcycle. The road on which I had travelled two days ago now seems worse and the potholes look larger. Elephant grass runs along one side of the road. The road gets progressively worse and suddenly Tezu seems very far away.

I come across a steep incline full of rocks that has no semblance of a road. I just can't remember how I had crossed it on the way to Walong. It is a long stretch and halfway through it I run into trouble. The rear wheel slips over a jagged piece of rock and goes into a spin. I kill the engine and check only to discover that the wheel has settled over small stones which offer no traction. My left leg slips on the loose rocks and the motorcycle tilts. I quickly get off the bike and hold it with both hands to stop it from tipping over to the left. I try to put the bike on its side stand but can't engage it because a large rock is stopping it. I have no choice but to stand and hold both the handles of the motorcycle and hope for a motorist or another biker to come along.

No one shows up for the next 10 minutes. My hands begin to ache from holding the motorcycle that weighs almost 200 kg to stop it from falling. I am reminded of the guest at the circuit house in Tezu who had warned me to be careful about what I wish for. I allow myself a smile and a voice inside my head tells me that nothing worth having in life comes easily.

I hear the sound of a motorcycle and look down the slope and see a biker heading up. He stops his bike and runs up the incline to help me and pushes my motorcycle out of the trap. I straddle the motorcycle and start the engine. The other biker keeps pushing until I steady the bike. I brake to stop and thank him. 'Your bike weighs a ton. Ride carefully because this road is tricky,' the Good Samaritan tells me.

I notice he is a wry, thin man in his early 40s. He goes back to his motorcycle and rides away.

I ride carefully through some more rocky stretches before I reach the border of Anjaw district. I am tired after that ordeal on the slope and stop for tea. The signboard says 'God Bless Hotel' and I have no doubt that both the hotel owner and I are running on faith. I stand and drink the tea.

The hotel owner tells me he is from Bihar. I ask him about the rent that he has to pay.

'It is Rs 3,000 a month. And the landlord wants to raise it to Rs 4,000 from next year. I have already told him I can't pay that much.'

The rent seems atrocious. I wonder if he makes that much of money. The only assured vehicle stoppage is that of a state transport department bus that plies on the Walong-Tezu-Walong route. Even then, not everybody would buy lunch at the hotel. SUVs which ply as taxis and private vehicles hardly stop there.

I cross a bridge just after the hotel and enter Lohit district. The road is relatively better for some time and then it is the same story of broken tarmac, rocks, and water crossings. Mithuns sit by the roadside and chew the cud. By now I know that these bovines are not aggressive animals.

The bad road is taxing my back badly and shortly before dusk I stop at a small settlement that has a couple of restaurants. I see the biker who had helped me an hour earlier. He is smoking a cigarette. I go up to him and ask his name.

'Sailum Tayang,' he tells me. 'I am going to Tezu where I work and live. I am returning from my village in Hayuliang where I had gone to check my cardamom cultivation.'

He finishes his cigarette while I sip my tea.

'There are two more bad rocky stretches ahead. I will stick with you until you clear those,' says Tayang. I am touched by his concern. I notice that his motorcycle's tyres are almost worn out and he must be a very good rider to undertake this trip. He has a small bag slung across his shoulder and a *dao* in a wooden sheath is tucked into the waistband of his trousers at the back.

We start together and soon reach the first rocky stretch which turns uphill. The surface is wet and slippery and despite my best efforts the motorcycle slips in the slush at the curve and topples to the right. I escape unhurt because the bike is in low speed. Tayang again stops his bike and rushes to help me pick up the motorcycle and pushes again till I clear the stretch and reach the tarmac.

I wait for him to appear but there is no sign of him. I can hear the sound of his engine as if it is straining to get out of a mess. I dismount and walk down the road to check and see Tayang trying desperately to steady his bike which is sliding in the slush. He is heading for a drain on the left and those bald tyres have no grip to stop the slide. I run down the slope and catch the hand grip at the rear to stop the bike and push him up to the tarmac.

It is completely dark now. At the next rocky stretch which is shorter, I make a wrong manoeuvre and find myself struggling to stop the bike from falling yet again. Tayang again rushes to my aid and pushes me to safety. He stops by my side and says, 'The road is more or less okay from here on. So I will leave. But ride carefully.'

He disappears into the night and I make no effort to catch him. The road goes mostly downhill. Almost half an hour later

I stop at Tohangam and see Tayang's bike is also parked there in front of a dhaba. I ask for tea. I take a seat at Tayang's table and see that he is drinking whisky.

'I thought you would be heading straight for Tezu.'

'I wanted to. But it is too cold so I stopped for a break.'

'We still have 30 km to go. Is it safe to drink?'

'Yes. I am used to it. And like I told you, it is cold.'

I buy two packets of snacks and give one to Tayang who orders one more drink.

Tayang tells me he works in a government department in Tezu. He has three school-going children. The eldest is a teenager.

I drink the tea and pay for Tayang's whisky. He protests.

'You don't have to pay for my drink. You have already bought me the snacks.'

'You helped me so much today. So the drink is on me,' I tell him as I leave.

I have not been able to speak to Subhash at the Tezu Circuit House and I am a little worried whether I could find a room there.

It takes me just over an hour to reach Tezu from Tohangam. There are a few cars in the parking and lot of people inside the circuit house. I find Subhash in the kitchen and ask if a room is available. 'I am sorry. We are full today,' he tells me and suggests that I try a particular hotel in the market.

I have better luck at the hotel and check in. My entire body hurts badly from the day's punishing ride. By 8:30 pm I eat dinner and sleep. The next morning I go out for breakfast. Before leaving Tezu, I go to a mechanic and ask him to tighten the chain and all nuts and bolts after the jarring ride to and from Walong.

'What motorcycle is this?' asks the mechanic. 'I haven't seen one like this before.'

He does the job pretty quickly and I leave for a town called Roing. Ron Duarah had suggested that I ride through Roing on the way back to Dibrugarh for my onward trip to another place in Arunachal Pradesh—Jairampur. The USP of the route is that I would be crossing India's longest road bridge—the 9-km-long Bhupen Hazarika Setu over the Brahmaputra.

I cross the Digaru river once again and stop at Hiralal Manjhi's dhaba for tea when I discover that my phone is not with me. I borrow Manjhi's phone and call up the hotel manager who tells me that I had left the phone in my room.

'Your phone is safe with me. Do you want to collect it now?'

'Yes,' I reply.

The back and forth cost me an hour and 30 km extra before I finally hit the road for Roing. Almost the entire stretch of the 60 km road to Roing runs through a reserve forest on a flat swathe of land. It is quite easily one of the best roads in Arunachal Pradesh.

I reach Roing in an hour and then slow down as the forest gives way to small towns and the road narrows. Another hour later I am in Sadiya in Assam and soon I am on the Bhupen Hazarika bridge which starts quite a long way off from the river.

There is heavy police presence at the entry to the bridge. At regular intervals, signages warn motorists not to stop on the bridge for photographs. But no one seems to care and on the bridge there are no policemen to stop motorists from taking photographs.

On the other side of the bridge is Dhola, a nondescript town in Tinsukia district that hit the headlines a month earlier when five Bengali speaking men were shot dead by gunmen suspected to belong to the rebel group ULFA. There are a few police pickets around Dhola and after some time there are no signs of any security.

I cross Doomdooma once again and ride through the tea gardens. By the time I leave Tinsukia, the sun is setting. Two hours later I ride into Dibrugarh and check into a hotel.

The Lohit flows fast and furious between two of India's easternmost villages—Kibithu and Kaho, a few kilometres from the Line of Actual Control with China.

Sunset on the Brahmaputra in Guwahati.

Monks practising a dance at Tawang Monastery in Arunachal Pradesh.

A morung in Kigwema village near Kohima, Nagaland.

The double-decker root bridge in Umshiang, Cherrapunji.

A half-frozen Sela Lake in Arunachal Pradesh.

A boat glides over a transparent Umngot river
in Shnonpdeng, Meghalaya.

Three of Kaziranga's patrol elephants raid
an Army convoy for lunch.

8

In General Stilwell's Footsteps

7 December 2018

I leave the hotel at 9 am and head for the office of the Deputy Resident Commissioner of Arunachal Pradesh at Mohanbari on the outskirts of Dibrugarh for a permit for Jairampur. The office is located near the airport. At 10 am I submit the form and the clerk tells me to collect the permit at noon.

With two hours to kill, I head to a restaurant nearby and order tea and take out my diary and write. By 11 am, the volume of traffic headed for the airport rises uncomfortably and it becomes too noisy to write. I ride out to nowhere in particular and stop in front of a stationery shop to buy a bottle of cold drink.

'Where are you going?' the shopkeeper asks.

'Jairampur.'

'Have you applied for the Inner Line Permit?'

'Yes. I have to collect it at noon.'

'At least the road to Jairampur is good. I worked near Tezu once many years ago and it was a nightmare,' says the shopkeeper who seems to be in his early 60s.

'What work did you do?'

'I was part of a road building crew about 40 years ago. The contractor had taken about 25 of us and we were given the task of chopping off a hill. Our food supply ran out in ten days and the contractor was not to be seen. We escaped from the labour camp and walked through a dirt track for four days to reach Tinsukia before climbing on a train and then jumped off it before it entered Dibrugarh station because we had no tickets.'

I look at the man carefully. His face is weather beaten but he seems to have made good in life. The shop is an indicator that he is doing well.

I ask his name.

'Kanak Das,' he says.

Like other parts of rural Assam, Mohanbari is also awash with posters and banners of rival parties for elections. I ask Das about who he thinks is likely to win.

'It is difficult to say. But if I had my way, I would make sure the BJP doesn't win.'

'Any particular reason for that?'

'They just talk and don't work. Have you seen the condition of the roads in Upper Assam? Jorhat, Dibrugarh, Tinsukia, Doomdooma...they are atrocious. They ought to lose the elections only on this count.'

His contention is strikingly similar to that of the restaurant owner's at Gaurisagar where I had stopped for lunch four days ago.

'This place used to be a Congress stronghold for years until 2014 when we elected a BJP candidate who went on to become a junior minister in the railways but did nothing for Dibrugarh. And what bugs me is the claim they make of doing so much work. All they have done is to carry on what the previous government had started. It is just a propagandist government.'

Das is politically very aware and tells me that there is a real danger to Assam because the state government was aligning itself completely with the Centre without a thought.

'The law that the central government wants to bring in to facilitate non-Muslims from Bangladesh, Pakistan, and Afghanistan get Indian citizenship is a dangerous proposition.

The state government should have opposed it from the start. But instead they backed it completely. Can't the chief minister see that Assam is sitting on a tinderbox?'

It is not only politics that bothers him. He also has other gripes against the BJP.

'This Central government favours crony capitalism. Take the airport privatization proposal, for instance. Why did they propose to include the Guwahati airport in the list? That airport handles about 60 flights a day and the Airport Authority of India makes a hefty profit there. So, why should the government put the Airport Authority, which is its own undertaking, out of business?'

I have had enough of politics so I change the subject and ask him about the road condition in Digboi and Ledo through which I would be travelling.

'They are mostly good. It is the Dibrugarh-Tinsukia stretch that is terrible.'

I check the time. It is almost noon and I ride back to the Deputy Resident Commissioner's office and collect my pass. My destination for the day is the coal town of Margherita, 100 km away from Dibrugarh. There is heavy traffic on the Dibrugarh-Tinsukia road and it takes me more than two hours to reach Tinsukia, where I stop for lunch.

After lunch, I ride through Makum towards Digboi, India's first oil town where petroleum reserve was discovered in the late 19th century and where India's first refinery came up in 1901. I lose some time inside the town in a traffic jam. On the outskirts of the town, I smell gas. There is a row of LPG tankers parked on the edge of the road and then I see a signboard that says 'LPG Bottling Plant'. I guess that explains the smell of gas in the air.

Margherita is about 20 km away. I am again riding through tea gardens which flank both sides of the road. Inside the town, I stop and ask a shopkeeper about hotels.

'The ones here are not that good. If you ride on for another 4 km you will find one called Bluemoon on your left on the highway.'

I cross a bridge over the Dihing river which splits Margherita into two parts. I come across another market at the end of which I find Bluemoon Hotel. I check in and order dinner. I watch television for some time and fall asleep. Around 11 pm I wake up after someone knocks on the door. I open the door to see one of the hotel employees standing.

'Will you be paying the rent now or in the morning?'

I am furious. I stomp down to the reception and give the manager a piece of my mind.

'Is this a hotel or an extortion racket that you are running? Is it your standard practice to wake up guests in the middle of the night to ask for payment? You have just earned yourself a very negative review. And I am never going to recommend your hotel to anyone.'

He apologizes profusely and then pulls up the bell boy. 'Why did you knock on the door when you saw the lights were off?'

I go back to my room and take some deep breaths to calm myself but sleep eludes me for much of the night. I check out of the hotel at 8 am. I want to see a coal museum in Margherita but it opens only at 10 am. With two hours at my disposal I head for Ledo, eight kilometres away and from where the Stilwell Road begins.

Some distance off the road, a few chimneys are belching smoke. Ledo is a sleepy little town. I head for the railway station which is India's easternmost station with a passenger service. The station is a small one with only four trains originating and terminating there. On the walls at the entry to the stations are murals depicting Ledo's history as a coal town. I walk up to the platform and see the tracks are empty. The next train is scheduled to arrive at 11 am.

A food stall is doing brisk business and I notice many local people who live near the tracks walk in for breakfast. I head for the exit when a man asks me if I am a passenger waiting for the next train.

'No. I am on a motorcycle expedition and I am just wanted to see this station. My father-in-law, who retired as a chief engineer in the railways, told me to check out this station since it is the last station in the East for passenger service.'

He warms up immediately. 'Yes. It is quite a historical station but very few people actually know about that aspect.'

And then he introduces himself.

'I am Sonowal. I am the booking clerk but I end up doing almost everything else in this station.'

'Like what?'

'Like keeping track of coal rakes from Tirap which pass through this station. I also have to keep track of consignments that are booked from here and I have been doing much the same work for the past 12 years at this station. I am also training a new booking clerk besides issuing the tickets myself.'

He has four more years to go before retirement.

I ask Sonowal about the chimneys I saw between Margherita and Ledo.

'They are *bhattas* or processing units before coal is dispatched to the buyers. I doubt if they are legal because there is a huge racket in coal business. The unprocessed coal which comes from the mines straight to the rail yard at Tirap for loading the rakes is legal. Everything else is a nexus.'

'Where do the rakes go?'

'Mostly to Haryana.'

But it is the illegal coal business that riles Sonowal.

'Greed is killing us. These chimneys belch so much smoke that the vegetation gets covered in a layer of ash. Imagine what it does to our lungs! The government is either incompetent or couldn't care any less for a place so far from the state capital.'

I ask him about Stilwell Road.

'That's the one you came on. You have to keep going ahead and turn right at Jagun for Jairampur. You will enjoy the ride.'

We shake hands and I head back to Margherita to see the Coal Heritage Park and Museum. It has just opened and I am the first visitor to buy a ticket. At the open air section of the museum are steam engines and rakes that were used to haul coal from the mines in the early years of coal mining in Margherita and Ledo. There is also a range of machinery that were used to treat coal but the highlight of the museum is an abandoned mine; complete with a trolley, rail track, and life size models of miners at work with helmet-mounted headlights and pickaxes. The mine is lit at regular intervals and gives a clear picture of what coal extraction looked like more than a hundred years ago.

There is also a large hall chronicling the history of the coal town of Margherita. Photographs, paintings, and newspaper articles adorn the walls. Mining equipment, safety gear, communication tools, typewriters, and cameras are among other exhibits displayed in glass boxes. One photograph on the wall that catches my eye is that of American General Joseph Stilwell who oversaw the road connecting Ledo to Kunming in China to circumvent the Japanese army after they cut off the Burma Road in the Second World War. Originally called the Ledo Road, it was later named after General Stilwell.

I spend some time in front of the sepia-tinted photograph. Wearing a trench coat, the spectacled General Stilwell is in full battle gear holding a map in his hands. He is looking at someone or gazing at something with a pipe dangling from a corner of his lips. His face is grim which is not surprising given that the Burma theatre saw some of the fiercest fighting in the Second World War.

On another frame near General Stilwell's photograph is a document in a golden frame that says that Margherita was given its name on 18 February 1884 in honour of the then Italian Queen. Margherita's Italian connection was a man named Chevalier Roberto Paganini, who as chief engineer constructed the first wooden rail bridge over the Dihing River, laid rail tracks on both its banks and founded the settlement around the bridge.

I spend more than an hour at the museum. At 11:30 am I start for Jairampur. Work has started at the coal processing units and almost all the chimneys are belching smoke. Boys are playing football in a field near one of the chimneys and girls are competing in sprints, seemingly oblivious to the pollution around them. I cross the Ledo station again and a little later the rail track runs parallel to the road. A short distance from the station, the passenger train which arrived at 11 am is waiting ahead of its return trip.

Further down the road, the air smells of coal and I soon reach Tirap where trucks are bringing in raw coal which is being loaded on a rake for its onward journey to North India. The trucks are coming down a hill where the vegetation has been completely destroyed by the mining in the Tirap collieries. I wonder if the extensive mining has polluted water sources in the area.

I notice that the vegetation is changing along the Stilwell Road. Tea gardens give way to paddy fields and betel nut cultivation for much of the way to Jagun. The presence of Assam Rifles also increases and I cross several camps of the paramilitary force.

At Jagun, there is relatively heavy traffic, compounded by police barricades, a busy market and buses heading for a place called Miao in Arunachal Pradesh. At a T-point in Jagun I turn right for Jairampur. It is past 12:30 pm when I stop for lunch at restaurant named Pangsau Pass.

The Pangsau Pass which leads to Myanmar is where I plan to go from Jairampur.

I am the only customer in the restaurant.

'Lunch will take time. I can serve you snacks quickly,' the young waiter tells me. I settle for a spring roll.

The manager comes and stands near me. 'May I ask you something?'

'Sure.'

'How does this motorcycle perform? I have been thinking of buying one but I can't decide whether I should buy a Himalayan or a Bullet 350.'

'I think the Himalayan is certainly better than a Bullet. I have covered 4,000 km on the trip so far and there is not a squeak from the bike. But then I am biased towards the Bullet, you see. I have seen too many of them give trouble to their owners. Of course, Bullet owners will give you a different opinion.'

'I think I will take test rides on both the bikes and then decide.'

Another customer walks in. He also asks me about the motorcycle.

'I have been thinking of upgrading to a bigger bike. I am tired of riding a 150 cc motorcycle,' he tells me.

Rajiv Das is in his late 20s and is from Ledo where he owns a small shop. He is visiting Jagun to see a relative. He sits opposite me and orders tea and samosa.

I ask him about the coal business in Margherita and Ledo and the illegal trade.

'The plunder of coal in mines around Ledo and Margherita is an open secret. But no government is willing to stop it. Daily wage earners are hired to dig out coal and at night, trucks loaded with coal head to different destinations including some outside the state.'

The North Eastern Coalfields, which owns some of the mines in the area, has lodged several complaints with the police, but illegal mining and smuggling of coal goes on, Das tells me.

'Illegal mining is carried out in remote areas inside dense forests along the hills of Namdang adjoining Tikak along the Assam-Arunachal Pradesh border. Some of them are shut down when they are discovered, but many illegal mines remain undetected.'

'How do you know all that? And, how can you be so sure?'

'Everybody knows it. It is a nexus of politicians, businessmen, police, and truck owners that has allowed smuggling and illegal coal mining to flourish. It will probably take a large human tragedy to shake up the government to stop it.'

I know illegal coal mining was once rampant in Meghalaya but I had no idea that it was much the same story in Assam. I wonder if corruption has developed such deep roots in Assam that it is endangering lives of the local people and the environment. Clearly, the central government's war on corruption which it never tires of tom-tomming hasn't had much impact around Ledo and Margherita maybe because like Rajiv Das told me, part of the government itself seems to be involved.

We finish our food and head in opposite directions. Civilization suddenly disappears and the Stilwell Road now begins to look like what I have read about it as it cuts through a dense evergreen rainforest.

The US spent almost $149 million to construct the road, which took over two years to build. More than 28,000 Americans and 35,000 Asian workers laboured through rain, landslides, and a hostile terrain infested with mosquitoes and leeches to build a seemingly impossible 800-km road at a terrible human cost.

The road was nicknamed the 'A man a mile road' for the number of lives it cost. More road builders died of malaria, dysentery, and accidents than from fighting. Ironically, General Stilwell had mooted the road after an air campaign to continue supplies to the army of nationalist Chinese leader Chiang Kai-Shek cost the Americans heavily.

The flight path required pilots to fly over 15,000 feet high mountain ranges of the eastern Himalayas that came to be known as The Hump. The Americans lost more than 600 planes over the mountains mainly due to bad weather while some were shot down by Japanese fighter planes.

The Stilwell Road till Jairampur is now a motorcyclist's dream. It twists and turns, climbs up and goes down and there are enough straight stretches to ride fast. I try to imagine the conditions when the road was being built in the 1940s and offer a silent prayer for the men who died making it.

There is hardly any traffic. At a few places there are dirt tracks off the road from where trucks carry rocks, probably for road building. At 1:30 pm I reach a police checkpost at the entry of Jairampur, show the policemen my permit and move on.

I ride slowly scanning the road for the Inspection Bungalow until I find it. There are a few guests in the lounge. The caretaker is in the kitchen cooking lunch for the guests. I ask him if there is room I can rent.

'There are vacant rooms but I am not permitted to let in guests without authorization from the Additional Deputy Commissioner.'

'Where can I find him?'

He comes out of the kitchen and into the parking of the Inspection Bungalow and points to the officer's house. I have to go through another checkpost, this time of the Assam Rifles. The troopers check my permit and ask me a barrage of questions about the purpose of my trip.

'I want to go to Pangsau Pass and I need a permit from the Assam Rifles Commanding Officer.'

'But civilians are not allowed these days to go to Pangsau Pass. You can ask the ADC and if he issues a pass, Assam Rifles will give you one too. Otherwise, you won't be allowed to go beyond Nampong which is 16 km from here.'

Bureaucracy, red tape or an unrealistic apprehension about security, call it what you will, but I find it absolutely illogical that you are not allowed to see parts of your own country.

I head for the ADC's residence. It is a second Saturday of the month and a holiday and he is relaxing at home. SS Choudhury is wearing a lungi and a shirt.

'What can I do for you?'

I tell him that I need a permit to go to Pangsau Pass and that the Assam Rifles won't give me one until he issues it first.

'I am sorry, I am helpless. There has been a change in protocol agreement with Myanmar and only locals from Nampong are given passes to go to Pangsau.'

I ask him the reason why outsiders can't be given permits for Pangsau Pass.

'I have no idea. We just have orders from the Centre.'

I am absolutely frustrated. And to think that the government never tires of advertising a much hyped Look East Policy. There is clearly a wide gap between its pronouncements and implementation on the ground.

But Choudhury tells me that I can stay at the IB. 'Just ask the caretaker to call me.'

I return to the IB and the caretaker shows me my room. It is so ancient that it seems like a relic. There are two beds, a dressing table, and an almirah. The linoleum on the floor is wearing off and looks like it has never been replaced. And no one has bothered to take off the old light switches and sockets made of ceramic and plastic. A contemporary switchboard that lies cheek by jowl with the old one accentuates the feeling of vintage in the room.

The almirah doors squeak like the ones in a horror movie. And the drawers of the dressing table are jammed. Not that I have any need for the drawers. The bathroom fittings include brass taps and an antique overhead flush with a chain that has to be pulled. The showerhead has disappeared and there is no geyser. Fortunately, the wash basin is new.

I want to take a bath and the caretaker brings a bucket of hot water for me. I head for the dining hall after the bath.

The caretaker is a dark, short man and certainly not a local. I ask him his name.

'Rama Rao. I am from Visakhapatnam in Andhra Pradesh.'

'How did you land here?'

'I came looking for a job 20 years ago and luckily I found it and have stayed put here.'

'And your family?'

'They are in Visakhapatnam. I go once a year. Sometimes they come over here for a couple of weeks.'

I wonder how he manages such a long distance family life.

Rao is a good cook and the fish tastes great.

'What fish is this?' I ask him.

'I can't remember its name, but I like its taste. It is found in the river nearby.'

I tell him about my bad luck with a permit for Pangsau Pass.

'The government is opaque, you know. But there is not much to see in Pangsau. I haven't been there myself, only heard about the place.'

I can't explain to him why I wanted to see and cross Pangsau Pass so badly. The immediate attraction is a border trade that takes place on the 10th, 20th, and 30th of every month. But the greater attraction was to see and try to understand if it is really that bad that it earned the sobriquet Hell's Pass. I also wanted to go to the Lake Of No Return, a few kilometres inside Myanmar.

Pangsau was called Hell's Pass by the Allied forces because mud and slush during the rains made the crossing a dangerous proposition. And, according to legend, the Lake Of No Return got its name due to the number of Allied aircraft which crashed into it on their approach to The Hump during the Second World War.

There are at least three other legends about the origin of its name. The common thread is that no one got out alive from the lake.

Now, at the dining hall of the IB, I tell myself that I will make it to Pangsau Pass and the Lake Of No Return some other time.

I decide to head for Nampong after lunch. The guards at the Assam Rifles checkpost stop me again to ask if I had any luck with the permit. I shake my head and tell them that I am going to Nampong.

Seven kilometres from the Assam Rifles checkpost, I see a war cemetery and stop. I had read that the cemetery was salvaged only in 1997 after it had been overrun by the jungle. A lone worker is painting the perimeter wall. I ask him if there is caretaker I can talk to.

'I haven't seen him today.'

I walk inside the cemetery on a tiled pathway. The place is heavily wooded. A plaque tells a visitor that the 'memorial is dedicated to the officers and the men who gave their lives that the Stilwell Road be accomplished'.

Near the plaque is the statue of a soldier in a running pose. The left hand of the statue is broken at the wrist. Further down the pathway, I spot the rows of graves. The concrete has worn off and the graves now look as if they were made only of bricks.

It is an eerie feeling to stand in a cemetery which is more of a jungle. There is a deathly silence which is only broken by birdcalls and the occasional rustle of leaves or a mongoose scampering in the undergrowth. The graves are withering away and there is no sign of any restoration. Most of the 1,000 men buried in the cemetery are Chinese and Kachins besides Indian, British, and Americans. The dead include both soldiers and road builders.

There are no headstones in the graves that are in my line of vision. But a small black signboard stands testimony to one of the men buried there. There are some lines in Chinese and in English, it says: 'Major Hsiao Chu Ching, Company Commander of 2nd Company of 2nd Battalion of 10th Regiment, Independent Engineers of Chinese Army stationed in India. He was born in July 1913 at Wei County of Hapeh province and died in December 1943.'

I walk around the cemetery a little more but can't see anything similar about any other man. I am apprehensive of going near the crumbling graves for fear that the ground may sink. As I leave the cemetery I wonder why the Commonwealth War Graves Commission which maintains the Kohima and Imphal war cemeteries did not take up the maintenance of this one at Jairampur. I can't help thinking that these men who died in the jungle never got out of it.

The worker who was painting the wall is not to be seen. I resume the ride to Nampong. A short distance from the cemetery I come across a picturesque tea garden that seems to have been landscaped on a hill. Nampong soon comes into view. It is a small town and very well spread out with no sign of any clutter.

Groups of women are sitting outside their shops or houses chatting among themselves. A few others are walking with little children on the road. I stop at a relatively large shop to talk to the shopkeeper.

He is from Rajasthan. I ask him if he goes to Pangsau Pass for the border trade.

'No. We are not allowed. Only local traders from Nampong are allowed to go to Pangsau Pass.'

'What do the Burmese sell at the border?'

'Stuff like these,' he answers and points to some packets of coffee, toy guns, blankets, umbrellas and a brand of mosquito coil called Godzilla.

'I wanted to go to see the border trade but I couldn't get a permit,' I tell him.

'Try to meet the Sub Divisional Officer just down the road. He could give you a permit.'

'I guess it is worth trying.'

But Pangsau Pass is meant to elude me this time. The SDO is not home and the gate is locked. I am an agonizing 16 km short of Pangsau Pass.

'Some other day,' I tell myself.

The shadows begin to lengthen and I decide to return to Jairampur. Dusk falls by the time I cross the war cemetery. I stop at a fuel station to fill up the tank before heading to the IB.

I go to the kitchen and ask Rao for tea which he quickly makes.

'I will go out for a walk in the market,' I tell Rao after I drink the tea.

I go to a shop to buy snacks. The shop is well stocked. The shopkeeper is about my age and I ask his name.

'Sitaram Saini. I am from Sikar in Rajasthan. I came here in 1996.'

'Twenty-two years is a long time. How do you like this place?'

'This is the most peaceful place in the country. No one bothers you here. No one gets drunk and picks up a fight like they do in North India. I love this place.'

'How about your children?'

'I have two sons. They completed their schooling here. They are now in college in Jaipur and stay with my mother.'

Saini tells me he has a warm relationship with his landlord for his house and shop.

'It's just a formality to renew the lease.'

I tell him that I met another shopkeeper in Nampong who is also from Rajasthan.

'Yes, there are quite a few of us from Sikar in Arunachal Pradesh and Manipur.'

I ask him if there is any security problem with militants of the ULFA or the Naga rebel groups given that the Assam Rifles maintains such an attitude to sanitize the entire area.

'No. There is no problem. I heard there could be movements of militants in the south around the Namdapha forests but I can't recall any showdown between the Assam Rifles and the rebels here. Like I told you, this is the most peaceful place in the country.'

A woman walks into the shop and asks for raisins and cashew. I take my packet of snacks and leave.

Further down the market are various shops, most manned by outsiders. The locals seem to be content in leasing out their properties. I see only a few shops with local shopkeepers including a boutique. But, like I saw in Bomdila and Tawang, most wine shops in Jairampur are also managed by local women.

A few shops are selling Christmas décor, mostly artificial Christmas trees and stars with lights inside. Along the pavement, migrants from Bihar and Assam ply their trade from handcarts and kiosks selling kebabs, fried fish, boiled eggs, and pakoras (fritters).

Jairampur is a place where time seems to move slowly. I walk across the length and breadth of the market in an hour and then there is nothing more to do. It is getting cold and

I walk back to the IB and head for the kitchen. Rao is cooking on a gas stove.

'What's for dinner?'

'Fish curry, mixed vegetables, and dal'

"I'll have fish curry.'

'I thought so. But there are two other guests who also want dal and vegetables.'

There is also a firewood stove where the embers are still burning. I sit on a stool by the stove and warm my hands. I tell Rao that I would be leaving in the morning since I can't make it to Pangsau Pass.

'What should I make for breakfast?' he asks.

'Roti and omelette will be fine. '

'Ok. Do you have kids?'

'One.'

'How old?'

'He will turn 14 in a few days.'

'He must be missing you.'

'Yes. I miss him too and sometimes it almost breaks my heart.'

'I know what it is like. I had the same feelings when my children were small. But I didn't really have a choice to go back to Visakhapatnam so we all suffered the pangs of separation. I am glad both my kids have grown up well.'

Suddenly, Rao seems like a brother or a best friend. He is much less privileged than I am but doesn't complain about anything and seems ready to take on anything life throws at him. Just like that saying: Not all heroes wear capes.

Rao lays the table for me and takes the dinner for the other two guests to their room. I finish my dinner and retire for the night when my phone rings. Aseem is on the line and he is barely able to conceal his excitement.

'Papa, can you guess what I have done?' he asks.

'Tell me.'

'I have adopted a litter of puppies.'

I am alarmed but he quickly tells me, 'Of course, Mummy knows about it. There are six of them.'

'Where did you get them?'

'Someone dumped them near our house. And they don't have their mother so I have decided to take care of them. They are really very cute and fluffy. I have made a kennel for them with cardboard and put it on the road divider.'

I tell him that I am touched by his kindness and ask him if he has named the pups.

'Yes. My favourite is Bruno. He has black and brown stripes. And there is also Doodle and Poodle. I haven't named the others yet.'

He ends the conversation saying he has to rush because the pups are crying.

I go to sleep. The alarm wakes me up around 6 am and I go to the kitchen to ask Rao for a cup of tea.

'I have also heated the water so you can take a bath,' he tells me.

'I will, after I finish the tea.'

I take the cup of tea and go out to the driveway and stand in the sun. The two other guests at the IB are preparing to leave and are loading their car.

'Is that you motorcycle?' one of them asks.

'Yes.'

'Where are you from?'

'Delhi.'

'I have been to Delhi only once. We were in a group and stayed for two days but couldn't make sense of the city. It is just too big.'

He tells me that he is a member of an organization called Arunachal Yuva Morcha. They had been to Ahmedabad for an event and had stayed in Delhi for a couple of days on their way back. He doesn't have fond memories of Ahmedabad either.

'A Gujarati man asked me if I was from China when he knew that I was a member of the Arunachal Yuva Morcha. Isn't this some kind of racism? We can teach those guys some manners.'

'So, what brought you to Jairampur?'

'Our kids study in school here and they stay in the hostel. So we come to see them once a month.'

He tells me that they stay near the Namdapha National Park and have to leave early to reach before dusk so that they don't run into wild elephants. Namdapha is 220 km east of Jairampur.

The mention of wild elephants brings alive the images of the herd I saw at the Nameri Forest Lodge just over two weeks ago.

Rao comes out to tell me that the hot water is ready and I head for my bath. By the time I get ready, he has served breakfast. As I finish eating he goes and gets the bill for a princely sum of Rs 750 out of which Rs 300 was for the second bed in the room.

It is 7:30 am when I leave the IB. I am planning to reach Jorhat, 250 km away, by evening. The Arunachal Pradesh police at the checkpost flag me down to record my exit in their register. Stilwell Road seems quieter than before. Despite the road being almost empty I resist the urge to ride fast simply because I want to savour the experience of riding through one of the world's most famous roads.

I cross Jagun, Ledo, and Margherita and then take a break on the outskirts of Digboi. I am just over 20 km from Makum and tell myself that I will try to find some descendants of

Chinese families who had come and settled in and around that town from the 1830s. Rubaiyat had suggested that I should try to meet some of them.

Chinese neighbourhoods were called China Patty (pronounced Cheenapatty) or Chinatown. By the 1960s they were no longer Chinese but had become Assamese Chinese. And then as if overnight, the Sino-India War of 1962 devastated the community. Most of them were rounded up and sent off to a detention centre in Deoli in Rajasthan while many others were deported to China. Those in Deoli were released from detention after three years. By then their lives were ruined and many simply came back to Makum to sell off their properties or what was left of them and then leave the place for good. Some simply abandoned their homes.

As I close in on Makum, I wonder if there would be any Chinese left in the town. Inside the town, I stop to ask a shopkeeper about China Patty. He tells me the direction and that I have to turn towards a Hindi school which once used to be a Chinese school.

'You can ask people near the school for direction to the house of some Chinese.'

I ride for some distance but can't spot the school. So I stop in front of a house where a man is reading a newspaper in the verandah. I dismount and go up to him and ask him about the school.

He takes a look at my motorcycle and asks, 'Why do you want to visit the school? It's Sunday.'

I tell him that I want to meet a Chinese man.

'Oh! Come and sit. I can tell you a lot about them. My name is Aggarwal.'

I learn that he is a contractor. He is in his mid-50s and was born in Makum.

'There is this man named Willy Ho. He is my friend. But he is not here now. He spends most of his time in Shillong these days after he married a Khasi woman.'

Aggarwal, who is a Marwari, calls out to his domestic help and asks for tea.

'Willy now looks after the family business of manufacturing tea sorting machines. He married recently and because Khasis are a matriarchal society he had to shift to Shillong. But he does come here to look after the business.'

'Did you and Willy go to the same school?'

'No. He used to be in a boarding school. But when he came home on vacations we used to play together every day. And then of course he came back to Makum after graduating from Mumbai to take up the family business. But our friendship has remained intact.'

Aggarwal's domestic help brings tea and biscuits.

'This is fresh tea from the local gardens,' Aggarwal tells me.

That has to be since I am in the heart of tea country.

'These guys were good.'

'Who?'

'The Chinese. They had become Assamese Chinese, spoke the language and some married Assamese or other tribal women in the state. It's a pity the 1962 war just scattered the community. They used to own shoe shops, some were dentists, and some ran saw mills.'

'Is there any other Chinese here whom I can meet since Willy is not here?'

'There is one guy. He is a mechanic. I will call him.'

But Aggarwal's phone doesn't connect. I try calling from my phone but the result is the same.

'Where are you heading today?' Aggarwal asks.

'Jorhat.'

'In that case you can meet John Wong in Tinsukia. He runs the Hong Kong Restaurant. You can't miss it. It is on the main road inside town. He can certainly tell you a lot of things.'

The information rekindles my hopes of meeting an Assamese Chinese.

I thank Aggarwal for the information about John Wong and get up to leave. I wait for some time to let a procession of political workers cross my motorcycle before heading for it. The procession has a few bikers riding with party flags.

Aggarwal shakes his head. 'Some things don't change. These rallies are money making exercises. They will come and collect money from businessmen and shopkeepers saying they need funds for a rally for 100 motorcycles. And then you will find just around 20 bikes. The others just fill up the tank and go home. Or take the money for the petrol and don't show up. And I have seen it since heaven knows when.'

I straddle the motorcycle after the procession passes off and take a U-turn for Tinsukia which is just 12 km away. But heavy traffic again slows down my progress. Half an hour later, I park in front of Hong Kong Restaurant and walk in and ask for John Wong.

A young waiter tells me that John is not in. I ask him when he would return.

'Wait, I will ask his wife,' he tells me and goes through the rear of the restaurant.

He returns a little later to say that John will take 30 minutes.

'I will wait and have lunch.'

I order noodles and take a seat. It looks like the restaurant has been recently renovated. The seats are covered in red faux leather. Chinese lanterns hang from the ceiling.

About 15 minutes later the waiter serves the noodles. I am about to finish when John arrives at my table.

'You wanted to meet me?'

'Yes.' I stand and shake hands and then he sits opposite me.

'I had gone to the rail station to see off my daughter. She is studying in the Agriculture University in Jorhat.'

I tell him about my journey and that I am curious to know about the Assamese Chinese.

'I couldn't meet Willy Ho in Makum. Someone suggested your name, so here I am.'

John Wong has quite a story to tell.

His grandfather Wang Teck Hong had come and settled in Tinsukia in 1945 and a few years later his family joined him. John's father, Wang Su Chin, was the headmaster of the Chinese school in Makum. He also helped his father run a saw mill called Lee Hing Yuang Saw Mill. The family was quite prosperous.

'My father had 14 General Motors trucks that carried the timber to the saw mill. He also had four elephants that were used for logging operations.'

John says the community had no inkling of the catastrophe they had to face in 1962. At the end of the Sino-India War, entire Chinese families were rounded up and were not allowed to take any possessions except their papers.

John has fading memories of the fateful day that changed their lives forever.

'I was a young boy then and vaguely remember the frightening incident of the last day of the war. Soldiers and policemen came in large groups and arrested almost all the Chinese origin people. We were first dumped in a cowshed in Makum and then taken to Dibrugarh jail before they put us on train to Deoli in Rajasthan. It was an internment camp. We were branded as spies. It was hard to believe that we had become enemies of the state overnight. My mother, Lee Su Chi, who came here in 1940, never went to China after that.'

John is the second among four siblings. He has a brother and two sisters. One sister died in the internment camp in Deoli.

By the time they were released three years later, Wang Su Chin was a ruined man.

'The saw mill had fallen into disuse and there was no chance of reviving the machinery. The trucks had rusted away and two of the elephants were stolen. We found the other two in the forest in Guijan about 10 km from here. There was one Jeep which survived because it was inside the garage. My father started running it as a taxi between Tinsukia and Guijan.'

I wonder if I did the right thing by asking about his past because it very obviously revived his most agonizing memories.

'I still feel so sorry for my father. He had worked so hard to build a small fortune only to see it being destroyed for no fault of his and ended up as a taxi driver for four years before he set up this restaurant in 1970.'

'Where was the saw mill?'

'It was here,' he says pointing towards the rear of the restaurant. 'This used to be a large place. Of course, the earlier structure was different. We still have our houses here. The restaurant next door—Ken's Kitchen—is my brother's. And the beauty parlour is my wife's.'

I ask him if his grandfather was also interned in Deoli.

'No. He was then in Kolkata and was somehow spared. My older cousins looked after him when we were in Deoli.'

John lightens up as he talks more about his family. His wife is of Chinese descent but now the clan's lineage is getting diluted.

'One of my sisters is married to a former policeman. He is a Bengali and they stay in Silchar. She also runs a beauty parlour and after my brother-in-law retired she convinced him to open a men's salon. So, both of them now run their own business.'

John's son is married to an Ahom woman.

'He was studying business administration in Gauhati University but left his studies and got married. So I told him to come back and help me run the restaurant.'

I want to talk to John some more but I have almost 200 km to go to Jorhat and more than half the day has already passed. I get up leave.

'Take my number, just in case if you need some help. And be careful when you come across the weekly markets along the highway. Some drunkard might stagger in front of you.'

'Drunkards during the day?' I ask him.

'Oh yes. There will be some of them, particularly those vendors who come from the tea gardens to sell vegetables or chicken or small tools. They sit and drink the local brew while waiting for customers and then they get tipsy. I had a bad experience a few months ago when a drunk woman almost fell in front of my car although I was driving slowly.'

He looks at the motorcycle and asks, 'What bike is this?'

'It's a Himalayan. Royal Enfield makes it.'

'I have a Bullet 350 but I haven't been on it for a few months after I injured my left shoulder and arm in a crash.'

'Invest in a riding jacket like the one I am wearing. It provides good protection against falls because it is armoured.'

'I think I will.'

John Wong will remain an enduring character for me. I watch him on the rear view mirror before I take a turn that sweeps him out of sight.

9

Back to Guwahati

10 December 2018

By 2 pm I am in Dibrugarh where I stop for lunch and call Ajanto.

'I guess you will take about three hours to reach. I will tell the maid that you will be reaching in the evening. I will come to see you around 8:30 pm and get you home for dinner,' Ajanto tells me.

I exit Dibrugarh and make good time till Sibsagar. And then I run into a massive go-slow on the highway where a sprawling weekly market is spread across one side of the road that is being laid to widen the current one. Two wheelers are parked haphazardly near the edge of road and shoppers spill into the main carriageway to slow down the traffic. For almost a kilometre the traffic moves at a snail's speed and there is no way I can weave my way out of the madness. Fortunately, I don't run into any drunk that John Wong had warned me about. It takes almost half an hour to clear the stretch and I know that I will not be able to reach Jorhat by 5 pm.

The sun sets, and the ride becomes difficult on the single-lane highway where there are no lights and drivers never seem to dip their headlights. I manage to reach Jorhat by 7 pm. The maid at Ajanto's house has gone out after leaving the key with another tenant. I call Nazneen and she tells me that mother's condition has worsened.

'Can you can return tomorrow? She is quite serious and had to be given life-saving injections. She's already had three so far. I have also asked Shahwar to come and he should be reaching soon. He started from Kohima today.'

'Okay. I will start early morning tomorrow,' I assure her.

At 8:30 pm Ajanto shows up to pick up his father who is playing cards with his friends. I follow him on the bike to his flat for dinner.

'How was Walong?' Ajanto asks as we wait for dinner in his flat.

'Very challenging, very satisfying and a ride I will never forget. I experienced a miracle of sorts when a local motorcyclist showed up and stuck with me to help me cross very treacherous road in the night.'

'Providence, I guess. God has some inexplicable ways of pulling us out of a mess. Did you go to Pangsau Pass?'

I tell him about my bad luck that put Pangsau Pass out of my reach.

'So, are you heading for Nagaland next?'

'I wanted to, but my mother is very ill so I will return to Guwahati and spend a few days with her. If she recovers quickly I will head for Meghalaya and then go to Silchar and then Manipur. I plan to spend a couple of days in Manipur before heading for Nagaland.'

The dinner is fabulous. His wife is simply a great cook.

Ajanto comes down to the parking to see me off. It is almost 11 pm when I leave his flat. I wake up early next morning and leave after handing over the key to one of the tenants. It is quite cold as I take the highway and ride at a modest speed before fog on the outskirts of the town forces me to slow down. After a tiring eight-hour ride I am home in Guwahati at 2 pm.

My mother looks terribly weak. Her voice is feeble and she has problem breathing. Years of suffering from asthma has weakened her lungs that make any exertion difficult. We talk briefly before she goes back to sleep.

The next day Nazneen and I take her to a doctor. We were worried whether she would need to be administered oxygen but the doctor says there is no need for her to be hospitalized. He prescribes new medicines for her which she has to continue for three months.

Over the next two days her health improves significantly. She can come out and sit in the sun and doesn't need to be in bed all day. I decide to stay two more days for her health to improve further before leaving for Meghalaya. Shahwar, who had returned from Kohima on a motorcycle, goes back to get his SUV.

I have already travelled 4,500 km since November 13 and I decide to service the motorcycle before starting the next leg of my trip. I ride to the Royal Enfield service centre near our home and leave the motorcycle and return at 3 pm to collect it.

There are six other men sitting at the customers' lounge to collect their bikes. But only one of them is talking. I gather that he is also from Delhi and has just returned from a road trip from some of the Southeast Asian countries. I presume he is the same man Sadiq Naqvi had told me about. For some reason that I can't fathom, the trip seems to have inflated his ego and modesty doesn't seem to be part of his makeup.

'Have you been to Ladakh?' one of the five other men finally asks him.

'Once. And twice to Spiti Valley in Himachal Pradesh. But in Ladakh roads are not what they used to be.'

I am a little surprised by his statement. If he has been to Ladakh only once, how does he compare the roads to the ones that were there earlier? I wonder if this all about optics. If one trip to Ladakh gives him such bragging rights, I wonder how much my nine trips, including a solo one to that region would give me.

A Royal Enfield executive comes and tells me that the motorcycle is ready for delivery. I make the payment and ride back home.

The next morning I head for the riverfront in Guwahati to shoot some photographs. It is cold so I decide to take a bus instead of riding the motorcycle. The bus takes about 45 minutes to cover a distance of just over 10 km, not because of heavy traffic but because the driver lingers at every stop in the hope of getting more passengers.

I get off the bus at Fancy Bazar. But there is heavy fog and mist even at 9 am and the sun is obscured. The ferries at the jetty look ghostly and the river is hardly visible. I decide to return home.

After breakfast, I head for the office of the Nagaland government's Deputy Resident Commissioner to apply for an Inner Line Permit. The guard at the gate tells me the office is closed on Saturdays. 'Come on Monday.'

I return home and spend some time with my mother and tell her that I would be heading for Cherrapunji the next day.

'It is so cold. Why do you have to go?'

'I'll be okay,' I try to reassure her.

But it is difficult to reassure a mother who herself is down with a bad cold and debilitating bouts of asthma. I was hoping Shahwar would be back by the evening. Then around noon, I see a WhatsApp message from him that he had to take a diversion because of a landslide and will possibly be out of mobile network coverage. I still hope he would make it by the night.

I head out for the riverfront once again after lunch. The sun is still bright and I am hoping to catch it set on the Brahmaputra. I take a bus once again, this time because I don't want to wade through slow traffic. I walk down from the main road through a dirt track to the river. Two large ferries that have been junked lie on a slope towards the river. Parts of the ferries have rusted and I wonder why the owners haven't scrapped them yet.

The river has receded and at the jetty across a large sandbank ferries are waiting for passengers for North Guwahati.

The riverfront presents a pretty picture initially. A fisherman waiting in his small boat after casting his net, ferries lined up and some approaching the jetty, a couple of small islands, a mid-river statue of Ahom general Lachit Borphukan who stopped a Mughal invasion of Assam and the Saraighat bridge at a distance combine to make the scene idyllic.

And then I begin to see the ugliness. As I get closer to the ferries and the fisherman's boat, I discover that the sandbank also serves as an open air toilet. There is also human hair wrapped in a 'gamucha' (thin cotton towel) dumped in the sandbank probably after some religious ceremony. Floral garlands also lie near the river's edge and some in the water.

I take photographs of the river, ferries, boats, and passengers. On one end of the sandbank, a group of boys are playing cricket with a tennis ball. The batsman whacks every ball with all his might but the sandbank is large enough to stop the ball from getting into the water.

An earthmover is working at a frenetic pace to carve an access from the main road to the jetty. I wonder what will happen when the river will swallow the sandbank in the monsoon. I retrace my steps and climb up to the main road and head for a restaurant that offers a view of the river from an elevated point. A double-decker ferry for joyrides is ready for departure and the last few passengers rush to board it.

I take a few photographs leaning against a railing over the river's edge and then I rush back to the sandbank to shoot the setting sun. It is also the evening rush hour and commuters are heading home to North Guwahati. In a couple of minutes a long queue of two-wheelers forms in front of a ferry. It moves slowly as one after another, the bikes roll over the gangplank into the ferry's deck. Other passengers board the ferry through another gangplank.

I ask a motorcyclist why he doesn't ride across the Saraighat Bridge instead of taking the ferry.

'That's a longer route. I will be doing about 25 km extra and the ferry crossing takes just 15 minutes.'

The sun sets behind a hill and dusk falls quickly. I leave the riverfront and head for one of Guwahati's oldest markets nearby—Pan Bazar—known mostly for its bookshops and which I used to frequent when I was in college. One of my favourites was a shop named Western Book Depot. I notice that the shop's layout has changed and it is not as crowded as it used to be.

Pan Bazar is also home to one of Guwahati's oldest bakeries—Shaikh Brothers. Business seems good and now there are tables for customers to eat inside the shop as well. Further down the road as I cross an intersection I see a familiar signboard at a corner—Mahamaya Restaurant. This time I notice that the signboard says 'Established in 1918'. There are no customers. A man is standing at the entrance and I presume he is the owner.

'Is this the original building or has it undergone some change?' I ask him.

'I wouldn't know. I am just an employee. The owner, Arjun Barman, will be here around 6:30 pm. You can talk to him.'

It is not yet 5 pm and I can't think of a way to spend one and a half hours before catching Barman. I decide to return home.

I get into a city bus and I am surprised to find a couple of empty seats during rush hour. Expectedly, the bus crawls through traffic. I close my eyes and try to visualize the rest of my trip. The man sitting behind me starts speaking in Hindi on the phone. I can make out he is talking to his wife. He tells her that he would be reaching his rented accommodation soon and then he would cook his dinner. He then asks to speak to his daughter.

The man tells the little girl that he would get her a doll when he goes home. 'A talking doll for the apple of my eye, you know. I am missing you so much. I just want to see you but I don't know how soon I will be able to go home. But be a good girl, eat your food and listen to your mother. And God bless you,' he ends the call.

I find a strange affinity with the man. I have been out for 45 days and I am missing Aseem too. The man gets off at the same stop where I alight and I notice that he is a travelling salesman, probably selling shawls that he is carrying in a large bundle. He hails a rickshaw and gets on to it. I walk home.

I remind my mother that I will be leaving in the morning and pack my bags. There is still no news from Shahwar and his phone is out of reach. I wonder if he has been stranded somewhere.

I eat dinner and got to sleep only to be woken up by a phone call. Aseem is on the line and sobbing uncontrollably.

'A rogue dog attacked the puppies and killed one of them. And Bruno is badly hurt. I have brought him home and dressed his wounds and made a bed for him under the staircase,' he tells me in a choking voice.

I console him and tell him that I am proud of him for his kindness for animals.

'I am going to kill the dog which attacked the pups,' he seethes in anger even as he sobs.

'But it won't bring back the pup. So it is better that you take care of Bruno, Doodle, and Poodle instead of trying to find out which dog killed the other pup,' I reason with him.

He relents and then asks, 'Papa, I got Bruno's blood on my hands when I was carrying him home. Will I need an anti-rabies vaccine?'

'No, you won't. Just wash your hands with soap properly.'

He has been a dog lover since he learnt to walk and is traumatized by the death of the pup and the injury to his favourite pooch and I wish I was home to console him.

I manage to calm him down and tell him to take care of the pups. I end the call after some time and sleep.

The next morning I finally get through to Shahwar. He says he is driving and will call back. At 11 am, I leave for Cherrapunji which is 150 km away from Guwahati.

10

The Abode of Clouds

16 December 2018

The Guwahati-Shillong road must rank as one of the best roads in India. The gradient rises and falls gradually and there are no blind curves, water crossings or a single broken stretch. The sun is shining brightly and the beautiful scenery accentuates the joy of motorcycling in the hills. At Nongpoh, 45 km from Guwahati, I stop for a break. Many years ago, there used to be a row of hotels but for some reason the numbers have fallen. I ask a restaurant owner about the road condition between Shillong and Cherrapunji.

'It is mostly good. The road is a little narrower than this highway. And you will find a few places with broken tarmac near Cherrapunji, but that's nothing to worry about.'

I resume my ride and half an hour later the majestic Umiam Lake comes into view, much below the road. I decide against riding into the Meghalaya Tourism's lakefront property that has a restaurant and water sport facilities and from where you can get a clear view of the lake. Instead, I ride a little ahead and stop at another viewpoint. But it doesn't allow a clear shot of the lake because too many trees get into the viewfinder of the camera. I put the camera back into its bag when a motorcyclist comes and stops near me.

'Are you from Tamil Nadu?' he asks.

'No. But I guess you are.'

'Yes. I am from Coimbatore. There are three of us on two bikes. We started the trip from Chennai and rode along the coastline before entering the Northeast.'

He dismounts and takes off his helmet. I can't see the other motorcycle which is obscured by other vehicles in the parking lot. I notice he is very young.

'I am Ajith and I have just graduated from college. I saw your bike's number plate and thought you are a Tamilian.'

He is on a Yamaha sports bike which has a crouching stance for the rider and is more race-oriented than long distance riding.

'You are on a wrong motorcycle. These clip-on handlebars are not for long distance rides and certainly not in the hills. Your arms must be aching by now.'

'Yes,' he concedes. 'I have a KTM 390 also which I have used for other long rides but for this trip to the Northeast I chose to ride this one.'

The three of them would be staying in Shillong for two nights before they head for Cherrapunji. As he rides away, I wonder why someone who owns a KTM 390 motorcycle and claims to have ridden it on long distance trips would ride a sports bike on such a lengthy trip. It simply doesn't make sense to me.

The four-lane highway effectively ends at Umiam after which there is no divider on the road till Shillong, 20 km away. The curves get sharper but not intimidating. It is Sunday and Shillong is virtually shut. There is very little traffic and I quickly get onto the road to Cherrapunji.

I cross a relatively less crowded Upper Shillong and ride through the sprawling headquarters of the Eastern Air Command of the Indian Air Force. Old fighter planes are placed in strategic places on IAF facilities along the road to catch eyeballs and particularly to boost recruitment into the Air Force.

A hoarding on the highway advertises a recruitment drive for the IAF. It says: 'Other companies want you to meet targets. We want you to take them down.' I think it is a great advertisement pitch and I hope it would have gotten the IAF the number of recruits it expected to get.

I reach a fork but can't see Cherrapunji's name on the signage and ask another biker for directions. I see a name 'Sohra' on the signage which I have not heard before. Twenty kilometres short of Cherrapunji, I stop for another break at a place where there are a couple of eateries and souvenir shops. A long steel railing runs along the edge of road to prevent a motorist from falling into a gorge surrounded by lush green mountains. Khasi women sit against the railing and sell roasted corn. I sit in the sun and eat noodles when my phone rings.

Shahwar is on the line and he tells me that he is in Diphu in Assam's Karbi Anglong district. His SUV has broken down and is waiting for a mechanic to repair it. He won't make it to Guwahati that night. He tells me that he has messaged me the name and phone number of a guest house owner in Cherrapunji where I could stay. He has also sent the number of another man named Rajesh Lymba who runs a camp site in Dawki where I would be heading after Cherrapunji.

Meghalaya literally means the abode of clouds and today it is living up to its name. As I eat the noodles I notice the clouds put on a mesmerizing display. I take a few pictures and then leave. At many places off the road I see abandoned limestone quarries that have been put out of business after the Meghalaya High Court imposed a series of regulations that many miners cannot meet. The court order came after widespread environmental damage that included contamination of water sources.

Half an hour later I roll into Cherrapunji. The highway forks at the edge of the town and I take the road which goes downhill. I stop opposite a petrol station and call Comanches Laloo, the guest house owner whose number Shahwar had forwarded. Comanches tells me that he is on his way back from Dawki and would take at least a couple of hours to reach Cherrapunji.

'But you go ahead and check in. The guest house is exactly three kilometres from the fuel station.'

I ride through the gently sloping road and pass some picturesque small churches. The guest house is on the main road and I find it easily. The signboard says Pumpkin Cherish Guest House. Two staff members at the facility welcome me and show me my room. It is a relatively new building and all rooms are vacant. I wonder if I am going to be the only guest that night.

It is 3:30 pm. I rest briefly and then go out to explore the town located on the quieter side of Cherrapunji. The road which goes down in a gentle gradient from the right of the gate of the guest house is almost deserted on the late Sunday afternoon. I can only see a few kids playing outside their homes. The houses seem small, almost uniform in size. A few shops along the road are closed. People take Sundays seriously, I guess.

Christmas is still nine days away but there are already signs of celebrations. Two busloads of young men and women are returning from a picnic. The cabin lights are on and the picnickers are dancing inside the bus to English pop music. By the time I return to the guest house, it is almost dusk. The staff members have switched on the lights on a Christmas tree and it makes a pretty sight against the backdrop of low hills across the road and a fading orange sky.

There is no sign of Comanches yet. An SUV with six passengers including two teenagers drives in. The guests take up two rooms on either side of mine. The staff members get busy attending the new guests and I go to my room and switch on the television. Comanches drives in around 7 pm and checks on me. He is probably in his late 20s. The short, young man has a smiling demeanour that makes him quite likeable.

'I had gone to Dawki to drop some customers who had come from Bangladesh. I left them at the border checkpost,' he tells me. 'Would you like to have dinner in your room or will you come to the dining hall?'

I tell him that I will take dinner in the dining hall. He goes back to the kitchen.

The new guests are quite noisy. The television is blaring from one of the rooms and I find it difficult to listen to the news. I switch off the television and take out my camera to review the photographs of the day when suddenly the television in the next room falls silent. The teenager complains to her father that the DTH subscription has to be renewed. The man calls Comanches and tells him about the problem.

'I'll get it done,' Comanches tells him and goes away. But the connection is not restored that night.

At dinner, I ask Comanches about the living root bridges of Cherrapunji which I plan to visit the next day. He tells me the direction to a village called Tyrna where I will have to park my motorcycle and start the trek through the forest for the bridges.

After breakfast the next morning I head for Tyrna, 16 km away. Shortly after leaving the guest house I see a group of people standing outside what looks like a factory. It looks like some kind of a demonstration by employees. Further down the road there are more signs of abandoned limestone quarries and contaminated water bodies.

The narrow road gets narrower about five kilometres ahead of Tyrna and much of the tarmac is broken. Traffic stops at a dead end in Tyrna. I park my motorcycle in the parking lot. Four young men who are coming back from the trek are sweating profusely and I begin to wonder if I did the right thing by wearing the riding jacket.

I ask one of the four young men about trek. 'It is tiring but doable. I suggest you take a walking stick. It helps on the way up.' Two of the four are from Delhi, one from Punjab and one from Odisha.

I rent a walking stick from a young boy for Rs 20 and start the trek. The sky is cloudy and after sometime a thick canopy blocks out the sunrays. The concrete steps seem never ending. There are about 3,500 steps one way so that makes a total of 7,000 steps to climb up and down for a glimpse of the root bridges.

A few villagers are heading up and some of the men have heavy loads on their backs. Two young female tourists sit on the stairs to catch their breath. A little later the staircase curves and I see a small shop in a tiny clearing. There is also a bamboo *machan* (platform) that provides a majestic view of the forest. I stop at the shop to buy a fruit drink and move on.

A group of tourists is behind me. At another viewpoint, one of them asks me to take a photograph of the group with his camera. I learn they are from Hyderabad and all of them are software engineers. A few tourists who are returning seem weary.

'How far is the double-decker bridge from here?' I ask one of them.

'Still quite far. May be an hour.'

I continue the descent. It gets warmer and I take off my jacket. I come across a small village called Nong Thymai and stop at a shop to buy oranges. There is no one inside. In a house built on stilts adjacent to the shop three toddlers are playing on the balcony with bamboo railings to prevent the children from toppling into the ground. The eldest of the three starts calling out to his mother after he sees me. The woman comes to the shop and I buy the oranges. She also sells biscuits, instant noodles, tea, chocolates, and water.

'How do you get the merchandise here?' I ask her.

'If it is less we carry it ourselves. Otherwise, we hire porters after we get the goods from Cherrapunji.'

It is a tough place to be in but she seems cheerful. Outside the shop there is a bench made of bamboo. I sit and eat the orange and throw the peel into a dustbin. Villages in Meghalaya take pride in cleanliness and Nong Thymai in the middle of a jungle is no different. Within the village limits dustbins are strategically placed so that nothing is littered on the ground.

I resume the trek and come to a small suspension bridge across a rivulet which has been shut. The only way to cross it is to walk across the rivulet but that is possible only because it is winter and there are enough large boulders to walk on. By the time monsoon sets in, the bridge must be repaired.

The climb has been downhill so far but the trek now is mostly uphill. I begin to feel hungry and my thirst increases. I see a small house with 'Restaurant' written on a wall and walk in. Two bearded young men are rolling *ganja* (cannabis) into cigarettes. I ask them where they are from.

'Kerala,' one of them replies. 'If you want tea or coffee you will have to wait. The manager has gone out for some time.'

The third man in the room is a European tourist. He is talking to the Malayalees who seem to be hippies and extreme right wingers.

The young man who spoke to me is railing against a threat that he believes Islam poses to India.

'Muslims in India will overtake the Hindu population and that is a real danger. Every Muslim has at least five kids. And they are not educated. South Asia will burn once India becomes a Muslim majority country.'

I am both angry and amused. The European is not convinced either.

'That's quite an alarmist view,' he says.

'Do you really expect a community of 14 per cent to overtake the population of 80 per cent of Hindus in India? How can you make such a sweeping statement? You are from Kerala where most Muslims are educated and pretty well off.' I tell him.

'Have you seen Muslims in Uttar Pradesh and Bihar?' he retorts.

'They are not representatives of Muslims of the entire country. And you know it as well. But if you want to believe your fantasies, I guess that's your privilege.'

'I am sorry if I have offended you but I think I am right.'

'I am not surprised that you think you are right. That's what you have been schooled in. But I wish you could see the country differently than the Hindu-Muslim binary that you can't seem to get over with.'

The two men light their cannabis. I find the smell repulsive and leave the place.

Another suspension bridge looms and this one is in working condition. I walk across the bridge. A river below the bridge has shrunk to expose huge boulders and a narrow channel of water fills up a few pools. The climb gets steeper before I come across a root bridge across the same river that I had crossed on the suspension bridge.

The village of Nongriat begins at this bridge and the trek goes up again. There are a couple of homestays in the village, one very appropriately named Serene Homestay. A little later the double-decker root bridge comes into view. It is a heady sight that makes me forget my hunger and aching calves.

I walk up and down the double-decker bridge and marvel at the villagers' ingenuity in building an all-weather bridge for generations. The shallow pools also seem to be laid out in decks. Fish swim in the transparent water with abandon because fishing is banned. I sit on a rock and spend almost an hour just listening to the sound of the water and the birds and watch little children frolicking in the pools. My legs hurt when I stand up. I walk to an eatery and ask for noodles and tea. I ask the woman running the shop about Rainbow Falls.

'It is more than an hour from here. But the fall is almost dry now so I won't suggest that you go.'

I eat the noodles and drink the tea and then start the trek back to Tyrna. At the suspension bridge a man is walking up with a bag of cement on his back. At least he is close to his home. The climb gets tiring. I set myself a target of climbing 40 steps at a time then.rest for five minutes. I manage to do it four times in a row and then I realize I can't climb more than 30 steps at a time. A few tourists are coming down the stairs but there is no one heading up.

I eventually make it to the parking lot and return the walking stick to the boy and go to a small restaurant and ask for tea. The restaurant is run by three young women and a teenage girl. Two of the women are sitting at a corner of the shop and one of them is doing up the other's hair.

The parking lot is almost full. An Assamese taxi driver comes in and starts flirting with the woman who is getting her hair done.

'Who are you getting decked up for?'

The riposte is quick and sharp. 'Certainly not for you. Christmas is round the corner and I better look good.'

It is two o'clock and I decide to head back to Cherrapunji. My legs ache badly and they hurt even more when I have to straddle the motorcycle. I start the bike and start climbing the broken road. The group of people outside the factory I had seen in the morning is still standing although the number has dwindled. I stop and ask one of them what it is about. A man tells me it is a government-owned cement factory.

'We are demanding a pay hike. We have stopped working and won't start until our demands are met.'

Another man butts in. 'The government doesn't care. This is one of Meghalaya's oldest cement factories. They had such a head start over all other cement factories but now they tell us that they can't raise our salaries because the company isn't making profit. There are conniving with private companies to rob us.'

I wonder how long this agitation will last.

Twenty minutes later I am back in Cherrapunji. I am not sure Comanches' kitchen is still open so I stop for lunch at a restaurant. The restaurant is on the first floor and I watch traffic go by as I wait for my food. A few old Jeeps, some of them with trailers, pass in front of the restaurant. Jeeps are so quintessential to Meghalaya that they haven't gone out of fashion despite the onslaught of modern cars.

A young man named Patrick runs the restaurant. As he serves me lunch he asks me about my profession.

'I am a journalist. I work in Delhi.'

'Then you should first write that Cherrapunji's name has been changed to Sohra.'

I guess that explains why all the signboards I saw had 'Sohra' written on them.

'How long has it been?'

'A couple of years. We fought hard to revert to the original name. Cherrapunji was a name the British gave. It made no sense for Khasis. We had been demanding for a long time that the named be changed to Sohra. All signage now says Sohra but officially the name is yet to change. It was important that we got Sohra's name restored.'

I think of Uttar Pradesh where the government has recently been on a renaming spree with hardly anyone asking for it. And here in Meghalaya they had to fight to get it.

'We didn't have alphabets for the Khasi language until Thomas Jones, a Welsh missionary, gave it to us towards the middle of the 19th century. And until then our history was oral. Like stories handed down from one generation to another, you know,' Patrick tells me.

I wonder why he is telling me all that. But it is interesting to know and I continue the conversation.

'Are there Khasi primary schools here or are they all English schools now?'

'There are both.'

'What about you? Where have you studied?'

'I went to a Khasi primary school and then to an English-medium school. I dropped out of college after my father died while I was doing my graduation course. I have been managing the restaurant since then.'

The weather is beginning to look bad. The sky gets dark and it begins to drizzle. I finish my lunch and hurry down to my motorcycle and rush for the guest house. I get in just in the nick of time as the drizzle becomes heavier. I am tired after the long trek to the root bridges and sleep for a couple of hours.

It is dark when I wake up and go out to the balcony. The drizzle has stopped. An SUV with six passengers arrives. The six men take a large room with three beds and then proceed to make a bonfire near the parking lot and sit around it and start drinking. The men are bantering and a couple of them are singing. I walk around inside the compound for the lack of doing anything better.

The songs end rather soon as the alcohol quickly gets the better of the men around the bonfire. It is a mixed group of Assamese and Bengalis. Two of them are extremely voluble and the subject of their discussion is the National Register of Citizens in Assam which seeks to detect foreigners and illegal immigrants in the state. One of the two loudmouths thinks that the NRC exercise is aimed against Hindus because many in the Bangla-speaking Barak Valley in southern Assam have been left out of the list. I can't make sense of it because many Muslims across the state have also been left out of the NRC list. Most illegal immigrants in Assam are from Bangladesh.

'I tell you, there is no unity among Hindus. If one Muslim man is attacked, 50 others will show up to retaliate. But if one Hindu is attacked, others will choose to stay inside their homes and not get involved,' he rails.

I wonder why his views are so coloured.

Another man chips in, 'Our leaders are useless. As long as their interests are served, the community can go to hell.'

The other man sounds even more ominous. 'There are going to be riots in a few months. Mark my words. The Muslims will start it and we will be at the receiving end of it,' he slurs and sways as he stands up.

A third man tries to make light of the apprehensions. 'We are going to die anyway. So why bother? Just drink and be happy.'

By the time two large bottles of whisky are over, one of the men can't get up from his chair. Two others sling his hands over their shoulders and carry him to their room. Comanches comes out to the balcony and announces that dinner is ready. One of the six men tells Comanches to serve the dinner in the room while I go to the dining hall. I eat quickly and head back to my room. It starts drizzling again.

I check the weather forecast on the internet and see that rain is predicted through the next day throughout Meghalaya. It means my trip to Dawki will be delayed by a day. I go to sleep and wake up to a cloudy morning. The drizzle is intermittent. There is no way I can ride to Dawki, about 85 km to the southeast in West Jaintia district, because I am not carrying a rain suit.

I go for a bath and discover that there is no water. Comanches runs to the roof and discovers that construction workers at the adjacent plot have siphoned off water from the overhead tank. He disconnects the offending pipe and I wait for the tank to fill. It takes quite some time for the tank to fill up to a decent level. The source of water is a stream and the flow of water is slow. And then I remember that Cherrapunji has been suffering from shortage of drinking water for years despite being the wettest place on Earth mainly because the rain water is not conserved. It also hasn't helped that rainfall has been erratic in Cherrapunji since the turn of the century.

I manage to take a bath and eat my breakfast. The drizzle continues for more than an hour. When it stops, I decide to explore the nearby areas on foot. The rain-washed hills look fresh. I walk to a nearby tourist attraction called Eco Park. It is a sprawling area from where you get a panoramic view of several waterfalls stretched across a mountain range. But most of the falls have dried up.

'You should come here in the monsoon to see the falls. They are awesome,' a guard, strolling from the opposite direction tells me. His lips are red and he is chewing *kwai*, a combination of areca nut and betel leaf (*paan*)with a dash of lime.

'That's Bangladesh,' he says pointing straight to a flat stretch of land where the mountains end. There is a thin layer of mist and view is slightly clouded. I walk around a little bit more and notice that a rainwater harvesting programme has been put in place. It seems to be a case of better late than never.

I walk out of Eco Park and head for one of Cherrapunji's famous caves at Mawsmai, two kilometres away, when I hear the most famous Christmas carol—'Jingle Bells'. Four little boys playing inside a garage in one of the larger houses in the area are singing at the top of their voices. Even after I cross the house I can hear their voices for quite a distance. The drizzle starts again and I take shelter in a small shop and chat up the shopkeeper. After the drizzle stops he tells me that it won't rain heavily.

'Mawsmai is one kilometre from here and you will find places to stop if the drizzle starts again. But the last half kilometre is open area and the only shelter is the trees. It is worth trying your luck.'

I start walking again. A couple of houses are being whitewashed and I notice that all houses are whitewashed with lime which I guess has to be natural because it is found so abundantly in the region. Barely five minutes later the drizzle returns and this time it is a little heavier. I take shelter in another shop and ten minutes later the drizzle stops. The pattern repeats itself twice more before I reach the Mawsmai caves.

The parking lot is almost full. There are many eateries and souvenir shops but most restaurants are packed to capacity and there are no places to sit. The temperature has plunged and I need tea. I finally get tea at another eatery but have to drink it standing. I learn that tourists are allowed to enter only one cave. An adjoining cave is for researchers and explorers and needs proper gear to enter.

I buy a ticket and enter the cave at the base of a lush green hill. Tourists stop at the mouth of the cave for photographs and selfies. Inside the cave, the tourism department which is responsible for its upkeep has installed lights at strategic places so that tourists can see the rock formations. At some places you have to sit and squeeze through small openings. In other places the cave widens enough to reveal layers of rocks and strange shapes. The air inside is slightly damp, probably because of the drizzle outside. I want to take a selfie but there are two women in the frame. I wait for some time for them to move away, but they don't. I take the photograph and when I review it I notice that the two women behind me were applying lipstick before taking their own selfies.

I spend more than half an hour inside the cave. Near the exit, two little boys play hide and seek among the rocks. The drizzle has reduced to a powdery stuff. I go to a restaurant and order lunch. The hot food feels great. Other customers also walk in and among them is a North Indian couple on their honeymoon.

The couple still has to visit the cave and I wonder how the woman will walk through it in high heels. Among all the tourists, she seems to be the only one with a wrong pair of shoes. The weather gets worse and the drizzle gives way to a spell of heavy rain which lasts for another 15 minutes before it stops. I make my way out of the restaurant and head for the guest house. The drizzle starts again when I am about 100 metres away from the guest house and there is no shelter where I can stop. I walk fast but by the time I reach the guest house, my jacket and trousers are wet. I quickly change and hang the clothes to dry.

The cold increases and I ask one of the staffers for a heater. The room gets cozy as I switch on the blower and fall asleep. I wake up later in the afternoon and check the weather forecast for the next day and I am relieved to find that a sunny day is predicted.

I call a colleague, David Laitphlang in Shillong and tell him that I would be heading for his town the next day after visiting Dawki. David asks me to meet Jason Lamare in a village called Shnongpdeng near Dawki. Shnongpdeng is where the Umngot river runs shallow and where the transparent water offers a fascinating view of the riverbed and creates an illusion that boats are gliding over a glass top on the water.

'Jason is a man of many parts. He is Meghalaya's cricket captain, also plays football, is an expert diver and a mountaineer and runs the first campsite that was set up along the Umngot river. I will forward you his number and I suggest you talk to him now.'

I call up Jason but the line is crackling. He gives me the directions to reach his campsite in Shnongpdeng before the line goes dead and I can't get through to his phone again.

I watch the news for some time on the television before Comanches calls me for dinner. I eat well and pay him the rent since I would be moving out early morning and he may not be at the facility. On some nights, Comanches goes home which is nearby.

I ask him about his father.

'He stays home mostly. He used to be in the limestone business until the High Court order stopped it. His customers were mostly from Assam and the other Northeastern states.'

The limestone business was pretty simple. Miners who were people who owned land in the limestone-rich areas of the Khasi and Jaintia Hills would extract the mineral and sell it to domestic consumers in other states or export it to Bangladesh through various export points along the border. There used to be a single-window clearance from the local forest authorities. The government's revenue came by way of a transportation tax on the extracted limestone that the miners had to pay. But the simplicity of the trade is now history.

Comanches tells me that he had been thinking of migrating either to the United States or Australia after his graduation but his father suggested that he would be better off building and running a guest house in their own land.

'So that's how I stayed put. I haven't even collected my degree from the college in Bangalore. It has been a few years since I graduated but I have just been putting off a visit to Bangalore.'

'Can't you ask for it on email?'

'I am not sure. They will probably want to see other original documents for which I will have to be there in person.'

I ask him about the guests who were drinking around the bonfire the night before.

'They left this morning for Guwahati around 9 am. It looks like they came here only to drink.'

I return to my room and sleep. I wake up at 5:30 am and get ready. But even by 6 am, it is quite dark and foggy. I wait for an hour before I leave for Dawki. Everybody else at the guest house is still asleep.

It is cold and the fog is still thick but as soon as I exit the town the sun breaks through in all its splendour. The mist rises from the valley around Cherrapunji and reaches the level of the road to create a surreal sight. A few kilometres down the road another spectacular sight forces me to stop. I dismount and walk off the road to take photographs of a sea of low clouds that has covered an entire valley and are slowly rising to the level of the road.

I notice a film crew. Two of them are checking a drone camera that they will use for the shoot. The drone is hovering overhead and one of the crew members is steering it with a remote control. I learn that they would be shooting a television commercial for a car rental company called Zoomcar.

A make-up man is working on a female model ahead of the shoot. She is wrapped in a thick shawl and is holding herself tight to fight off the cold. But she is shivering in a mini-skirt and it beats me why on earth the director would want her to wear such a piece of clothing in such a cold place in December. Glamour extracts a strange price, I guess.

I continue my journey downhill before I reach a fork and take a turn for Dawki. For a few kilometres it is as picturesque as it can be. Hills with pine trees, massive rocks and rolling pastures and a clear blue sky combine to make the ride a pleasure. But it is too good to last. The fog sets in suddenly and gets thick in no time. On the twisty road with blind curves, the pleasure of motorcycling quickly turns into a pain.

I see a milestone which says Dawki is still 55 km away. I pray that the fog lifts quickly but God doesn't seem to be in a mood to listen to me. My helmet visor gets foggy so I lift it and ride on for some time before my glasses also suffer from the same effect. I take off my glasses and put them in my pocket. The ride tires me but I am apprehensive of stopping in the fog just in case a vehicle bumps into me from behind.

The fog lessens near the outskirts of a small town called Pynursla. I stop the moment I see a small restaurant and walk in. The cold seems to have frozen my knees temporarily and the first few steps are painful. I ask for tea and an egg cutlet. I walk up and down the verandah of the bamboo structure to get the circulation back in my legs. Three dogs are playing near the shop. One of them—a black and white pooch—is wearing a collar. I soon find out that it belongs to the owner of the restaurant.

Dawki is still 30 km away. But the fog is in no mood to give way as it sets in again after I cross Pynursla. The fog finally lifts 10 km ahead of Dawki but now the road is narrower. I see trucks lined up on the edge of the road. Some of them are loaded with coal. I wonder where the coal has come from since mining has been banned in Meghalaya. The scene repeats itself a few times till I reach Dawki.

I cross a Border Security Force (BSF) outpost in the final approach to Dawki and can make out Bangladesh beyond the sandbanks of the Umngot river. A group of young men try to flag me down as I approach a bridge over the river. I slow down and each one shouts over the other to ask if I want a hire boat. A ride costs Rs 500 an hour. I am not interested and I ride on.

The Umngot river becomes uniquely transparent in the winter and allows a clear look of the riverbed and the fish.

I take a road uphill to Shnongpdeng. The other side of the road is lined up with trucks loaded with rocks headed for Bangladesh. The border at Tamabil is just a kilometre away. From the main road, a narrow lane leads to Shnongpdeng. Loose stones, slush, and potholes filled with water combine to make the road an obstacle course but the Himalayan takes it all in its stride and keeps me firmly on the saddle. I finally reach Shnongpdeng at noon. The fog ensured that I took at least an hour more than I should have. The sky is partly cloudy and the sun plays hide and seek.

I stop near a small shop and dismount. I want to call Jason but there is no signal on my phone so I ask the shopkeeper where I could find Jason but draw a blank. At the car park near the riverfront, I ask a woman at a shop if I could borrow her phone to speak to Jason. She knows Jason and calls him and hands her phone to me.

'Where are you?' Jason asks.

'At the car park,' I tell him.

'Okay. Please walk down the stairs to the boat counter and wait. I will send a boat to pick you up. My campsite in on your right, the red tents that you can see.'

I take the stairs down and reach the boat counter from where tourists hire boats for Rs 500 an hour. A few minutes later a young man comes up and asks, 'Are you Sabir Hussain?'

I nod and he asks me to follow him to a boat.

The Umngot river makes Shnongpdeng a minor paradise. The water is crystal clear. The rocks and sand on the riverbed are clearly visible. And there is plenty of fish. A few tourists are on canoes while others splash around in the shallow water. Some tourists jump from a moderately high rocky platform into the water at a relatively deeper stretch of the river.

There is a suspension bridge high above the river under which the boat passes. Tourists pose on the bridge for photographs. The boatman manoeuvres the boat to the bank near the campsite behind which is a hill of evergreen forest.

'Come, I will show you your tent,' he tells me.

'My tent? But I am not staying here. I came to meet Jason.'

'Oh. Jason is not here,' says the boatman as we walk towards a tent. It is a large, three-man tent and seems comfortably pitched on the sandy surface. 'I'll get somebody to talk to you.'

I wait for a few minutes before another young man comes down from an elevation behind the tents and introduces himself as Adrian.

'Jason told me you are a guest.'

'I am not. There has been some misunderstanding. I wanted to speak to Jason about this campsite. David Laitphlang had told me about Jason.'

'Jason is in Shillong for a Ranji Trophy match which begins tomorrow. And yes, David helped setting up this campsite.'

Adrian takes me on a tour of the campsite. The dining hall which is made of bamboo is at an elevation. Further down are the bathrooms and toilets. The bathrooms have showers but no roofs probably to lend a touch of the wild. And there are no geysers. Everything is neat but by now I have seen that much of Meghalaya is squeaky clean.

From the elevation there is a trek that goes into the jungle which more adventurous tourists take. And there is a rockface that offers rock climbing thrills. Adrian also takes tourists for scuba diving. What sets this campsite apart from others is its exclusive location. You can't reach it without taking a boat.

Adrian gives me his number and asks me to call him if I return to Shnongpdeng to stay as we head back to the river bank.

As I wait for the boatman, I see the Hyderabadi tourists I had met on the trek to the double-decker root bridge. They are also getting ready to leave for Shillong and ask Adrian where they can hire an SUV for their onward journey. The boatman comes and I get into the boat along with another couple from Odisha who also has to catch taxi for Shillong.

We get off at the boat counter from where a bamboo bridge runs across the shallowest part of the river to the opposite bank. There are three more campsites on that side. I walk across the bridge to try to find Rajesh who runs one of these camps and whose number Shahwar had given me. But he is not there and there is still no signal on my phone. Near the campsite a boy of about 12 is sitting in a kiosk selling fruit drinks and chewing gums. I ask him where I could find Rajesh Lymba.

'He is my father. He has gone to the other side of the river.'

Like Jason, Rajesh also turns out to be elusive but for an altogether different reason.

I walk back to the parking lot and go to a restaurant and ask for noodles. The woman takes quite some time to make it. Another man walks in and sits near me while I wait for my noodles. He takes a look at me and asks, 'What motorcycle?'

'Royal Enfield Himalayan.'

'I haven't been on it but I heard it is good.'

'It is. I have very little to complain about.'

'Ah, that's life. I have a lot to complain about.'

'Like what?'

'Oh, I used to be a coal trader. I sold coal mostly to small businesses. But after the court stopped coal mining I ran into a dead end. I used to drive my car for my own work. But now I run it as a taxi. The earnings are much less than what I used to make selling coal.'

'If mining is banned then where is the coal coming from that I saw on my way here?'

'They say it was excavated before the ban came into effect and can be transported before the 31 January 2019 deadline imposed by the Supreme Court.'

Coal mining has been a contentious issue in Meghalaya, mostly because of the method used to extract the fuel. 'Rat-hole' mining became infamous after frequent accidents that claimed the lives of many miners over the years. The primitive style of mining that entails digging a vertical shaft and then boring parallel tunnels is prone to sudden flooding that leave miners with virtually no chance to survive such an accident.

Mining of coal by hand has been going on in Meghalaya for over 150 years, mostly for local use. Large-scale illegal and indiscriminate mining of coal by private landowners and the local community started in the late 1980s. Many miners are minors. Others come from neighbouring states and Nepal as well. They work many metres underground in unsafe conditions, mining coal with their bare hands.

A week earlier, 15 miners were trapped in an illegal coal mine which suddenly flooded in East Jaintia Hills and eventually died. Illegal mining had been rife in that area despite a blanket ban on such activities ordered by the National Green Tribunal to restore the environment damaged by years of such activities. Poverty and the lack of alternative livelihood have apparently continued to fuel rat hole coal mining in Meghalaya.

I leave Shnongpdeng at 2 pm and see that the trucks loaded with rocks and bound for Bangladesh have started moving. The long convoy rolls in slow motion. At a T-point, the trucks turn left for the border at Tamabil while I turn right for Shillong. I stop at the BSF post I had seen on my way to Dawki and ask one of the troopers to show me the boundary. From the post high on the road, no formal markings are visible.

'The green part vertically down here with vegetation is ours. The sandbanks and beyond is Bangladesh. The river flows into Bangladesh after that turn over there,' he tells me and then asks, 'Where are you heading?'

'Shillong.'

'It's going to be a long ride today. Just heard on the radio that it is quite foggy.'

I moan. Another foggy spell is the last thing I wanted.

I run into the fog sooner than I expected. And it is even worse than what it was in the morning. I take almost two hours to reach Pynursla. I stop at the same restaurant where I had tea in the morning. As I walk into the restaurant I see the three dogs playing in the road when a large truck that was behind me crosses the stretch and the dogs scamper. But it is too late for the restaurant owner's dog to avoid the truck. After the truck passes I see the dog lying motionless on the road. The owner joins me as I run to check. The dog is dead but there is no blood anywhere. It must have taken a knock on the head and died instantly.

The owner kneels and mourns. 'Let's remove it from the road,' I tell him and help him lift the dog from the middle of the road and put it on the grass near a railing. 'He was such a playful chap,' the owner says, almost choking with grief.

He picks up his dead pet in his arms and goes down the slope of the hill. I return to the restaurant for my tea and by the time I finish it, the fog thickens. Visibility drops drastically and all vehicles crawl at snail's pace. The next 20 km take another hour to cover before the fog lets up to allow some decent speed. But visibility drops again on the outskirts of Shillong as a trademark powdery drizzle envelops the hills during rush hour. I crawl through lengthy queues of traffic before I reach Assam House in the heart of the town at Dhankheti.

It is 6 pm and it has taken me four hours to cover 80 km from Dawki. I walk to the reception to confirm if my booking is still valid because state guest houses are known to cancel the booking of a civilian who is not a government employee if some VIP shows up. Fortunately, my booking is valid. I return to the parking to unload my luggage. A man in his late 50s is strolling on the balcony of the building near the parking.

'Where are you from?' he asks.

'Delhi.'

'And you have been riding from there?'

'No. I started the ride from Siliguri. I have been living in Delhi for 30 years. I hail from Guwahati.'

'A fellow Assamese, I see. I am with the statistical department of the central government and I am posted in Shillong.'

I ask him his name.

'Bipul Bordoloi. I am the grandson of Gopinath Bordoloi, first chief minister of Assam.'

I was beginning to like him until he mentioned his grandfather. Something snaps inside me and I wonder why he can't be his own man and must invoke his grandfather in a simple conversation with a stranger. I pick up my bags and go inside the building.

Once inside the room, I realize that I am very tired. It is very cold and my knees are stiff and my body aches badly. I ask room service for tea and snacks and then call David. He tells me he will be there in an hour.

I almost doze off when the bell rings. It is David. He tells me he had been busy for the past week running to and from a hospital where a close friend is under treatment. I tell him about the miscommunication with Jason and how I couldn't meet him in Shnongpdeng and ask him about the recent coal mine tragedy.

'Illegal coal mining is a huge nexus in Meghalaya. It will take a political leader of great courage, conviction and integrity to stop it or introduce modern mining,' David tells me.

He wants to know my plans for the next day.

'I have to go to the Nagaland House for an Inner Line Permit. I will move around, meet locals and check out the archery competition in the afternoon. And I want to meet Lou Majaw.'

'Let me check with Lou,' says David and calls up Shillong's most famous singer, song writer, and musician.

'You can meet him at around 2 pm at Dylan's Café down this road. And I suggest you go to the Polo Ground to check the Baby League football competition in the morning. It is actually great,' he tells me.

We talk some more. He tells me he has to drop his younger daughter at the airport in the morning to catch a flight to Kolkata where she will spend Christmas with her older sister. After David leaves, I go out for dinner and head for a particular restaurant near Assam House that he had recommended.

I walk barely 200 metres when I see a group of men huddled on the pavement. As I get closer I notice that three men have cornered another man and one of them is holding the victim by his collar. I run to break up the fight and see a young strapping Sikh rushing in from the opposite direction. The two of us separate the three men, all locals, from the other man who is a North Indian and ask what the fight was about.

'He is smoking *ganja* (marijuana),' says the young man who had been holding him by the collar.

'And you think that gives you the right to beat him up?' the Sikh asks.

The victim is bleeding from a cut in his lips after he was punched and is on the verge of tears.

'I was just walking down the pavement and smoking when they stopped me and started beating me and tried to snatch my wallet.'

'Where do you people work?' I ask the three men.

Two of them are unemployed and the most aggressive of the three says he is a caretaker at a company guest house. There is a police checkpost nearby and I suggest that we go there but the proposition scares the three men.

'No, there is no need. We will leave,' says the hothead and tries to walk away.

The Sikh stops him. 'Listen, if you really want to fight, hit me. How would you feel if I just stop you on the road and whack you? Don't pick on someone who is disadvantaged.'

The three men sober up. I ask the victim if his wallet is with him. 'Yes,' he replies and walks away into the night. The three men head in the opposite direction.

'These guys were after some easy money,' the Sikh man tells me and thanks me for being with him to break up the fight. I wonder if mugging is a common crime in Shillong.

It is 9 pm and almost time for the restaurant to close when I walk in for dinner. I eat well and return to Assam House and go to sleep.

I wake up to a sunny morning and clear blue sky. After breakfast, I leave for Nagaland House for an Inner Line Permit. I choose to walk since I am not familiar with roads and traffic restrictions that include many one-way roads. It feels invigorating to walk under a bright sun and breathe in the crisp air. I cross Shillong's most famous boys' school—Saint Edmund's—on the way to Nagaland House and notice that the city's love affair with Jeeps has continued. Most Jeeps still ply with a trailer carrying goods but I also see a few of them now lug small water tankers.

Nagaland House is a two-storey building in a sprawling area with a beautiful garden in the front but it is under renovation and there is no official to talk to. I walk to the rear of the building and discover that there are quarters for minor staffers. I ask one of the men about the Inner Line Permit.

'The Resident Commissioner has gone home to Nagaland. I don't know if anybody else will show up today. I can give you the form but you will have to come back around 11 am and check if there is any official to sign the form.'

I have no choice but to take the form and go out. I head for a taxi stand to go to Polo Ground. I notice that there are several small shops along the pavement with just a table and a chair and a board with some numbers. I learn that they are booths run by bookmakers to accept bets on archery. You bet on a number between 0 and 99 and buy a ticket and if that number is declared the winner that day, you can collect the money by submitting the ticket.

A punter has to predict the last two digits of the total number of arrows hitting the target. For example, if 1220 arrows hit the target, then the winning number is 20 and if 1107 arrows hit the target then the winning number is 07. I don't bet so I just move on.

The first taxi in the row at the taxi stand is empty and I get into front seat. I notice that there is padding between the two front seats that effectively converts it into a middle seat. The driver tells me it will take about 10 minutes before he gets all the passengers. In five minutes, four passengers squeeze into the rear seat but the driver is still standing outside. A few minutes later a young man gets though the driver's door and inches towards the middle before the driver gets in. So in a four-seater car we have seven people. I can't push my seat back because the rear is already cramped. My knees touch the glove box as the driver takes us through a long downhill stretch to Polo Ground where everybody disembarks.

I walk to the stadium complex and head for the football ground. The cricket ground is adjacent but there is no one watching the Ranji Trophy match between Meghalaya and Mizoram. I look at the manual scoreboard and make out that Meghalaya is fielding but can't recognize Jason Lamare. I enter the football stadium and find the atmosphere completely different—it is electric and infectious.

Little boys and girls in different age groups in bright colourful jerseys and shorts are ready to fight it out. There are two matches going on simultaneously—one between coaches and the other between parents of the kids who would be playing a little later and the mood is that of a carnival. Every goal and save is celebrated with whoops of joy and loud applause.

I sit near a little boy in blue jersey and shorts. His boots are lying in front of him. He is eight years old and his name is Malcolm. He tells me his father is playing in the parents' match underway and points him out.

'There he is. And that's my mom on the sideline.'

'What time is your match?' I ask him.

'I am not sure. But it is after the kiddies finish. Our age group is the next.'

The stands are getting filled up, mostly by young people and middle school students. A man comes with his two daughters and they take the seats in front of us. The younger girl is dressed in yellow football gear. I ask the man his name.

'I am R Phawa. I am a government employee and I have taken leave today to bring my daughters here. The younger one is mad about football but the older one is more interested in arts.'

Football has long been Shillong's favourite sport. In recent years the performance of Lajong FC in I-League, India's top football league, has fuelled the passion for the game even more in the city and the state.

The two matches end and the organizers announce that the first of the Baby League finals will start. The announcement is greeted by a roar from the crowd. The two kiddies' teams are still on the stands and their parents and coaches organize them in a queue to go to the ground. It is a heartwarming scene to see the mixed team of little boys and girls walk together to play. Ahead of the match, there is a minor ceremony.

I check the time and see it is 11 am. I have to return to Nagaland House to try my luck for the Inner Line Permit and reluctantly leave the stadium. On the cricket ground, there is a drinks break. And there are still no spectators to see the match. Cricket may be a religion in the rest of the country, but here in Shillong it just can't hold a candle to football.

I wait for ten more minutes before taking another taxi which drops me near Nagaland House. There is still no official inside. I wait for half an hour and then go for lunch near Assam House. I call up David and tell him that I have drawn a blank at Nagaland House.

'Let me see if I can do something. I will call you back,' he tells me.

After lunch I head for Dylan's Café. I am well ahead of the two o'clock meeting with Lou Majaw. On the first floor of a two-storey building, Dylan's Café is an idyllic hangout for western music lovers. Lou, who publicly acknowledges that he loves Bob Dylan's lyrics, had helped set it up.

The décor is minimalistic and impressive. On the stairwell leading to the café, vinyl records of Dylan's albums are mounted on two walls. A row of old-fashioned lanterns hang from a cable on the balcony which also has lounge chairs. Inside the café are normal restaurant seats, a guitar hanging on a wall and Dylan's photographs. I sit on the balcony and wait for Lou.

At 1:45 pm, David calls to say that an official has reached Nagaland House and I should hurry to get my Inner Line Permit.

'But I am waiting for Lou at Dylan's Café.'

'You go to Nagaland House first to get your permit and then go to Shillong Café. Lou will be there. It is near Nagaland House,' David tells me. 'That official at Nagaland House had called in sick but I got a Naga friend of mine to request him to show up for half an hour so that he can sign your permit.'

I am at a loss for words to thank David as I rush to Nagaland House. I can't find a taxi so I walk as fast as I can. It still takes me about 20 minutes to reach and another 20 minutes for the officer to complete the formalities of checking my identity papers and writing my name in the office register. It is 2:45 pm when I reach Shillong Café. A few customers are drinking coffee and reading books on Lou. I find the man standing on the balcony with an irritated look on his face and I apologize for the delay.

'I was trying to call David to tell him that I am leaving,' Lou tells me.

'I am sorry. I was actually waiting for you when David called and I had to rush to Nagaland House for my Inner Line Permit. There was no one in the office in the morning.'

He cools down almost immediately. 'These government chaps! I tell you, they just don't want to work. How can the entire office be empty on a working day of the week?' he says as he orders two cups of tea.

He is known for his trademark shorts but this December afternoon he is wearing jeans and a jacket and a woollen cap with a grey ponytail sticking out of it. He looks much younger than his 71 years.

We sit in the balcony and talk. Young people on the opposite side of the road wave and wish him as they cross the stretch and I quickly find out why. Lou Majaw's charm is infectious and I soon forget that I had planned to meet him for 15 minutes.

He warms up even more when I tell him that I am on a motorcycle expedition of the Northeast.

'That's really great. We need free spirit like that.'

I also tell him that I had been to the Polo Ground in the morning and watched the football matches for some time and how the kids were thronging the stadium.

'Yes,' he clenches his fist just like a goal scorer does in celebration, and gives a wide smile. 'There is no game like football, man. Fast, furious, action-packed. I just love it.'

I ask him about Shillong Café.

'Someone asked me to help set it up as a place where music lovers and young musicians can meet. We meet once a week where budding musicians are encouraged to sing their numbers and strum the guitar.'

'How many of them stick to music given the pressure of finding a job and keeping it?' I ask.

'Unfortunately, only a few do. It takes a lot of courage to pursue your passion, particularly in arts and music. Parents worry too much that their children should earn well and believe there is no money in music. And so many talented young musicians end up burying their passion and take up jobs they do not like.'

Lou acknowledges that money is important to make ends meet and that his concerts are a source of income for him but detests lure and greed of it.

He tells me that there have been times during his concerts when people have suggested to him ways to make more money.

'I told one of them that there is a mint which makes money for the country. What will I do with more money? I can't take it with me when I die. When my concerts are fully sponsored, they are free for fans to attend. When they are not completely sponsored, we sell tickets to pay for things like hire charges for the venue, lights and sound system and stuff like that.'

He falls silent for a while, as if in deep thought and then says, 'The lust for money is ruining us. Everyone wants money without honest work. A simple example, Shillong is no longer as clean as it used to be. Why? Because the money is not spent on what is necessary. I may be wrong but sometimes I think politicians just don't care.'

I mention the illegal coal mining in Meghalaya which has claimed so many lives and ask, 'Have you ever thought of taking on the government over corruption? Have you ever wanted to write songs to launch a mass movement?'

He looks at me for a while and then says, 'Well, they have got promises when you are uncertain. They will help you, yes, to win your confidence. They will choose you, they will use you, they will abuse you and they will refuse you. And they will blind you if you start seeing too far.'

'Are those your lines?'

'Yes. From a song I wrote in 1967. It is called "Chains of Freedom". But no, I am not interested in becoming a mass leader of sorts to lead protests. I do my bit to help those I feel strongly about, like residents of an old age home and an orphanage.'

Lou's life, including his struggles in Kolkata (then Calcutta) in the 1960s, is well documented. I ask him about his days in the City of Joy.

'Calcutta was a madhouse. Noisy, cluttered, and full of traffic jams. But there was a kind of energy in that city that fired me and connected me to music. Even now it is like a second home for me and I have many friends with whom I strum the guitar and sing when we meet.'

The musician is also a fitness fanatic and had celebrated his 70th birthday in 2017 by walking 65 km from Shillong to Jowai to promote a healthy and responsible lifestyle.

'Was it a stunt?' I ask him.

'No. I just wanted to underline that walking is good for health. We are getting too soft by always choosing the easy way out to travel or commute. I may be a little biased because I just love to walk.'

'You are 71. Have you ever thought of slowing down?'

'I never went overboard that I have to slow down now. Music is my life. I have no one in the family. My parents and brother have long been gone. I live alone but by God's grace I am in good health and I am not worried.'

I check my phone and see that I have already spent 90 minutes with Lou. It is time to leave. Lou quickly disappears while I check out the CDs and books in the café before taking another taxi to Polo Ground once again to check out an archery competition.

I am little late and I rush in to find that the day's competition is in its last stage. It is a small area hidden from the main road behind a garage and wine shops. The ground is crammed with spectators and bookmakers on one side of the enclosure are still accepting last minute bets. I am just in time to see the last three archers shoot their arrows at a cylindrical target about 30 yards away. The target which is made of wicker looks like a pin cushion by the time all the 50 archers have shot their arrows. There is no fancy equipment and only traditional bows and arrows are used in the competition.

The archers sit in a semi-circle on their haunches chewing *kwai*. A few officials begin the counting process and once the finally tally is made, they announce the winning numbers.

The lucky ones go to collect their payments. The others shrug and leave. I wait near a bookmaker's table where a man comes to submit his ticket and collect his payment. He counts his booty and puts it in the inside pocket of his jacket. I ask him how often he bets.

'Not more than twice a week. I am a retired government employee so I don't go overboard with betting. And when I win, it's a bonus of sorts.'

'How much do the archers make?'

'They get Rs 300 to take part in the competition. They are also members of archery clubs. The shooting is conducted by the Khasi Hills Archery Sports Federation. Every day, 50 archers take part in the competition in two rounds at 3:30 pm and 4:30 pm. They shoot 30 arrows in the first round and 20 arrows in the second,' he tells me.

I also learn that betting in archery used to be illegal until the Meghalaya government realized that it could be a good source of revenue and so legalized it in 1982.

I want to speak to one of the archers but by the time the senior citizen has enlightened me about archery and betting, all the archers have left. I take a taxi back to Shillong Café and start walking to Assam House.

A short distance from Shillong Café, shoppers throng a road side market selling vegetables, fish, fruits, and areca and betel nuts. Along the narrow pavement, I notice one of Shillong's perennial problems. Light posts and electric poles are smeared with lime as people wipe the excess mineral from their *kwai*. Like the Jeeps, lime smeared light posts seem to represent quintessential Shillong.

Irrespective of age and gender, *kwai* is hugely popular among locals in Meghalaya and is an integral part for formal and informal gatherings. Most are addicted to it and it is associated with red lips and a constant chomp.

Christmas shopping is in full swing and the roads are crowded with cars. Traffic moves slowly but no one drives rashly. Roadside eateries and bakeries are packed with customers. I walk leisurely and it takes me about half an hour to reach Assam House. Next door, a large church—The Mary Help of Christians Cathedral—is illuminated with blue lights and Christmas carols are wafting from it. I stand on the driveway and listen for some time before the cold forces me indoors.

I have to leave the next morning for Silchar in southern Assam and I pack my bags and keep them aside. It is only evening but I have had a long day and I doze off in my chair. I wake up at 7 pm and call David. He doesn't answer the call but sends a message that he is in a hospital to see the friend who is in intensive care and that he wouldn't be able to show up for a dinner we had planned. I eat dinner at 8 pm and go to sleep.

By 8 am next morning, I eat breakfast and leave Assam House and stop at a fuel station to tank up. Silchar is 218 km away and I am hoping to make it in six hours. The sun is shining brightly but the cold increases as the elevation rises. On the outskirts of the town meat shops selling pork have just opened but there are already a large number of customers waiting to buy the best cuts. The road is great to ride on and it is certainly a marked improvement since I last drove through it in 2000. For much of the way, there is thin traffic as the gradient rises and falls.

Locals drive their cars into minor streams and rivulets in the hills to wash them, another trademark feature of Meghalaya.

As I get closer to Jowai, the first major town on the way to Silchar, I see abandoned coal mines. Rat-hole mining once used to be rampant in the area. Beyond Jowai, I pass a small town called Khliehriat that once used to be a dot on the map. It is now a bustling small town with shops, banks, a large school, and small cars. The town has grown up on either side of the highway and it throttles traffic. I get stuck behind a truck and have no chance of overtaking it because of equally heavy incoming traffic. Twenty minutes later, I finally overtake the truck on the outskirts of Khliehriat.

I cross a few more abandoned limestone queries. Six kilometres later I stop at Ladrymbai, once a small outpost but now expanding along the highway like Khliehriat. I have taken almost three hours to cover about 90 km. I walk to a restaurant and ask for tea and snacks. My neck begins to ache and I massage it standing near a table.

'Sit down,' a waiter tells me as he puts the tea and snacks on the table.

'I have been sitting on the bike for almost three hours. I want to stand.'

I keep my helmet on the table and take the tea and snacks in my hands and walk out to stand in the sun.

A local man standing in front of his fruit shop adjoining the restaurant walks towards me.

'Where are you going?'

'Silchar.'

'You are lucky that this road is almost new. If you had been here last year you would have turned back. The road was that bad. There were so many accidents including quite a few fatal ones.'

'Like you said, I am lucky.'

I ask him about his shop and how business is like.

'I get by. The buses stop here and the passengers are my customers. The truck drivers also buy the fruits sometimes. But it is nothing compared to what I used to earn earlier.'

'What did you do earlier?'

'My family has land in Khliehriat where we used to extract limestone and sell to buyers in Bangladesh. Now we can't touch it after the court banned mining.'

He is sore at Meghalaya's political class for not standing up for limestone mine owners. 'When the Supreme Court banned bull taming in Tamil Nadu, the government passed a law to restore it and overturn the court order. But our government is not interested.'

'The ban can't be permanent. I think the court will lift it once the government comes up with a blueprint for environmental protection,' I try to console him.

He doesn't seem convinced. 'The government doesn't seem to be trying at all for limestone miners. But it is turning a blind eye to illegal coal mining. It may have stopped along the highway but if you go into the interiors, you will see coal mining in the forests. The cops are involved in it and that's how the trucks can pass off in the night,' he tells me and goes away to attend to a customer.

I resume my ride and wonder what the next stop on the way—Sonapur—would be like. Sonapur used to be notorious during monsoons for deadly landslides. I notice some of the hills have been sheared and retaining walls built along particular stretches to stop landslides. Close to Sonapur trucks are parked along the highway.

Ninety minutes after starting from Lydrambai, I ride into Sonapur. Unlike Khliehriat and Lydrambai, Sonapur hasn't changed at all. There are still a few restaurants and the only difference is that one of restaurants is now a concrete structure. The aquamarine Sonapur river flows below the road and behind the restaurant. The restaurant is crowded with taxi passengers bound for Jowai and Shillong but I find an empty table and ask for rice and fish curry. I barely start eating when I feel a tug on my trouser and look down to see the restaurant's resident cat prompting me to part with some fish. I give a fishbone with some flesh in it which it finishes in no time and goes away.

I am still 100 km away from Silchar and 60 km of that stretch will be through the hills. A convoy of five trailer trucks carrying heavy machinery slows me down towards the end of Meghalaya's boundary. I get a glimpse of corruption on the highway as the trucks slow down at police barricades to hand over some money to the policemen on guard duty and drive on without their papers being checked. The scene repeats itself at the first checkpost in Assam.

11

Heartbreak in Silchar

21 December 2018

By 4 pm I am inside Silchar and the traffic is maddening. From the top of a flyover near the railway station, the town looks like a vast slum and bears almost no resemblance to the place where I lived between 1978 and 1982 to complete high school. Every empty plot along the road has been filled up with shops and vehicular traffic which has increased exponentially, can't move at more than 20 km per hour.

Hospitals, pharmacies, phone shops, and wine shops have mushroomed along the route that I am taking. The last two kilometres take almost half an hour before I reach the house my grandfather had built almost a century ago. The double storeyed house built of red bricks and wood is getting a fresh coat of paint and it looks gorgeous. My youngest uncle, Aminul Hossain, who has flown in from the United States welcomes me as we meet for the first time in 36 years.

A young man named Ashiq who is overseeing the paint job tells me his mother used to work in our house when we stayed in Silchar and she is in poor health. I promise him that I will go to see her before I leave for Imphal.

The afternoon passes into evening as I chat with my cousins and their wives and children. A hospital has come up opposite the house and I learn that a classmate of mine, Sumit Das, who is a paediatrician, visits the facility in the evening. I send a message to Sumit and we agree to meet after his duty ends. Another classmate, Abhijit Das, an engineer, also sends a message that he will also be there.

At 8:30 pm, I meet Sumit and Abhijit for the first time since we passed out of school in 1982. Sumit suggests that we go and sit in his chamber. Both have put on weight. We exchange notes as we catch up with each other. I have already travelled more than 6,000 km and Abhijit seems to be in awe of it.

'I must salute you. How could you do it, and that too alone?' he asks.

'A lot of other people do it too. Some ride across the whole country, others even go across other countries. There is nothing exceptional about it. It is just like following a passion,' I try to explain to him.

'Yes, that may be true. But they would be much younger than you. I am really impressed that you are doing it when you are on the wrong side of 50. If I had to ride from Shillong to Silchar, I wouldn't be up at this hour talking to you.'

I squirm at the compliment because I have never felt that my age could be a hindrance.

Sumit saves the day for me asking about my family. I tell him about Sudha and Aseem.

'How old is junior?' he asks.

'He will turn 14 in a week.'

'That's nice to hear. At least I am not the only one among the batch of 1982 to have married late.'

I ask about a few other classmates and learn that one particular classmate, Bijon Singh, who was also a doctor, died a few years ago in a freak accident. Bijon and I were in the school cricket team. Sumit tells me that Bijon had fallen off the roof of his house and was fatally injured in the head. He had been a fitness fanatic but his death was a reminder of the fragility and uncertainty of life.

We talk for an hour before parting ways. There is a get together with the class of 1982 the next evening at another classmate's house but Sumit and Abhijit tell me they won't be able to make it.

Next morning, I go for a walk and see the ground where I played cricket passionately is still there but I can't see the pitch because grass has covered it. I learn that kids now play cricket with a tennis ball so there is no need to curate a pitch. Further down the road, I reach the Barak river. At least some things haven't changed here. Two men are tying a consignment of bamboo that they will take downstream as a raft. Small boats still carry passengers across the river and fishermen still cast their nets like they used to years ago.

I return home and ask one my cousins, Akbar, about some of my cricket team mates because I want to meet them.

'Most have died of excessive drinking. And they were not even 40 when they passed away.'

What a waste of life, I wonder.

Shortly before noon, I ask Akbar to take me to the cemetery because I want to offer prayers for my grandfather, uncles, and aunts buried there. The traffic has already scared me and I don't want to ride myself. I sit pillion on Akbar's scooter as we head for the cemetery. There is a traffic policeman at a busy intersection and Akbar points to him.

'That's Kamrul.'

He used to play cricket with us and was known as a pinch hitter and a fielder with a great throwing arm. The traffic is crawling and as Akbar passes the traffic point, I wave at Kamrul and he does something absolutely unbelievable. He abandons his post, runs across the road and hugs me as Akbar stops the scooter.

'It's been such a long time. How have you been? Where do you stay? I am so happy just to see you. Do you still play cricket?' Kamrul's queries come out in a torrent.

The traffic is piling up and horns are blaring but Kamrul is seemingly oblivious. 'Don't worry, I will sort it out. So, how long will you be here?'

'I am here today. I will be leaving for Imphal tomorrow.'

'What a pity. I wish we could have met for a longer time. Have a nice trip to Imphal,' Kamrul tells me and rushes back to his post and starts directing the traffic.

Kamrul's warmth overwhelms me. Akbar starts the scooter and the crawl begins all over again. The entire town seems to have turned into a huge market with all kind of shops clubbed together. Hawkers have taken over the pavements and pedestrians have to weave their way through stalls of hawkers and the traffic on the road.

We get stuck in one of the most congested part of the town. The municipality department had cleaned a drain and dumped the sediments on the side, narrowing down an already narrow road. Vegetable sellers sit on the edge of the road making it a precarious position both for themselves and motorists and riders. I thank myself for not taking out my motorcycle because it would have been difficult to ride a heavy bike in such crowded condition.

We finally reach the graveyard which has been recently revamped and fresh soil laid over it. There are no signs of any tombstone or headstone for the older graves. A few new graves have been fenced with bamboo. We offer our prayers and leave. Fortunately, Akbar takes a different route which is less crowded.

Ahead of the reunion with my classmates in the evening, I decide to check out the heart of the town. A movie hall has been converted into a mall and two others have been shut. Two book shops that I used to frequent changed business and have turned into apparel outlets. On this particular stretch, there are no pavements and pedestrians have to dodge traffic as they walk on the edge of the narrow road.

I walk towards the river front near which a row of shops that sell cane furniture still exist in almost the same form I last saw more than three decades ago. The products still look good and the craftsmanship is of a high order. At one end of the road, a large banner announces a sale of winter wear by a group of Tibetan refugees inside the walled compound of a government department. I am a little surprised by the Tibetans because I did not expect to see them in this part of the country.

The compound where the Tibetans have pitched their shops is near the home of a classmate named Sudha Mundra, who is the hostess for the evening's reunion. I see Kamrul at another traffic point a short distance from where I had seen him earlier in the day. But this time I don't disturb him and walk to Sudha's house and knock on the door. She doesn't recognize me after three and a half decades and I can't blame her.

Four other classmates arrive after some time. Like Abhijeet, they also praise me for undertaking a solo expedition. After two hours of going down the memory lane, Sudha serves dinner. By 9 pm we disperse.

I wake up early and get ready to leave. But I have to see Ashiq's mother before that. Akbar takes me on his scooter once again and rides through a narrow lane to reach the house. She is lying in bed and is quite frail. Ashiq tells me her eyesight is failing. But she recognizes me when I speak to her. She sits up in bed and pats me on the head and is almost in tears.

'I never thought I will see you again. All of you were so young when you left. How are your mother and siblings?'

I tell her we are fine and that I wanted to see her after Ashiq told me that she was not keeping good health.

'I don't know how long I will live. I want to meet your mother once. She was so kind to us.'

'I can't promise that my mother will come to see you but I'll try to get her here once,' I tell her.

I get up to go and realize that she is sobbing. 'You are leaving without even a cup of tea?'

'I just had breakfast before coming to see you.'

We return and I leave for Imphal, 265 km away to the east.

12

Through Manipur and Myanmar

23 December 2018

It's a Sunday and traffic is thin as I head east and cross the Barak river over an old bridge while a new bridge parallel to it is almost ready to be inaugurated. After about 45 minutes of riding through the countryside, I cross into Jiribam in Manipur where the elevation rises and the road begins to wither away. Some of the stretches are complete blacktops but interspersed with massive craters mostly filled with mud and slush as hilly streams carry sediments down and flow over the road. Trucks crawl through the craters to avoid the risk of breaking an axle. On some stretches I have to stop and search for a narrow strip of tarmac to avoid riding through the muddy craters.

I cross several checkposts with armed policemen on duty but no one stops me. The road gets progressively worse and the ride becomes tiring. Trucks struggling to climb uphill slow me down as I trail them through clouds of dust and smoke. About two hours into the ride I cross a rickety bridge over a river and stop at a dhaba. The bridge is in bad shape and the trucks that had been ahead of me have stopped because the drivers seem apprehensive of crossing it.

I ask the dhaba owner about the condition of the road ahead.

'For the next five kilometres it is okay and then the road is bad. You will reach a place called Barak in an hour and after that the road will be relatively better.'

The hills along the highway are thick with evergreen forest. I ask him what the monsoon is like here.

'Sometimes it rains like it will never stop. But normally it rains heavily for a few hours when the temperature and humidity reach certain levels. I haven't seen such heavy rain in my place.'

'And, where is your place?'

'I am from Katihar in Bihar. There are no jobs there. I came here as a road builder many years ago and then as I grew older I decided to open this shop. Business is okay and it is certainly better than what I could have earned in Bihar.'

An hour later, like the dhaba owner said I reach Barak, an outpost kind of settlement. I stop for lunch and check out two restaurants but they are very grimy and don't inspire any confidence. I decide to ride on but can't find any other place to eat lunch so I fall back yet again on my emergency ration of biscuits, chocolates, and fruit drinks. The road is largely downhill from here. There is a massive construction activity going on with the highway being rebuilt and a railway bridge being constructed to connect Imphal to Jiribam and there is a constant traffic of trucks carrying road building materials.

The hours roll by. The road finally improves but I am still in the hills and about 80 km away from Imphal when dusk begins to fall.

I cross small villages along the way where small kiosks list their wares on a signboard. Most of them say: 'Tea, Petrol, Diesel available here', which reminds me of Walong although the shops there do not advertise selling petrol. I finally hit the plains about 20 km ahead of Imphal.

It is 7 pm when I ride into Imphal. A cousin had told me that I would find hotels at Thangal Bazar, one of Imphal's commercial areas. Thangal Bazar also hosts Nupi Keithel or Ima Keithel (Mothers' Market), a sprawling market spread across three large buildings and run exclusively by women. The market has now spilled onto the road under a flyover and triggers sporadic traffic jams. I park the motorcycle and decide to check out the market that is said to be 500 years old. It is also Asia's largest and singularly unique all-women's market. A variety of goods are on display including clothes, snacks, fruits, vegetables, dry fish, handicrafts, groceries, and utensils among others.

In normal times, the market would have been shut by 7 pm. But Christmas is two days away and so Ima Keithel continues to bustle with a gaggle of shoppers. The aroma of fresh fruits, spices, and food fill the air.

Ima Keithel came up in the 16th century out of necessity dictated by Manipur's territorial fights as a kingdom. As men were sent to fight battles mostly against the neighbouring Burmese to maintain Manipur's independence, it was left to the women to take care of everything else such as farming, selling the crops and vegetables, and managing the family's finances.

Over the centuries, Ima Keithel has acquired a legendary status and it is now more than just a market. It is also a protest site and women are usually at the forefront of such activities. In the late 1930s, they protested successfully against the export of a major portion of the local rice to British battalions in other regions. In 2003, they forced the state government to shelve a plan to replace Ima Keithel with a shopping mall. The government gave up after the women protested with sit-ins for three months. The Imas (Mothers) simply cannot be taken lightly. The women have also been at the forefront of protests against excesses by the armed forces.

I walk past rows of shops and stop at one selling women's garments such as shawls and a type of sarong called *phanek* that locals wear. A woman in her 60s who is minding the shop is stacking her merchandise in a corner.. But she stops when she sees me and asks if I want to buy something.

'Would you like to buy a shawl or a stole for your wife?' she asks.

I tell her that I am just window shopping. But she doesn't give up and insists that I see some shawls and takes down half a dozen of them and spreads them in front of me.

'I have no space to keep anything else on my motorcycle so I really don't want to buy anything,' I explain. She finally relents and then tells me, 'Next time bring your wife. She won't let you walk away without buying anything. I hope you will remember this shop and me. My name is Bina Devi.'

I smile at her and pull down my balaclava over my ears. 'Feeling cold?' she asks and I nod.

'Then you must eat something to warm you up.' She comes out of her shop and tells another woman in the next shop, 'Leina, give this man a plate of *singju*. He is feeling cold.'

Leina Devi is almost of the same age as Bina Devi. She serves me *singju*, a salad made of an assortment of vegetables of which I am only familiar with cabbage. It is tangy and spicy and different from any salad I have ever eaten. She watches me eat and asks where I am from and whether I am aware of the iconic status of Ima Keithel. I tell her that I had heard of the market.

Like most of the Northeast, Manipur is largely agrarian. The lack of industries and manufacturing sector has meant that many Manipuri men move out of the state to seek employment. It is also one of the reasons why Ima Keithel continues to grow in stature as the women of the market anchor a large section of the Manipuri society. Only married women are allowed to run shops in the market. Ima Keithel is self-financed and facilitates borrowing by traders from the market's union instead of any other financier.

Leina Devi asks if I want another helping but I decline and tell her that I must be on my way to find a hotel. I start the motorcycle and scan both sides of the road but a couple of hotels that I can see do not have parking space so I stop and call Sobhapati Samom, the *Hindustan Times* correspondent in Imphal. He tells me to wait for a few minutes and then calls back to tell me to head to Nagampal and check into the Sangai Hotel, named after an endangered species of deer found only in Manipur.

'I made a booking in your name,' Sobhapati tells me.

Nagampal is near Thangal Bazar but I lose my way near the hotel and stop again and scan the other side of the road when a man comes over and asks me if I am from Tamil Nadu. I am exasperated with that question and tell him that I am from Delhi.

'I saw your motorcycle's number plate and thought you are from Chennai. I had worked there for some time a few years ago. By the way, where are you heading to?'

'Sangai Hotel.'

'You have overshot it. Follow me and I will take you to the hotel. I will walk so ride slowly.'

I am floored by the stranger's gesture but I can't even ask him to sit pillion because of my luggage. I take a U-turn and start following the man who is walking quite fast. A few minutes later he turns to face me and points to the hotel. It is on the main road but the entry is through a small lane. I ride into the parking and go to the reception with the stranger following me. I tell the receptionist that I have a reservation. He checks the bookings, gives me the key, and asks a bell boy to take the luggage to my room.

The stranger introduces himself. 'My name is Samarjit. I used to work in a realty company in Chennai for a couple of years before I returned here. I now work for a local company.' And then he turns to the receptionist. 'I hope you have given him a good room. He has come from very far.'

Samarjit is still not done with me. 'Take my number. Call me if you have any problem.' I thank him and we shake hands before he walks away and melts into the night.

I follow the bell boy into my room. He opens the door, puts down my luggage and then asks, 'Do you want anything to drink? Beer or whisky?'

Manipur is a dry state and I am suspicious of unsolicited offerings like these and so I tell him that I want tea. I call Sobhapati to tell him that I have checked into the hotel and he promises to show up in an hour. I check a few local newspapers and notice that there is anger against the state government after a journalist was arrested and jailed for a Facebook post against Chief Minister Nongthombam Biren Singh.

Kishorechand Wangkhem was arrested in November after he uploaded a video criticizing the BJP and its ideological parent, the Rashtriya Swayamsevak Sangh (RSS) and called the chief minister a 'puppet of Hindutva'. The arrest had drawn widespread criticism for disproportionate punishment by a government that is now being seen as extremely touchy to any kind of criticism and intolerant of dissent. Wangkhem had been arrested under the National Security Act which empowers the government to detain a person to prevent him/her from acting in any manner prejudicial to the maintenance of public order. It is only one of the several reasons for which a person can be detained under the NSA.[1]

An hour later, Sobhapati arrives and tells me that my ride had taken longer than it should have. I tell him about the road conditions and the unending highway constructions which had slowed me down.

'I can imagine that. Manipur is now India's biggest diesel consumer for infrastructure projects. Roads are being built across the state,' he tells me and asks me about my plans.

'I wonder if I can meet Second World War veterans here. I also want to go to Moreh.'

'There is no WWII veteran alive here. A couple of them are in remote districts. But there is a man who is setting up a museum dedicated to the Imphal campaign of WWII and you can meet him. And, as for Moreh, I suggest you leave early so that you can be out of there before dusk. It may not be safe to start late from Moreh because someone can potentially stop and harass you.'

---

[1] Kishorechand Wangkhem was released on 10 April 2019 after the Manipur High Court quashed the detention order.

'Like who?'

'Like militants, although that area is a sort of ceasefire zone for security forces and rebels. Militants are not supposed to carry weapons in the area but you never know if someone is carrying a small arm looking to extort a solo traveller. So it is better to be safe than sorry.'

Sobhapati leaves after half an hour and I go to the hotel's roof-top restaurant for dinner. Most of the guests are tourists. The food is good and since I didn't have lunch, I eat almost ravenously. I return to my room and go out like a light.

The morning is slightly foggy. I get out of the hotel at 8 am after breakfast and head for Moreh, 110 km away to the south on the Myanmar border. The roads in Imphal are wider than in any other town in the Northeast. The traffic is modest. A canal runs along the road for a few kilometres and the fog begins to thicken on the outskirts of the town but it is not as bad as the one in Dawki. A little outside Imphal, there are signs of heavy security. Police stations are fortified and policemen are armed with automatic weapons.

Insurgency was once a major problem in Manipur. Although insurgency has waned considerably and many rebel groups have withered away, there is still a huge deployment of security forces in the state.

The tarmac is broken at a few stretches on the highway but it is largely a decent road. Paddy fields stretch on either side of the highway and some farmers are setting paddy stubble on fire. The cold increases and my fingers start getting stiff. About 50 km into the ride, I stop at a small town called Pallel for tea. The managers at the first two restaurants tell me there is no tea. I see two other restaurants with the signboards saying 'Chak Hotel'. I walk into one and ask, '*Chai?*'

A young waiter looks at me and says, 'Chak.'

I realize there is a language problem and I explain to him again and try to communicate with gestures that I want tea. 'Chak, chak,' he repeats and gestures of eating with his hands. I head to the next restaurant and run into the same problem. The waiter and I can't understand each other. A woman comes out from the kitchen and I ask her.

'No *chai*, only chak. Chak is rice. Chak hotel meaning rice hotel,' she tells me and points to another eatery where I can get a cup of tea. I stand outside the eatery and drink the tea and watch the traffic. There seems to be quite a lot of cars and SUVs headed for Moreh. I finish the tea and start riding again. The road begins to climb and I get a bird's eye view of Imphal valley. A few villages that I cross have put up Christmas gates decorated with stars of different colours sprinkled with glitter. Teenagers, some with guitars, sit near the gates and sing carols.

The road is largely good and I maintain a decent speed. The Assam Rifles is in charge of the security of the area and I see signboards at regular intervals proclaiming itself as 'Friends of the Hill People'. India's oldest paramilitary force has been accused of atrocities including rape and murder against civilians in Manipur in the past and has been trying to project a humane face dedicated to serve the people where they are deployed.

I stop at an Assam Rifles checkpost in Tengnoupal. The sentry at the gate asks me where I am from.

'Delhi,' I tell him.

'I am also from Delhi,' he replies and we shake hands.

He points to a booth and asks me to take a token from there which I will have to submit in another checkpost at Moreh.

I am still wearing my helmet when I approach the soldier at the booth to take my token. But he is not willing to listen to me. He points to another booth across the road and tells me to go there which I find a little odd.

I take off my helmet and hang it on the motorcycle's handle and cross the road. A trooper is standing outside the booth and two are inside. I ask them for a token.

'Where are you from?' the soldier outside the booth asks me.

'Delhi.'

'Then you should have taken it from that booth,' he says pointing to the one from where I have just come. 'This one is for foreigners.'

'But the soldier in that booth told me to report here.'

'Come with me,' he tells me and I follow him across the road. He asks his colleague why he sent me to the other booth.

'Sorry. I saw the motorcycle and I thought he is a foreigner. I haven't seen a bike like that until he came,' says the trooper at the booth and then gives me a token after writing down the motorcycle's brand and its registration number.

Close to noon I stop at another checkpost outside Moreh to deposit my token and ride into the town. Moreh is a crowded border town. Shops stretch one either side of the road for quite a distance. I ride straight at a fork before an Assam Rifles trooper at another checkpost stops me and asks a few questions.

'I am on a day trip to Moreh. I wanted to see the main market in this town,' I tell him.

'You should have taken the left from the fork instead of riding straight. But since you have already come this far, I suggest you go see Tamu in Myanmar and then go to the Moreh market on the way back.'

It made good sense. He tells me the direction to the Myanmar border which is just a kilometre from his post. I cross the India-Myanmar Friendship Bridge over the Chindwin river and stop at the border checkpost. Other two wheeler riders from Moreh are standing in a queue for a permit to go to Tamu, the first town inside Myanmar. The riders collect their permits and ride away. I submit my driving licence as security and pay Rs 20 for the permit.

'Bike?' the clerk asks me as he hands over the permit. I point out my motorcycle to him.

'No. No. No. No bike,' he shakes his index finger at me.

'Why?'

'No. No. No. No bike,' he repeats.

I wonder if he doesn't understand English so I ask him in Hindi. But the response is the same.

'No. No. No. No bike.'

I am exasperated. A man standing behind me to submit his driving licence for his permit taps my shoulder and says, 'Don't worry. Leave your motorcycle here. You can ride pillion on my bike. They won't let your bike through because it doesn't have a local registration.'

I heave a sigh of relief and go to lock the motorcycle handle. 'Leave the helmet on the handle. No will take it from here,' my saviour tells me. I do that and climb on his ancient Yamaha RX 100 motorcycle. It feels strange sitting on a small motorcycle after riding the substantially bigger Himalayan almost every day for more than a month. I also take some time to get used to traffic driving on the right hand side. The road to Tamu is wide and well maintained.

'My name is Mohammad Hasan. I own a furniture shop in Moreh,' the Yamaha owner tells me.

I introduce myself and tell him that he doesn't look like he belongs to Manipur. He laughs.

'My father came from Tamil Nadu 60 years ago and settled here. I was born and brought up here,' he tells me.

'So, why are you going to Tamu?'

'I have to meet someone.'

I see a lot of Chinese motorcycles and scooters and ask Mohammad about them.

'They are cheap and cost about Rs 50,000. But they don't last and break down easily. My Yamaha is a thousand times better. It is almost indestructible.'

I can understand his passion for his bike. It is the model that the Japanese company launched first in India in the late 1980s and it had become a rage for its powerful engine and high speed.

'What do Indians go to Tamu for?' I ask Mohammad.

'Traders go to buy clothes, cigarettes, and electronic goods. Individuals mostly go to buy petrol because it is Rs 20 cheaper per litre.'

Mohammad drops me at the market in Tamu, three kilometres away from the border checkpost, and tells me to take a shared autorickshaw on the way back. The autorickshaw stand is on the other side of the road.

'They charge Rs 20 in Indian currency. Look for the one going to Gate Number 1,' he tells me as he leaves. The exchange rate was 22 kyat for one Indian rupee.

I walk around the market which is more orderly and cleaner than the one in Moreh. Motorcycles are parked along the pavement but there are very few cars, among them a couple of Toyotas. I see something which looks like a shawl in a shop window and go to ask. It is not a shawl, I am told. It is a sarong. The next one is a jewellery shop where a few women are sitting looking at gold necklaces. Most shops are packed with goods but the ones with customers are the general stores.

Many shops are run by women and quite a few of them have their daughters with them. Some of them have rectangular, pale yellowish patches on their cheeks. I buy a bottle of water from a shop and ask the woman about the yellow patches.

'It is sandalwood paste…sunblock cream. Tamu very hot, no? Sandalwood paste keeps us cool,' she tells me. I nod and walk away.

There is a small, red, three-door SUV parked on the road. I notice that a small, embossed 'Jeep' plate is screwed on the metal panel below the windscreen. I have never seen a Jeep like that and I wait for the driver to show up. I look through the window and see that the instrument panel on the dashboard is ancient. A couple of minutes later a man comes and opens the SUV's door.

'Is this a Jeep?' I ask him.

'Nah, nah. Chinese car, Chinese car,' he tells me and drives away.

I explore the rest of the market. Some shops sell only conical bamboo hats that Myanmarese use during the rains. Lungis and umbrellas are also bestsellers. Apparel shops are stuffed with winter wear and I am tempted to buy a camouflage jacket but I have no space to carry it. A couple of wine shops are dominated by the Dagon brand of beer and whiskies. A large bottle of beer cost 1,500 kyat or Rs 70, but since Manipur is a dry state, I decide against buying one because getting caught in a random check could mean a jail term.

I stop at a fast food joint and try out some round-shaped snacks made of sticky rice, black sesame, and jaggery. They taste good. I try to pick up a conversation with another customer who is eating fritters.

'Excuse me, are there any Rohingyas in Tamu?'

He looks at me as if I have committed some blasphemy. 'Not here. They are in Rakhine in the south. They are bad people.'

'Why are they bad?'

'They kill Myanmarese soldiers.'

'But Myanmarese soldiers have killed hundreds of them and thousands have fled to Bangladesh and India to save their lives. They hardly have any rights here. Why do you think they are bad?'

'They are just bad. That's all,' he puts it very simply. 'I don't want them here and neither does anyone in this town.'

The man puts down his half-finished plate of fritters and walks away and I really wonder if I had upset him so much. I go to pay my bill and the senior citizen who runs the shop bends over at the counter and tells me, 'No one will speak against the government on Rohingyas if that's what you want to hear about. Anyone who does and sounds like he is supporting them can end up in jail.'

I wonder if this is what a semi-police state has done to the ordinary people in Myanmar.

'I don't want anyone to go to jail. But tell me, are drug runners better than Rohingyas? Drugs have flourished in Myanmar for such a long time but you hardly hear of extensive crackdowns on the drug mafia in the country. Drug lords push the stuff across the border and Manipuris who act as couriers keep getting caught.'

Conflicts in Myanmar's border areas that have raged for decades have fuelled the drug trade and rebel groups of all shades have benefitted from it. Although Tamu is far from any conflict zone, it has now become a conduit for narcotics to enter India through Moreh.

'Drugs are different, you know,' he tells me. 'There's a lot of money for everybody involved and they certainly wouldn't want drug trade to stop.'

'Aren't you now afraid of going to jail for telling me all this?'

'But I am not telling you anything new or a state secret,' he grins. 'You know what it is like.'

A large van stops near the eatery and the passengers, all white foreigners, troop out and head for different shops. I cross the road and go to the autorickshaw stand but the vehicle which is leaving for Gate Number 1 is full. There are two other autorickshaws in the stand and I decide to wait for other passengers. No one shows up for ten minutes and then one of the drivers asks me where I want to go.

'Gate Number 1,' I tell him.

'Kyat or Indian rupees?' he asks.

'Indian rupees.'

'Two hundred rupees.'

I smile at him and shake my head. It is a rip off at 10 times more than the normal fare that Mohammad had told me. It is 20 minutes now and there are still no passengers. I decide to walk back.

The driver sees me walking off and makes another offer. 'Hundred rupees.' I walk away.

The weather is pleasant and I am not worried about sunburn. About 200 metres from the autorickshaw stand I see a fire station and stop because it has a strange looking, ancient fire engine. There are no gates at the facility and I walk in before a fireman in dark blue uniform runs towards me and asks me something in Burmese that I can't understand but I tell him I want to see the fire engine.

He gestures me to wait and runs inside the building and comes back with another young man who is also dressed in the same uniform. He introduces himself as Yell Zar Ni Kyau. I ask him about the old fire engine which stands with relatively two modern ones. The old one is the largest of the three and has a long nose like lorries of yore with large external headlights mounted on the bumper. The new ones have rectangular front with integrated headlights.

'This one Japanese...very old, 50 years. Just made new,' Yell tries to explain that the fire engine has been overhauled. I notice it is a Hino truck, a Japanese brand. Oil has dripped from the engine block and the axles and there are dark patches on the floor.

Yell tells me the other two fire engines are Chinese and then asks, 'Where you coming from?'

'Delhi,' I tell him.

'Oh! Very far. How you like Tamu?'

'Nice. Quiet place unlike Moreh.'

'Yes. Moreh very crowded. Very noisy.'

'So, have you been out on firefighting missions?'

'Once. Last year. Small fire, two kilometres away.'

Yell has a smiling countenance and I ask him if I can take a photograph of the old fire engine.

'Yes. Sure.'

I take a couple of pictures and then the three of us pose for selfies in front of the ancient Hino fire engine before I start walking towards Gate Number 1. I cross a double-storey building which looks like some kind of a government office with large pictures of Aung San Suu Kyi on flex posters draped over its walls. Further down the road I cross a few motorcycle garages with bikes lined up for repairs. I guess Mohammad was right about the quality of the Chinese bikes but the number of two-wheelers dumped for repairs seem quite large by any yardstick. The garages also service three-wheeler goods carriers which are Chinese made as well.

A small shopping complex has an assortment of stores including a grocery shop, a pharmacy, an electrical goods store, and a wine shop. A man in a shirt and lungi and a woman in a sarong and T-shirt are sitting outside in the open between the grocery shop and the road, frying snacks. The woman who is quite heavily built is sitting on a stool, a cigar dangling from a corner of her lips as she wields a large perforated spoon to stir the snacks in a big wok. She orders the younger man who is sitting on his haunches, to put in more snacks into the oil.

I finally reach the border post and surrender my permit to collect my driver's licence and ride across the Friendship Bridge to Moreh. I take the turn to the main market and immediately run into chaos. The road is choked with two-wheelers and cars. Every rider and driver honks and there is no traffic policeman in sight. Volunteers struggle to put things in order. After being stuck for 15 minutes, I park the motorcycle along the pavement and start walking.

The market is haphazardly built with different kinds of shops clubbed together. It is more crowded in front of the wholesale shops as small traders buy goods in bulk and load them in pick-up vans and SUVs. I see many small traders buy mattresses, blankets, plastic items and stuff them in the SUVs. Retailers sell different types of food, fruits, cigars, coconuts, clothes, toiletries, and shoes which are mostly Myanmarese while electronic goods are almost exclusively Chinese. Unlike other parts of Manipur that I have seen, the market in Moreh is quite dirty with the street littered with different kinds of wastes.

I walk back to my motorcycle and ride a short distance to a less crowded part of the market and stop for lunch. I ask for rice and fish curry and a little later the waiter arrives with an enormous quantity of food. There are two kinds of fish—the first time in the trip that I have been served such a fare. The food is tasty but the rice is too much for me and I leave a small portion.

'Didn't like the food?' the manager asks when I go to pay.

'I liked it. I finished the fish. But the quantity of rice was too much for me.'

I mention the Assam Rifles and ask him about the local people's relation with the paramilitary force.

'I doubt if anyone likes them. There have been many extrajudicial killings and fake encounters and not a single man in uniform has been prosecuted. I tell you, the Armed Forces (Special Powers) Act gives them a licence to kill with impunity. Now I know why the Kashmiris want this law to be scrapped. It makes you feel like you are living under an occupying force.'

'What have they done to you?'

'Not to me. But I have seen awful things happen to others. It is always a sledge hammer approach to swat flies. And I can't figure out why no state government has demanded its repeal. I feel so sorry for Irom Sharmila who spent the best years of her life on a hunger strike to end this law.'

Irom Chanu Sharmila, also known as the Iron Lady, is a civil rights and political activist who began her 16-year hunger strike on 5 November 2000 and ended it on 29 August 2016. She was 28 years old when she began her fast. But the government simply did not budge.

'Politics is strange, you know. It is as if the government has a lot to gain by keeping alive the draconian law for the armed forces,' he tells me.

'But the government feels it is necessary to stop insurgency.'

'We have bigger problems than insurgency and that is ethnic tension. There is an undercurrent of hostility among various ethnic groups in Manipur—the Nagas, Kukis, Meiteis, Paites. We have had violence earlier on ethnic lines but no government has bothered to find a permanent solution to these problems. They think an Army flag march will control every kind of trouble,' he sighs. 'But I am hopeful that the AFSPA will not be around for long now that the matter has gone to the Supreme Court.'

In July 2017, the Supreme Court directed the Central Bureau of Investigation or CBI to investigate the alleged encounter killings in Manipur by the police and security forces after an organization called Extra Judicial Execution Victims' Families Association filed a case. It claims it has as members the wives and relatives of individuals killed in alleged fake encounters.

'The trouble is that the government thinks it can do no wrong. Have you heard of the journalist who has been jailed because he criticized the chief minister on social media? Imagine sending that chap to a year in jail under the National Security Act. I mean, are they really so touchy? If they won't listen to anybody, how will they ever know the angst of the people?'

I have no answer to that question but it is a familiar failing with many politicians and chief minister N Biren Singh is certainly not the first politician to be accused of it.

The manager isn't done yet. He brings up the issue of the central government's peace talks with Naga rebel groups of neighbouring Nagaland. Among other things, the Nagas have been demanding that parts of Manipur be included in their version of Greater Nagaland.

'Why would Manipur give up its land for Greater Nagaland? I tell you, we are sitting on a tinder box of ethnic fault lines and territorial claims,' he says, ominously.

It is 2 pm and time for me to leave. I start the motorcycle and exit Moreh quickly before I find myself at the end of a long queue of vehicles at the Assam Rifles checkpost. Fortunately, a trooper asks me to bypass the cars and report to the booth to collect my token. I wait behind five men to collect my token and notice that the cars are being thoroughly checked. It is at this checkpoint that many drugs consignments and other contraband are seized. I collect my token and continue the ride. I complete another formality at the other checkpost in Tengnoupal of depositing the token before moving on to Imphal.

The last 10 km of the ride becomes a pain through slow traffic and my back and neck begin to hurt. It is past evening by the time I reach my hotel. Shahwar calls and tells me to try to meet a man called Zit Saikhom, the founder of a biking club named Royal Riders Manipur.

I wake up early morning on Christmas, eat my breakfast and head out for The India Peace Memorial at Red Hill in Maibam Lokpa Ching about 20 km towards the airport. It is also called the Tiddim Road which ends in the south at Tiddim village in the Chin Hills of Myanmar. Tiddim was one of the three launchpads from where the Japanese started their invasion of Manipur in 1944.

The India Peace Memorial is a relatively recent construction, built by the Japanese Government in 1994 to commemorate the 50th anniversary of the Battle of Imphal.

The memorial is built on the site of the Battle of Red Hill which saw nine days of bitter fighting between the British and the Japanese as part of the much larger campaign for Imphal. It was the closest the Imperial Japanese Army got to Imphal from the south. Plagued by poor logistical support and depleting supplies and rations by that time, the Japanese army suffered one of its biggest losses in the battle of Red Hill. By one account, only 40 out of the 500 soldiers who took part in the battle survived.

It is 10 am. I park my motorcycle at the base of Red Hill where a large flex banner mentions a brief history of the battle. There are still many trees on the hill but the grass and shrubs have turned mostly brown in December. I walk to the gate of the memorial only to see that it is locked. Momentarily, I think it is closed for Christmas. About 50 yards away a man is standing on the edge of the road and I go over to ask him if the memorial is closed for the day.

'No. The caretaker will show up. He is around somewhere here.'

We talk while I wait for the caretaker. The man is in his mid-30s and is a small businessman. I ask him if the India Peace Memorial draws a large number of tourists.

'Tourists certainly come here but their number is not really big.'

I ask him if he has any family members who had witnessed the battle of Red Hill.

'No. My family settled here much later. But there are a few elders in the village who were kids during the Imphal campaign.' He points to an old man walking towards us with a slight limp and says, 'That's the caretaker.'

He tells him in Manipuri that I have been waiting to see the memorial. The caretaker asks me to follow him. He walks slowly to the gate and unlocks it. He looks around 70 years old.

'I can't sit at home and do nothing. So I volunteered for his job,' he tells me.

Dedicated to Japanese soldiers who lost their lives at this site and the Battle of Imphal, the memorial consists only of concrete walls, a red sandstone floor, and three large uncut sandstone blocks at the far end of the site. There are two circular plaques embedded on two opposite walls. The one in English says 'The India Peace Memorial'. The other one is in Japanese and presumably says the same.

'What are the sandstone blocks for?' I ask the caretaker.

'I am not sure. But I heard that they symbolize the blood spilt by the Japanese, Indian, and British soldiers in the Battle of Imphal.'

Outside the memorial, there is only the noise of continuous traffic, a far cry from the sound of shells and gunfire that rocked Red Hill between May 21–29 in 1944. I had hoped there would be some more information about the memorial in the form of a citation, but there is none.

The caretaker then takes me to another memorial nearby, dedicated only to Japanese soldiers who were killed in the larger Battle of Imphal in different theatres. Enclosed in a small plot fenced by an iron grille, it is a white, concrete structure with a few steps and a rectangular block topped off with a small conical roof. On the two pillars of the gate and in front of the structure are inscriptions in Japanese. On the right of the memorial are a heavy machine gun and a small artillery gun.

A senior citizen with a walking stick strolls in and starts talking to the caretaker.

'Were you around during the war?' I ask him when he ends the conversation with the other man.

'Yes. I was less than ten. I live in Maibam village just down this road which the Japanese had briefly occupied. I don't remember much except the noise of gunfire and seeing army vehicles and ambulances. My father used to tell me that the

Japanese had run out of food but they fought ferociously almost to the last man. There was no one to claim the dead bodies of the Japanese. The villagers cremated a lot of them. So much bloodshed, and for what?' he shakes his head.

'But you know, the Japanese did not misbehave with the locals for the short time they were here or anywhere else in Manipur. Maybe that's why there is still a lot of goodwill for the Japanese among the Manipuris,' the old man tells me.

'Do you know any Manipuri who fought in these battles?'

'I knew some of them. Most have died. But there were not Manipuris like Meiteis. They were mostly Nagas and Kukis from other parts of the state. Manipuris refer to the Imphal campaign as Japan Lan or Japanese war.'

A bus arrives with a load of tourists and the caretaker goes out to guide them to the India Peace Memorial. The senior citizen asks me where I am headed for and I tell him that I would be going to Kohima the next day.

'You will find a lot of war stories in Kohima as well. This entire route is so historic but so few Indians know that this is the place that stopped the Japanese invasion of India.'

We leave the place and go our separate ways.

Half an hour later I reach the hotel and call Zit Saikhom to ask if we can meet.

'Sure, but not right away. It is Christmas and I am visiting a few friends. But we can meet in the afternoon. I live close to your hotel.'

It turns out that Zit is quite well known in the area. I ask the hotel receptionist about a motorcycle garage near which Zit lives so I could check it out and won't lose time looking for it when I have to meet him.

'Go straightly from here and then turn right at the chicken market and then ask someone. But first you go straightly from here. Ok?'

I go 'straightly' and take the turn like the receptionist told me and ask a couple of men who can't help. I check out Google maps but can't get a fix on the location. I finally find someone who directs me to the location. As I approach the garage on a narrow lane, another biker on a Bullet motorcycle with a little boy on the pillion rides in from the opposite direction. I stop behind a stationary car to let him pass but he stops in front of a pharmacy parallel to me. He is a strapping man in his 40s with a beard. I tell him that I am looking for Zit Saikhom.

'I am Zit. I am going to my friend's place with my son. I will see you around 3 o'clock at the hotel,' he tells me.

We shake hands and I leave for the Imphal War Cemetery, a few kilometres away. On the way I see a huge poster advertising sumo wrestling bouts in the ten-day Sangai Festival that was held in November. I am quite surprised by the advertisement and tell myself that I must find out more about it. Manipuris are passionate about sports but they are mostly into football, hockey, and boxing.

The war cemetery, which is maintained by the Commonwealth War Graves Commission, is located at a quieter part of the town about 100 metres off the main road. Ahead of the cemetery is an open area where I park my motorcycle under a tree. There are a few small houses and some of the residents are still sitting in the sun with their children and pet dogs. I walk past them and cross a small bridge over a canal and walk into the cemetery.

The sprawling cemetery is immaculately maintained. Hedges along the perimeter are trimmed and trees are pruned. Straight down the gate stands a cross almost at the far side. On either side of the gate, among the perfectly manicured grass are the markers with brass plaques of more than 1,600 men including 828 who were buried and 868 others who were cremated.

Many of the dead were never identified and all that their epitaphs say is: 'A Soldier Of The 1939–1945 War. Known Unto God' or 'A Soldier Of The Indian Army 1939–1945 Is Honoured Here'. Some epitaphs are more personal, more touching like the one a woman wrote in her son's memory: 'Roses May Wither. Leaves Fade And Die. If Others Forget You. Never Will I.' And, then there is that immortal one: 'There Is Some Corner Of A Foreign Field That Is Forever England.'

I walk along the rows of the plaques reading the epitaphs of the men who died so young and so far away from home. Most of the men were in their 20s and the cemetery is home to soldiers, engineers, radio operators, cooks, pilots, and navigators among others who perished in some of the fiercest fighting of the Imphal campaign.

There is no other visitor but the silence of the cemetery is suddenly broken by the laughter of six little children who start running around the trees at the far end of the complex before they troop out of it as quickly as they had arrived. I spend another hour to check out the entire cemetery before walking out of it.

The locals are still sitting in the sun. I ask one of them about the advertisement for sumo wrestling that I had seen earlier in the day.

'Are there sumo wrestlers in Manipur?'

'No. They were Japanese. They came here for exhibition matches during the Sangai Festival. A private group called Salai Holdings arranged their participation. I am told a lot of people went to see the bouts,' the man tells me as he cradles a baby sleeping on his lap.

'I didn't know sumo wrestling has a fan following in Manipur.'

'I am not sure it is about fan following. But there is a soft corner for the Japanese among Manipuris and for the past many years, efforts have been on to forge some kind of partnerships despite the bitterness of the Second World War. Have you been to the India Peace Memorial? The Japanese built it. I think it was some kind of reconciliation with the people of Manipur. Or maybe it was a diplomatic move to pave the way for Japanese investments in infrastructure projects in Manipur which has been rising.'

The baby wakes up and starts to cry. The man pats it for some time before he stands up and goes inside his house. 'Excuse me, I think he is hungry.'

It is 3 pm when I return to the hotel and call Zit. He says he is on the way and arrives a few minutes later.

'So, who told you about me?' he asks.

'My brother did. He said Royal Riders Manipur is a different kind of bikers' club.'

'Yes, it is. The club was set up to provide a forum to Royal Enfield riders and create awareness for responsible motorcycling and the need for a good biker image. But we are not just into rides. We are essentially into philanthropy. And it is serious business. Riff raffs are not allowed in the group. Gentlemen can also be bikers, you know.'

He tells me that members of Royal Riders Manipur include doctors, government servants, artists, independent filmmakers, media persons, and other professionals. Of course, every member is a Royal Enfield Bullet owner. People younger than 24 years of age are not allowed into the group.

'And, what kind of philanthropic work does the club undertake?' I ask.

'We conduct quite a few free medical camps in remote parts of the hill districts of Manipur. And the most satisfying part of these efforts is that the people in those far flung areas call us Angels on Wheels. There are no government health facilities in many of these remote places.'

But everything doesn't always work out smoothly for the Royal Riders.

'There was one particular instance where we were confined in a remote village for two days because of heavy rain. We had finished the medical camp and then we left some generic medicines with the villagers to use if they were needed. But when we were returning, the Assam Rifles stopped us and told us to go back to the village and retrieve the surplus medicines because they did not want any rebels to benefit from them. It was such a hare-brained idea but they refused to budge. So we had to ride back in the slush and take those medicines back.'

The Royal Riders are also passionate about the environment and have carried out several tree plantation drives in Manipur. And they also find time to go on long rides to the rest of the Northeast and Bhutan. Local rides, rallies, and road shows are organized around contemporary themes to ensure maximum public interaction.

I ask Zit if the club ever ties up with the government for its various initiatives.

'No, because that would probably mean the government would be dictating terms to us and we don't want that. We are involved in all these activities because we feel passionately about them.'

He is not very enamoured of the government. The arrest of the journalist has touched a raw nerve across Manipuri society.

'They shouldn't have arrested that guy for his Facebook post. It was just a rant of a man in rage.'

He asks me about the Himalayan.

'I have fallen in love with it. I have never ridden a Bullet so when I took delivery of the Himalayan I was slightly apprehensive. But when I straddled it I just loved riding it. It does its job of going through bad roads very well. I did fall a couple of times but I think that is par for the course for a trip this long.'

'Yes, no biker can claim he never had a fall.'

Zit has to meet another friend and leaves after we have tea. I call up Sobhapati and ask him to join me for dinner. I also ask him about the contact details of the man who is setting up a museum dedicated to the Imphal campaign of WWII. He sends me the phone number of Arambam Angamba Singh who agrees to meet me and sends his coordinates. I ride to a residential part of Imphal and find him waiting for me outside his home.

There is a Mitsubishi Pajero and a KTM 390 motorcycle parked in the driveway. The SUV has stickers of a rally on its body and Arambam tells me that he is also a member of a motor sport club which organizes rallies. He leads me to the drawing room. It is modest and cozy. An old, large radio rests on a table. It doesn't work but he has no intention of throwing away a family relic that he has inherited.

Forty-five-year-old Arambam is also the co-founder of the Second World War Imphal Campaign Foundation. I ask him about his efforts to set up a war museum.

'The Second World War changed Manipur forever in a way. One of the objectives of the foundation was to showcase the rich World War II heritage and its connection with the state. The construction of the museum is almost complete.'

A history buff, Arambam had started collecting WWII relics since he was 20. In 2012, he left his job as a telecom engineer to devote himself full time into the setting up the museum along with another researcher named Rajeshwar Singh.

He is racing against time for the museum's inauguration on the 75th anniversary of the Battle of Imphal in the summer of 2019.

The museum is being funded by Nippon Foundation and Arambam has flown a few times to Japan to discuss the matter. There have been hiccups about the concept with some anti-war faction in the foundation opposing what they believe is glorification of war.[2]

---

[2] The museum was inaugurated on 23 June 2019.

'But that's not the case. We wanted our younger generation and future generations to know what really happened in the Imphal campaign,' say Arambam.

He goes away for a short time to make tea. When he returns, he tells me that one wing of the house used to function as a makeshift museum. But it is my bad luck that I can't see any of the exhibits because they are packed. They have just arrived from an exhibition. He tells me that the exhibits include rifles, artillery shells, grenades, and helmets among other things. The only exhibits that I can see are the rusted frame of a Norton motorcycle that was once used by British soldiers and the engine of an Allied transport plane that had crashed. The two were found in different places.

'The motorcycle was completely buried when we found it. We have managed to convince many villagers to hand over war materials to us for the museum. Most of them have been gracious enough to oblige us.'

Arambam is also some kind of an archaeologist and has been on several excavations across different battle theatres in Manipur after receiving news of a find. He is also associated with the Japan Association for Recovery and Repatriation of War Casualties or JARRWC that visits Manipur to complete formalities when the remains of Japanese soldiers are found or identified.

'The Battle of Imphal was fought at different places, some of which are still very remote. That partly explains why the remains of Japanese soldiers are still found,' Arambam tells me.

Dusk begins to fall. I tell him that I would be leaving for Kohima the next morning and ask him about the condition of the road. I get the answer I did not want to hear.

'Not very good. There are a lot of broken stretches but it is certainly not as bad as the Kohima-Dimapur road which is simply atrocious. By the way, where will you be staying in Kohima?'

'I haven't fixed up anything but I will try to find a place.'

'I know someone who runs a hotel in Kohima and you can speak to her. I will give you her number.'

It is evening when I leave his house. Thangal Bazar is less crowded probably because most people are celebrating Christmas. I pack my bags for the next morning's ride and then call Sobhapati to check when he would be coming for dinner. But he says he has just gotten out of a long meeting of the local journalists' union for a plan of action to protest the arrest of Kishorechand Wangkhem for his Facebook rant, and wants to rest. I had planned to eat at the hotel's restaurant but with Sobhapati opting out, I decide to check out some local street food and go out.

Most of what I see is not to my liking. About half a kilometre away from my hotel, I finally see a vendor with 'Rolls' written on his cart and ask him for chicken roll. He takes out something which resembles a seekh kebab wrapped in polythene packing. He extracts it from the packing, heats it, puts it in a paper plate and gives it to me along with a large vegetable sandwich.

'What is this? I asked for a chicken roll.'

'The chicken is the roll. It is eaten with the sandwich.'

I realize that my quest for street food has turned out to be a misadventure but I try to make the most of it. Another customer comes and asks for a chicken roll to be packed. The vendor serves him quickly and the customer rides away.

The chicken is tasty but very spicy. The vendor appears to be in his late 50s. I ask him if he is a local.

'No. I am from Ukhrul.'

Ukhrul is about 80 km northeast of Imphal and used to a hotbed of insurgency. It is largely populated by Tangkhul Nagas.

'But what was the need to come from Ukhrul for this business? You could have done the same thing there,' I tell him.

'No, I couldn't have. I moved here ten years ago because things were very difficult there. Insurgents would demand money as some kind of tax and no one could protest for the fear of being killed. If you go to the police to complain you would be a marked man.'

'Is it better here?'

'Yes. Maybe because it is the capital and there is more security. Also there are more economic opportunities. I sell poultry during the day and in the evening I run this shop.'

'Will you ever go back to Ukhrul?'

'I may return in a few years. It's my home and I would like to grow old there.'

I finish my meal and compliment him and walk back to the hotel as a cold wind sweeps through the road.

13

In The Land of The Nagas

26 December 2018

I leave the hotel at 8 am after breakfast and head north to Kohima, 135 km away. It is cold and there is thick fog on the outskirts of the town. Out of Imphal the road begins to worsen like Arambam had warned. The cold rises, the fog gets worse and riding soon becomes almost impossible as visibility falls drastically. I am forced to stop at a small town called Sekmai, about 20 km from Imphal. Shops have just started to open and tea stalls are crowded with people.

I stop at one such stall and buy a glass of tea, cup my hands around it, and stand near one of the stoves. The sun is struggling to cut through the fog. Other customers, most of them wrapped in shawls and wearing thick woollen caps are sitting on two benches and eating breakfast.

A truck carrying small rocks for building roads is parked nearby. A man walks in and orders tea, comes and stands near me and asks where I am going.

'Wait for some time for the fog to clear. It won't last long.'

He wants to know what I do for a living and where I have been riding from.

He tells me his name is Tam Psa Jao and spells it out. It sounds quite unlike any Manipuri name I have heard.

'My ancestors came from Thailand and settled here. They came to work in the royal court more than a century ago,' he tells me as he takes his glass of tea from a waiter.

'And what do you do?'

'I am a small contractor. I am building one of the road stretches here.'

He asks me about the motorcycle and the company which makes it.

'Royal Enfield,' I tell him.

'I didn't know Royal Enfield makes this kind of bikes. I used to ride a Bullet earlier but that was a long time ago. Now I mostly take a shared autorickshaw to travel.'

I ask him how long it would take for the road to be completely built.

'It will probably take less than a year if we manage to build most of it before the monsoon starts. We have to build the road till Mao after which it is Nagaland territory. And Mao is about 80 km from here. Work will be slow until the end of the month because of Christmas holidays.'

The fog begins to clear and I wait a little longer before I start the ride again. My luck improves and about 15 minutes later the sun finally shines brightly as the fog lifts completely. The road goes mostly uphill as Kohima's altitude at 1,444 metres is almost double that of Imphal's. On my right the Sekmai river snakes through the picturesque valley.

A little after Sekmai the Christian influence in the state becomes more evident. There are Christmas gates along the highway in the approaches to villages and towns. The road alternates between a blacktop for short stretches and long stretches of rocks and earth where it is being rebuilt. Along the way, I cross minor war memorials dedicated to fallen soldiers of WWII. There had been various small battlefronts along the entire Imphal-Kohima road.

Close to noon I ride into Senapati town, the headquarters of the district by the same name. The highway runs through a market in the town. I stop at an eatery for snacks and see banners advertising the first ever two-day Barak Festival that had concluded 11 days earlier on December 15. The festival was held to raise awareness for the conservation of the Barak river which originates in the hills near the town and flows down through Senapati and Tamenglong districts before crossing into Assam's Cachar district and then into Bangladesh before it empties into the Bay of Bengal.

The road stays good for a few kilometres after Senapati town before the familiar broken tarmac reappears and this time it seems never-ending. Mao, the last town in Manipur before Nagaland begins, is just over 40 km from Senapati but the road condition conspires to slow down my progress. An hour later I make another pit stop in the middle of nowhere. There is a large wooden restaurant with a long verandah where it seems truckers normally stop. I ask for tea and sit on a bench inside the eatery. A family from Bihar runs the joint.

A short while later three small cars drive in and stop in front of the restaurant. A dozen people including children and women step out and walk to the restaurant. They are headed for Kohima with their guru—a saffron clad, Hindi-speaking man with a streak of vermilion on his forehead. It seems such an unlikely place for a godman to show up.

The restaurant owner tells me that the next 20 km to Mao is also in bad shape. But by now I had stopped expecting good roads. Mao is a small town with a busy market. It is almost lunch time and I toy with the idea of stopping for lunch. But since Kohima is just 35 km away, I decide to eat after checking into a hotel in the Nagaland capital. Policemen at a Manipur Police checkpost in the market stop a few vehicles exiting the town but they don't bother about me. The road finally gets better and I ride faster again.

I cross a small town and see a large crowd watching a football match. I stop and watch the match for a few minutes. The footballers are wearing sneakers, not boots, and one of the teams is topless. It is the first time that I have seen all 11 players of a team play without jerseys. And I find it amazing that on a cold December day they could be doing it, a bright sun notwithstanding.

I roll into the outskirts of Kohima and call Nino, the woman whose number Arambam had given me. She doesn't answer the phone so I call up Shahwar's friend, Thejakielie Zuyie, who is also known as Akielie. He also knows Nino and gives me another number to call. There is no answer on that phone either. I call Akielie once again.

He asks me my location and then directs me to turn back for about a km and look for a signage called Greenwood Villa. 'That's also Nino's place. You will have to turn in from the highway. There will be someone there.'

I find the place easily, park the motorcycle outside a large iron gate and walk in. A handsome dog comes running towards me and starts wagging its tail. I bend down and pat its head and it follows me as I take a cobbled pathway through a beautiful garden that leads to a two-storey building with the front door open. It looks like a reception with a few chairs. A young foreigner is parking his bicycle inside the room. I ask him if there is anyone to talk to.

'I couldn't find anybody. I was staying with a few friends at another facility called Morung Lodge that these people own in the town but we had bookings only till today. So they asked us to shift here. My friends will be here in an hour. But it is strange that the door is open and there is no one present.'

He and his friends are from Britain and are cycling through the Northeast. We wait for some time before he decides to go out for a walk. I wait for some more time but no one shows up. I come out of the gate and see a signboard that says 'Dawn Homestay' with an arrow pointing to the direction parallel to Greenwood Villa, about 50 yards away.

I walk towards it and discover a cluster of three buildings in a horseshoe layout, one of them double-storeyed with a small garden and large parking. An SUV is parked and a man in his 50s is pruning a tree. I ask him if there would be a place to stay. He asks me to wait and goes in and comes out with a woman following him. She looks like she is in her late 40s.

'I am looking for a place to stay for two days,' I tell her.

'Yes, you can certainly stay. The rent is Rs 800 per day, meals included. Would you take a look at the room first?'

I nod and she takes me to one of the buildings which is at a slight elevation compared to the other two. I climb a small flight of stairs through a garden with colourful flowers and notice that a hill rises behind the building. We walk through a lounge for guests and reach the room. It is neat and clean. There are two beds, a table, a small almirah, and a clothesline.

'You are the only one in this quarter. No other guest in this room. There are three guests in the building at the front. The bathroom and washroom are common. There is no geyser but we will give you hot water for bath.'

I nod again. The bathroom and washroom are clean too.

'I will stay. Let me go and get the motorcycle,' I tell her.

It is 2 pm. I unload the motorcycle and take the luggage to my room. I rest for some time and then freshen up and go to ask if lunch is ready. I learn that her name is Akieno.

'Lunch is almost ready. I have cooked noodles and scrambled some eggs. Do you want to eat right away or would you like to wait for ten minutes? The other three guests have also returned.'

'I'll wait. Ten minutes is not a problem.'

The dining room is large with a six-seater table. I pull out a chair and sit. On one side of the room along a wall is another long table where Akieno keeps the food before putting them on the dining table. The next room is the kitchen which is as big as the dining room and also serves as a store room. Another woman comes out of the kitchen and introduces herself as Rovi Tono Yhoshii, Akieno's younger sister. I learn that they are from the Angami tribe which is dominant in and around Kohima.

Three young men troop in after some time and take their seats. We introduce each other. Mohammad Shaheer, Sharath, and Mahesh are friends from Shimoga in Karnataka and work in the IT industry in Bengaluru. They have just returned from a trek and are hungry. And so am I after a six-hour ride through broken roads. We eat to our heart's content.

Rovi serves chutney and says it is made of wild apple that grows abundantly in Nagaland. A little spicy and sweet and sour, but it certainly enhances the taste of the food.

The three young men and I exchange notes and I learn they are headed for Imphal the day after. Shaheer is also interested in photography. I tell them that it is my second long-distance solo ride after the one to Ladakh in 2013 and that I am planning to write a book on my travel.

'Did you start the ride particularly to write a book?' Shaheer asks.

'Not really,' I tell him. 'I had wanted to ride across the Northeast for a long time but it is only now that things fell in place so I could actually be on the road. And I have had such diverse experience along the way that I might as well write about it.'

'I'll wait for it,' Shaheer says. I tell them that I had already written a book about my travel through Kashmir and Ladakh and they seem to be genuinely interested in me. We keep talking for some more time after finishing our meals. Rovi serves tea after which we disperse.

I call up Akielie and we decide to meet at the Kohima war cemetery. On my way I notice signage of the recently concluded Hornbill Festival which has become Nagaland's top tourism draw since it began in 2000. I also notice that much of the city is closed the day after Christmas. Unlike the cemetery in Imphal which is on a flat stretch of land, the one in Kohima is built on a hill and its area is bigger although it contains 1,420 Commonwealth burials compared to the 1,600 plus in Imphal. Also unlike Imphal, the Garrison Hill on which the cemetery is located was the site of one of the most ferocious fighting of the Burma campaign as a small Commonwealth force repulsed repeated attacks by a Japanese Division. At the highest point in the cemetery is the Kohima Cremation Memorial where the remains of 917 Hindu and Sikh soldiers were cremated.

At the lower end of the cemetery, near the entrance, is a monument to the 2nd Division of the British army with an epitaph that has become the memorial's signature:

'When you go home
Tell them of us and say,
For your tomorrow,
We gave our today.'

The Japanese advance into India was halted at Kohima in April 1944. In 2013, Britain's National War Museum chose the Battle of Imphal/Kohima as Britain's greatest battle.

There are a few other tourists at the cemetery. I walk out after some time and wait for Akielie at the parking. He rides in a little later on a red BMW motorcycle which the German auto major had just launched in India. It is the smallest of BMW motorcycles with a 313 cc 34 bhp engine but it still looks big for its size.

'Let's go sit at a restaurant where we can talk,' he tells me. I follow him as we ride to the heart of the city. We stop in front of a fast food joint and walk in only to discover that the eatery section is closed and only its ice cream parlour is open where a few youngsters are eating the frozen dessert. I find it pretty strange that an ice cream parlour is open at the peak of winter but there is no hot beverage to buy.

Akielie and I ride to a different part of the town past the bus stand and stop at a large, upmarket club and restaurant. We walk in and sit and talk. He tells me that he runs an event management firm which had organized the opening and closing ceremonies of the Hornbill Festival in the first week of December. The festival is overseen by the government's

Tourism and Art and Culture Departments and showcases a mélange of cultural displays under one roof.

I ask him about prohibition that has been in force in Nagaland for a long time and whether it has actually achieved what it had intended to.

'Yes, to quite an extent. But Nagaland is probably the wettest dry state. Name a brand you want and you will get it.'

I am not really surprised at Akielie's answer but it makes me wonder why some governments think that prohibition is a good idea.

He takes out his phone and shows me a photo of a prize distribution ceremony of a car rally during the Hornbill Festival which he had won. We have been sitting for ten minutes and no waiter has showed up. Akielie gets up and goes to the reception to enquire. He returns shaking his head. 'I can't believe it. The club is open but there is no service at the restaurant today. Let's go.'

It is already dark when we step out of the restaurant and start our bikes. I stay behind Akielie as he leads the way to a coffee shop which is fortunately open. We stand and drink the coffee and I ask him about his motorcycle. He tells me he had to buy it from Kolkata because there is no dealership anywhere else in the Northeast.

'Where will you service it?'

'I don't know. It has a service interval of 10,000 km and I am hoping that by then a BMW dealership will probably come up in Guwahati. But the first service has to be done at 1,000 km and for now YouTube tutorials are my service engineers.'

I notice that the bike doesn't have a crash guard and I ask him why he hasn't fitted one.

'I will get one. But I can't figure out how to fix it because there doesn't seem to be a proper place in the frame to install it. And accessories for this bike are too costly.'

I tell him that I plan to visit Mon, home of the Konyak tribe who were once the fiercest of the headhunters in Nagaland.

Mon is northeast of Kohima towards Myanmar. He tells me about three different routes and all of them would partly involve offroading and would be largely through dirt tracks.

'Shahwar and I took one of these routes twice—once on bikes and another time on Polaris ATVs,' Akielie tells me. If I had been on an ATV I wouldn't have bothered about the road conditions. But after my experience on the Imphal-Kohima road I have no inclination to go offroading.

It is time to go. Akielie leads me to a particular place from where he points to the road that goes straight to Dawn Homestay. There are no street lights and I ride slowly. The road is illuminated only by headlights of vehicles or the occasional Christmas decoration along the way. A chilly wind starts to blow and by the time I park my motorcycle, the cold is numbing. I rush to my room and keep my bag, helmet, and gloves and go to the dining room where Shaheer, Sharath, and Mahesh are sitting around two heaters fired with charcoal. I take a chair and Akieno brings another heater and keeps it near me. The room begins to get cozy.

I get up after some time and walk into the kitchen and ask Rovi about dinner.

'I am cooking fish, chicken, dal, vegetables, rice, and rotis,' Rovi tells me as she stirs the chicken on a gas stove. On one side of the kitchen there is another earthen stove fuelled by firewood. Above both the stoves are thin iron roads where strips of meat have been hung to dry. A few children of the two sisters are also present in the kitchen helping with the cooking.

'Is this pork?' I ask.

'Yes,' Rovi answers. 'Do you eat pork?'

'No. I eat chicken, mutton, and beef.'

'We have run out of beef or I could have cooked some.'

'No problem. You are making quite an elaborate dinner anyway.'

I return to the dining room and sit. The conversation with the three young men from Bengaluru briefly moves to politics and corruption. No one in the room believes in any politician's call to fight graft.

'I am from Shimoga. And so are Yediyurappa and Eshwarappa, two of the BJP's top leaders in Karnataka. Between the two of them they virtually own Shimoga. That's how rich they are.'

It is probably an exaggeration but I get the point. B.S. Yediyurappa and K.S. Eshwarappa had been chief minister and deputy chief minister at different times. In 2011, Yediyurappa was briefly jailed in two cases of corruption for illegally denotifying land in and around Bengaluru and whispers of his wealth allegedly acquired through shady means never quite died down.

Rovi and Akieno finish cooking dinner and come and sit with us.

'What are you planning to do tomorrow?' Rovi asks me.

'I would like to meet any surviving soldiers of the Second World War.'

'There is no one nearby. You can try Khonoma village although I am not sure there would be anyone there either. I would suggest that you visit Kigwema which is my village a few kilometres down this road. It is quite historical because Japanese commander General Kotoku Sato stayed there for a couple of months during the war. The house is still there.'

That sounds interesting. Shaheer and his friends have decided to visit Khonoma. 'You can check out Kigwema in the morning and then head to Khonoma,' Rovi tells me. The three friends from Bengaluru have already hired the SUV I saw at the parking for the Khonoma trip. I ask Rovi about the man who was pruning a tree when I checked in.

'That's our brother, Neiphrazo.' Rovi is the more articulate of the two sisters.

One of the children opens the door to go out and a blast of cold wind enters the room. Akieno gets up to close the door. The charcoal in the heaters has burnt out and Akieno replenishes them with a fresh supply to ensure that heaters keep burning and keep the room warm.

'Is the house where General Sato stayed still owned by the same family?' I ask Rovi.

'No. It has changed hands. There is a new owner now but you can go and see it. I heard stories from my father and other elders in the village of the time when the Japanese lived there and some of it is quite terrifying.'

'Why? Did the Japanese kill or torture the villagers?'

'No. They didn't do anything to the villagers. They were mostly bothered about food because their supply lines had dried up. But the villagers were caught in the fighting. When the British attacked Kigwema many of the villagers including women and children headed to the hill behind this building to take shelter among some huge rocks. But the trouble was they couldn't light a fire to cook for fear of being targeted by British artillery. I don't know how those people survived.'

Kigwema is about 20 km away from Garrison Hill and the fighting was not as fierce. But like many other parts of Kohima, artillery fire had destroyed quite a lot of the village.

At 8 o'clock we decide to eat dinner. The two sisters are good cooks and the food tastes great. All of us take several helpings. The room is very cozy and none of us want to leave it. Rovi asks if we would like to have tea and all of us raise our hands.

'I will draw a map for you in the morning so you can ride easily into Kigwema,' Rovi tells me. We finish our tea and head for our rooms. I get under the blankets quickly and go off to sleep.

I wake up in the morning and laze around for some time before I force myself to get out of the bed. The sky is clear and the sun is shining brightly but it is very cold. I go to the dining room and ask for tea which Akieno quickly serves.

'The hot water is ready if you want to take a bath.'

I drink the tea and then take a bucket of hot water to bathe. I get ready and ask for breakfast. Rovi gives me bread, butter, jam, and omelette. She serves another cup of tea and as I drink, she sits down with a large sheet of paper and starts drawing a map. When she finishes, she comes over to me to explain.

'Turn left on the highway about a kilometre from here when you see a huge gate with Kigwema written on it. A little later you will see a road going uphill on the right,' Rovi explains.

And then as if to stress that I have to cover some distance, she says, 'Ignore that road and go, go, go, go, go, go straight and take the next right turn and you will reach Khamima Khel, which is a small open space in the village. You can park there. I have asked two of my nephews to be there and they will take you to the house where General Sato stayed.'

I am truly touched by her concern that I should not be wasting time to find General Sato's house. I leave the homestay and turn left towards Kigwema. The road is narrow and on my left I see terraced cultivation of paddy on the slopes of the hills that stretch for miles. The road withers away quickly and soon I am riding only over bare earth, rocks, and cobblestones. Kigwema is a large and prosperous village. Cars are parked in front of many houses. The final access to Khamima Khel is quite narrow, barely enough for two small cars to pass each other. I park the motorcycle near a signboard and see three little boys standing.

Two of them are Rovi's nephews and the other one is their friend. The brothers are aged 13 and 5 and their friend is 11. The older nephew is Neizezo. I hang my helmet on the motorcycle's handlebar and walk with the three boys. They take me through a narrow alley downhill with houses on both sides. Most houses have some vacant space in the compound, usually along the boundary with the alley which is used to store firewood in a very systematic way that makes it easy to access them.

Most families also have chicken that forage in their gardens. A few minutes later my three young guides stop in front of a wooden house on a platform and with a sloping tin roof. Five slabs of rock form the stairs to get into the house. The new owner has built a long, double-decker shelf along the front wall where he has put flower pots. Different types of flowers are in full bloom. The front door is closed.

'Hello,' I call out, hoping someone will open the door. But there is no response. There is another small house nearby with its door open. I knock on the door and a man in his mid-30s comes out with a baby in his arms.

'I am looking for the owner of that house,' I tell him.

'That's mine,' he says and asks me to come inside. The two-room structure is just a kitchen and storeroom. His wife is sitting on the floor cooking on an earthen stove.

I tell the man that I wanted to see the house where General Sato stayed.

'It's an ordinary house. It is probably a coincidence that the Japanese commander chose to stay in this one.'

'Can I see the inside of the house?'

'Yes. But it is very untidy right now.'

He leads the way up the stairs and opens the door. The first room has a few chairs and clothes and toys strewn about. I wonder if this room served as General Sato's office or dining room. The next room is the bedroom and it is much larger with a couple of windows. One of the windows opens to the view of the hills not far away while another opens parallel to an alley in the village. Everything in the house including the floor and the ceiling are made of wood.

'Have you made any alteration to the house?' I ask the owner.

'No. And none of the previous owners did either. All owners took care of it. An annual coat of polish has ensured that the wood hasn't decayed. The only repair done was to fix the roof after shrapnel from an artillery shell punctured it and left this mark on the floor,' he tells me pointing downwards. 'Somehow no one seems to know where General Sato was when the shrapnel hit the house.'

I notice a small depression on the floor as if wood had been scooped out. That scar has remained ever since 1944 and now it almost seems like a badge of honour.

'I don't know much about the war but from what I heard it seems the Japanese fought ferociously despite heavy odds,' the house owner says.

'Yes, that's recorded history,' I tell him.

I take a few photographs of the house and the house owner with his kid and leave. Neizezo tells me that he will take me to see traditional houses in the village. We trudge uphill and take another alley as the three boys guide me to another part of Kigwema. We stop in front of a house with a horn like structure at the gable end of the roof. Not every house has that sign and not everyone is allowed to put it up.

'It is a mark of stature for a resident who has hosted feasts for the villagers four times. And it is for a man who commands respect,' Rovi had explained. 'It is called *kika*.'

Smoke rises from the kitchen of the house. In the courtyard, women of the family are sitting and chopping leafy vegetables. Two men sharpen machetes. Further up the alley, I hear Rod Stewart sing 'Maggie' as we cross another house. A young woman in jeans, jacket, and sneakers walks past us with a large wicker basket on her back supported by a headband across her forehead.

'Where is she going?' I ask Neizezo.

'To collect firewood.'

A little girl, not more than seven, stands at the community water tank to fill up a small bucket. The alley leads to a fork where three teenagers are playing football. We turn right and I find myself looking at two oblong houses with curved designs at the gable ends of the roofs. Wood carvings decorate the facia set slightly inwards along the roofs' gradient.

I learn that these two are Morungs or community halls where young boys of the village are taught the tribe's way of life and moral values. The front wall is studded with skulls of animals, mostly bulls and mithuns. Angami art and paintings in red, white, and black decorate the wooden wall. It is the holiday season so there are no boys at the morung.

I spend more than an hour walking around the village before I start for the homestay. The exit from Kigwema is even more challenging. The road is steep and large, uneven cobblestones make it difficult to manoeuvre the motorcycle through sharp turns. But I reach the homestay safely.

Shaheer, Sharath, and Mahesh are preparing to leave for Kohonoma and Dzuleke in Neiphrazo's SUV. Shaheer asks if I would like to join them and I tell him that I will follow them on the bike. Rovi also joins them to visit a hospital on the way to see an aunt.

Khonoma is about 30 km from the homestay and Dzuleke another 15 km away on the outskirts of Kohima, a little off the road to Dimapur. The SUV stops a few kilometres from the war cemetery and Rovi gets off the vehicle to go to the hospital and we start again. The road soon disappears. The entire 75 km Kohima-Dimapur stretch is being rebuilt and riding soon becomes a pain. The road is full of stones covered with a thin layer of earth. It is wet in many places and the water has washed away the soil along those parts. After about five kilometres on the atrocious road, Neiphrazo turns left from the highway and the road starts going uphill. For some time the road appears good before the tarmac wears off and we go through some rocky and watery stretches. The tarmac appears intermittently but the rocky stretch is overwhelmingly longer.

We stop at a view point and Sharath and Mahesh get out of the SUV. We take a few photographs and I decide to leave the motorcycle on the road and tell the three men that I want to join them in the vehicle. Mahesh volunteers to ride the bike. I am a little wary because he is not wearing shoes. He is in a pair of sandals and is wearing two pairs of socks to ward off the cold.

'I will be fine. I am used to riding like this. Even in Karnataka I normally ride in this outfit when we go out for weekend trips,' he tells me. I am still not convinced. Mahesh refuses to wear my riding jacket either. 'Not now. If I feel cold I will take it.' I give him my helmet and gloves and he guns the motorcycle to life and we start moving.

Neiphrazo is a cautious driver and drives slowly even when he is on a good stretch of road. We reach a fork from where one road goes to Khonoma and the other to Dzuleke. A signage with an arrow mark says Khonoma Green Village. We decide to head to Dzuleke first. The road continues to alternate between broken tarmac and extreme rocky stretches. Neiphrazo drives as if he has all the time in the world and I begin to wonder if we have made the right choice heading for Dzuleke, a small village of about 200 people, which wasn't on my original itinerary. The only bright spot is the landscape. Neiphrazo had been to Dzuleke only once many years ago and has blurred memories.

The village got its name from the river Dzuleke which flows underground in the village. 'Dzu' mean water and 'leke' means underground in the local language.

In the end, the place turns out to be a disappointment. There is a barrier on the road and Neiphrazo stops the vehicle. On one side on the road there is a Nagaland Tourism office and Sharath and Mahesh go to get some information. The two of them spend about 15 minutes inside the office before they return.

'It is Rs 500 per head to cross this barrier and we need to hire a guide to go anywhere and that cost is extra,' Sharath informs Shaheer and me.

It is already past noon and we decide it is no use to spend more time in Dzuleke because we would end up rushing through Khonoma. We request Neiphrazo to drive a little faster but the SUV's engine seems fatigued. It takes us over an hour to reach Khonoma barely 10 km away, around 1:30 pm. We park in front of a church. Neiphrazo decides to stay put in the vehicle. We can't find a guide but begin to explore the village that is said to be 700 years old.

Khonoma was once considered the cradle of Naga insurgency. Angami Zapu Phizo, regarded by insurgents as 'father of the Nagas', hailed from this village. It was under Phizo's leadership that the Naga National Council and Naga Federal Army launched their secessionist movement in the late 1940s.

At first look, Khonoma is deceptive and it almost seems deserted. Shaheer, Sharath, and Mahesh walk ahead while I stroll slowly along a cobbled pathway checking out the architecture. Three women are sitting in front of a house washing clothes in large wooden tubs. Outside another house two old women are sitting in the sun and a man is trimming hedges along a stone staircase on a slope behind the house. I climb the stairs and ask him if there are any WWII soldiers left in the village.

'It is unlikely any of them are still alive. But I am not sure. I don't stay in this village anymore and come here sometimes to see my mother. I have settled in the town after my retirement.' He says he is 70 but doesn't look older than 60.

I climb down and start walking again. It is very quiet and most houses are locked. A little later on my left a staircase goes down. It had been decorated with colourful ribbons and festoons for Christmas. On one side at the top of the stairs is a miniature house with figurines of Jesus and Mary inside. On the ground outside the house are miniature gifts in wrapping papers with golden ribbons. I walk down the stairs at the end of which are two large concrete water tanks around which a few villagers are standing in the sun. I ask them about the soldiers.

'There's no one alive,' one of them tells me.

'Are their families and relatives here?'

'Some have left the village, some are here. But you won't find anyone at home now. They have all gone to their farms.'

I notice a morung with a red façade studded with skulls of bulls and mithuns. Two guns, one of which is six feet in length, are mounted on the front wall along with other tools and fishing gear. On a circular open space near the morung a woman is spreading out paddy to dry in the sun. Like Kigwema, every house has a stockpile of wood.

I retrace my steps and climb up the stairs and join my three co-travellers and go up to see what looks like the ramparts of a fort. The village continues to sprawl out as we keep walking. I notice a few houses have tombs in front of them with names of the deceased inscribed on them. We finally reach what seems to be one end of the village where many women are sitting in an open space and their children are playing.

There is also a hotel built of stone and concrete with red tiles on the roof. It is called Dovipie Inn. Adjacent to it is a large, wooden single-room that serves as a restaurant and a viewpoint. A large group of tourists has already arrived and filled up the restaurant. We ask for tea and wait our turn. We learn that a man who is standing near us is a guide the tourists had hired and he is waiting for his payment. The four of us decide to hire him.

The guide is a young man named Viko. We finish our tea and Viko starts the tour. I ask him about the tombs.

'It's an individual's wish that he wants to be buried at the particular spot and so the family makes a tomb. And sometimes families want to bury a person in their own land and so they build a tomb.'

We learn that Khonoma is a very large village with about 3,000 inhabitants. Viko takes us to the top of Khonoma fort once again. It had borne the brunt of British onslaughts in the late 1800s and had been repaired each time. But very little of the original structure remains.

'Angamis are a warrior tribe. We were once headhunters. A headhunter was acknowledged as a man who could protect the women and children of his family. Headhunting stopped with the advent of Christianity here. There are different denominations of Christianity here.'

Viko then leads us to the morung. He explains that the big gun is a ceremonial weapon and it takes three men to hold it and one to fire it. It is a muzzle loading gun and used once a year. He takes us inside the morung and shows the dormitory where the boys stay for a particular number of days. During the stay the boys make their own beds, take care of their belongings and do tasks assigned by elders.

'If a boy didn't come to a morung, he would be called a weakling. If a married man came, he would be called a henpecked husband. A few elders adopt a few boys each to guide them and pass on the tribe's wisdom and skills.'

'Have you stayed in a morung?' I ask Viko.

'I did. Morung is a place where elders teach youngsters various things and give them moral lessons. I was told never to give wrong directions to a stranger and to volunteer for the hardest work if I had to do something for the community.'

On the opposite side of the morung is a large, single-room house. Viko takes us there to show handicrafts, tools, and dummy wooden guns made by boys at the morung on the advice of their elders. All the items are exquisitely carved. The exercise also serves to hone a spirit of competitiveness among the boys.

Near the morung stands a monolith in memory of a warrior named Judelie Hiekha for his role in opposing British forces who were trying to get a foothold in Nagaland in the 19th century. The citation hails Hiekha for his role in Khonoma's victory over a British expeditionary force. The warrior is said to have initiated an attack in which British Political Officer G.H. Damant was shot dead on 13 October 1879.

British incursions into the Naga hills began in the 1840s but it took nearly four decades for them to conquer a territory that is less than 10,000 square kilometres. It underlined the stiff resistance from the independence-loving Nagas, who had never been conquered by any empire before. Eventually, a truce between the British and the Nagas stopped further bloodshed and by then Khonoma had earned its spurs for its resistance to colonial invasion.

'There is a memorial for Damant also in the village,' Viko tells us as we head for another part of Khonoma.

Viko is quite well known in the village and we frequently run into his acquaintances. Most houses have an assortment of colourful flowers in the porch and I notice butterflies hovering over the small gardens. I mention the Green Village signboard to Viko and ask him what it means.

'That's because we have banned hunting and felling trees and have taken up large scale projects for conservation and protection of nature and biodiversity. The vegetables we eat and those we cook for tourists come from kitchen gardens.'

Viko tells us that the conservation story started in the mid-1990s following the slaughter of around 300 Blyth's tragopan, a pheasant with stunning plumage and the state bird of Nagaland. 'Some village elders recognized that such large-scale hunting would pose serious danger to the ecology and convinced villagers to stop the age-old practice of hunting and chopping trees. In 1998, the Khonoma village council reserved an area of 20 sq km as Tragophan Sanctuary.'

It was a herculean achievement given that hunting is a cultural right of the Nagas. Khonoma was declared India's first Green Village in October 2005. I would later learn that the Indian government's tourism department and the Nagaland government also backed the campaign for the conservation efforts.

We keep walking uphill and cross a memorial to Damant. Viko leads us to the ramparts of another fort from where there is a clear view of an entire mountain range and an expansive valley lined with terraced farms. A thin layer of mist hangs in the air over the valley.

Viko points to a particular hill straight ahead. Amid the lush greenery of the hill is a rockface. 'That structure looks like a human face. It is supposed to be the guardian of animals. In earlier times, hunters used to look at it to invoke its blessings before going out on a hunt. And according to legend, if it looked happy it meant the hunters would find very few animals or none at all. If it appeared to look sad, it was thought that the hunters would return with many birds and animals.'

We strain our eyes to see if the rockface resembles a human. But the mist doesn't allow a clear sight of it. Viko leads us down a flank of the rampart that eventually opens up at the parking. The sun is waning and it would be dark much before we reach our homestay. My shoulder had been aching for some time and I request Mahesh to ride the motorcycle till the highway from where I would take it. It is getting cold and Mahesh and I exchange our jackets. I climb into the SUV with Shaheer and Sharath while Mahesh starts the bike, overtakes us and disappears. We rock and roll through those potholes and ditches before we finally reach the highway.

I can't see Mahesh at the spot I had asked him to wait and I am worried. Shaheer and Sharath tell me that Mahesh is probably enjoying the ride and that's why he hasn't stopped. We finally see Mahesh a few kilometres later sitting on the stationary bike. I get down as soon as Neiphrazo stops the vehicle. I ask

Mahesh to get into the SUV but he insists on riding it to the homestay. We make a brief pit stop at an ATM to withdraw money before we return to Dawn Homestay. A blast of cold wind stings my face as I disembark. We head for the dining room where Akieno and Rovi had already lit the heaters.

We sit and drink a few cups of tea. There are two different voices in the kitchen that I can't recognize and ask Rovi.

'A couple. A Frenchman and a Tamil girl,' she tells me. Shaheer goes over to chat with the new arrivals.

Rovi also tells us that the menu for dinner is fish curry, dal, vegetables, soup, and a dish of bamboo shoots.

'The bamboo shoot is a Naga dish. We play safe with food so we use spices while cooking for guests. If I were to give you food cooked the Naga way you wouldn't like it because we don't use spices. You will find it bland.'

She has learnt to address concerns about food for all kind of guests.

'Sometimes both vegetarians and non-vegetarians can be difficult to serve. We had a Muslim guest once who insisted that he would slaughter the chicken until he saw us do it the same way as Muslims do. For most non-vegetarians fish and chicken are safe bets so we normally stick to them.'

She returns to the kitchen to join Akieno. They finish after about 15 minutes and return to the dining room and fill up the heaters once again with charcoal. I ask the sisters about prohibition.

'In most villages people brew their own drink. Prohibition wasn't meant to stop people from drinking it and it didn't stop. It was meant to stop easy access to alcohol because at one point of time alcohol abuse was quite high in Nagaland. I think prohibition has largely achieved its goal although bootlegging has always been there,' Rovi tells me.

That's not exactly what Akielie had told me the previous evening but I guess there is a difference in the situation inside

Kohima and a village like Kigwema which is on the town's outskirts.

I was also curious to know why despite being highly qualified there are no women in politics in Nagaland. There are doctors, professors, journalists, and cops but no politicians. I ask Akieno about women's rights in Nagaland which has never elected a female lawmaker since it became a state in 1963 and which witnessed violent backlash in the beginning of January 2017 against reservation for women in civic elections. The protests in 2017 were led by the Naga Hoho, an apex body of 16 Naga tribal groups.

Tribal bodies had claimed that reservations disrupt Naga customary laws that are protected under the Constitution and are distinct from state laws. Under the constitutional provision, no act of Parliament that interfered with Naga customary laws or social and religious practices would apply to Nagaland unless the state assembly passed a resolution allowing it.

Akieno does not seem much bothered about it. 'I am not very interested in politics. Maybe it will take time for the Naga Hoho to accept the changes that women's reservation will bring about. Sometimes, a change in the social set up takes longer than expected.'

She gets up and joins Rovi to lay the table. Shaheer and the Indo-French couple also join us for dinner. I learn that the two of them had left their jobs in France to travel across South Asia. They had crossed over to India from Nepal and were planning to celebrate Pongal in Chennai with the woman's parents. The man is an engineer and his wife is a software professional.

I stick to rice, fish curry, and vegetables. Everybody else tries almost everything on the table and the dinner stretches for quite some time before we top it off with tea and head for our rooms.

I wake up early to see off Shaheer, Sharath, and Mahesh who are heading to Imphal. They had booked a taxi to drop them at the bus station. After they leave, I too get ready and leave for Mokokchung, about 160 km away.

'Next time, bring your family,' Rovi tells me. I promise her that I will.

By the time I exit Kohima it is almost 8 am. The road is good for a change but the right hand side of the road is wet mainly from dew falling off trees from the hill slopes or small streams flowing onto the road. I cross a few villages where women are going out with baskets to collect firewood. Outside one such village I see a man with a gun and a bag slung over his shoulder walking ahead of me. He is looking at the trees on the hill on the right as he walks. I stop near him and ask him where he is headed.

'I am out on a hunt. I am looking for birds. But rabbits will also do.'

'What gun is this?'

'Winchester .22. It used to be my father's. I hope I am lucky today.'

'How much time do you spend on a hunt?'

'Not very much. If I get out of my house early like today, birds are easier to find.'

Unlike Khonoma, there is no ban on hunting in this part of Nagaland. He agrees to pose for a photograph and I wish him luck before I resume my ride. The road remains a blacktop for about 50 km till a hamlet called Botsa after which it begins to deteriorate. Half an hour later I make a pit stop outside a village. I see an Assam Rifles patrol walking down the road. One of the troopers has a dog on a leash. I notice that there is a pattern in the patrol with successive troopers walking on either side of the road. One of the soldiers in the middle stops to ask me where I am heading for.

'I hope you make it in time. The road is not very good,' he tells me. I wait for the last trooper to cross me before I start again.

Ahead of Wokha, the road becomes atrocious with very rough and rocky gradients and straight stretches. I reach Wokha, home of the Lotha tribe, around 1 pm and stop for lunch. The 80-km ride had taken me almost five hours, three of which were spent on the last 30 km.

The restaurant is large and spacious and most of the tables have been taken up. Almost every customer is eating pork. A woman walks up to me and asks if I would like to order a pork dish. I shake my head.

'Would you like Lotha style chicken or plain chicken curry?' she asks.

'Just plain rice, dal, and mixed vegetables.' She looks at me as if I am an oddity, but serves me quickly. The food is fresh and tastes great.

I am halfway through my meal when three other motorcyclists in leather jackets walk in. The only three vacant chairs are at my table.

'May we share this table?' one of them asks me.

I nod and they pull the chairs and sit. All of them are in their 20s.

'I am David. And that's Ezung and Tumben,' the young man introduces himself and his friends. 'I guess the Himalayan motorcycle is yours.'

'Yes. I am about to finish my ride across the Northeast,' I tell him.

'Did you like Nagaland?'

'I have visited the state twice before and I have always liked it. I find Nagas very hospitable and kind and I like the way they have preserved their culture.'

'Preserving culture is the difficult part. And I find it so paradoxical because the younger generation hardly follows the culture. But what bugs me even more is what you hear in other parts of the country, particularly in the North, that Nagas are savage and uncivilized people who eat any living thing. Many people make it sound like we just stop short of cannibalism,' David says with a wry smile.

He reminds me of Sonam Lobsang who told me the same thing at a restaurant near the Tawang monastery a month earlier.

The waitress serves pork curry and rice to the three men who start eating. I ask them about what they think of a peace deal that the central government has been trying to hammer out with an assortment of Naga rebel groups. The dominant faction of the National Socialist Council of Nagaland or NSCN, the largest insurgent group has been insisting that Nagaland be allowed its own flag and constitution. It is a demand that the Indian government has not accepted. Despite a 'framework agreement' signed between the Centre and the NSCN in 2015 to end insurgency in the state, a concrete deal has remained elusive.

Tumben stops eating to say the Centre is not serious about the peace talks and suspects that it hopes to wear out the NSCN with endless negotiations.

'You just can't hold talks and decide to sign a peace deal. You need to be a statesman with a vision to make a deal to end India's longest running insurgency. And Narendra Modi is anything but a statesman,' Tumben says and shakes his head.

David nods. 'The Centre thinks it can sugarcoat a deal and get the NSCN on board to sign it. I don't think the NSCN can be bought over. The way the government has been insisting on a peace deal makes it look like the cure could be worse than the disease. In any case, the government keeps extending the Disturbed Areas Act every six months which ensures that the

Armed Forces (Special Powers) Act remains in force. We are actually walking on thin ice but it is not apparent to many people.'

'I hope peace remains here. We can do without bloodshed,' I tell them.

'Every Naga wants peace. But everyone has a tipping point. And so the peace deal has to be something genuine and not one that the Nagas have sign under coercion,' David says.

I finish my lunch and order tea and ask Tumben about the condition of the road ahead.

'It is bad until 30 km ahead of Mokokchung.'

And I am still 80 km away. I take leave of the three men and resume my ride. The road goes downhill for quite some time but it is peppered with large craters that slow down every kind of vehicle. Long stretches of roads have been dug up for miles to lay stones before they are tarred. In the stretches where road rollers have flattened the stones, it is relatively easier to ride. But in the stretches where the road rollers haven't been used, the ride becomes dangerous. I finally reach the point from where the road improves. The initial stretch is through a thick forest and after an hour of starting from Wokha, I take another break in the middle of a jungle. Elephant grass forms a buffer between the road and the forest. The wind makes strange whistling noises as it runs into a barrier of trees. The road becomes wider as I approach Mokokchung and I reach the town by 3 pm. Mokokchung is also a district and home to the Ao tribe, one of the major Naga tribes. They were the first Naga tribe to embrace Christianity in the state.

I stop at a fork inside a market to review the situation. Although I had planned to stop for the night at Mokokchung, there is still plenty of daylight left and despite the fatigue I feel I can reach either Jorhat or Amguri in Assam by the evening. I ask a shopkeeper about the road condition.

'They are as good or as bad as the roads in the rest of Nagaland,' he tells me.

That's not an encouraging reply. Both Jorhat and Amguri are equidistant at about 100 km from Mokokchung and I opt to head for Amguri because it would cut the distance to my next destination Mon by 30 km.

Outside the town, the nightmare of the road returns quickly. I find myself behind a small car but I make no effort to overtake it and instead let it work as a pathfinder for me. The car has an Assam registration and after some time it becomes clear to me that the driver is not comfortable driving in the hills and is slowing me down. I overtake the car but the road worsens with slush and water crossings that crop up frequently. The sun begins to wane and the last of the daylight comes through the gap between the mountains before dusk falls. For a long time there are no milestones and I have no idea how far away I am from Amguri. I had made the mistake of not checking the odometer reading when I left Mokokchung.

By 5:30 pm I begin to feel that I had been riding through much of the night. I pass through a small hamlet still aglow with Christmas lights and slow down in the market hoping to find a tea stall but almost every shop has downed the shutters. There had been a full moon six days earlier and it is waning now. Clouds often obscure it and the night becomes darker. There is no sign of the road condition improving and it becomes clear that I had made a bad decision by not staying the night in Mokokchung.

The motorcycle stays faithful as I negotiate broken tarmac, rocks, slush, water, and sand through what is supposed to be a road. I finally see a dhaba which is open and I stop. It has been four hours since I left Mokokchung and the road has already taken a toll on my body. My neck and the back of my thighs hurt badly. I walk in and I am surprised to see that there are two women running the dhaba in such a remote place at night. I ask for tea and biscuits.

Beyond the dhaba I can see the lights of another hamlet down the road and ask the woman about it.

'That's our village.'

They have to go back to the village later in the night and do not seem bothered at all that they will have to walk.

'How far is Amguri from here?'

'It is about 45 km. You will reach Tuli which is the last town in Nagaland before you cross into Assam and Amguri will be another 15 km away from the border.'

I stand and drink the tea and ask her how long has the road been in such bad condition.

'When was it good? It is not as if the government has no money to fix these roads. But these politicians siphon off all the money and the roads remain like this.'

Nagaland has been notorious for a culture that has encouraged politicians to host feasts for villages and dole out cash for votes ahead of elections while infrastructure work like roads lags behind.

'Our people are also to blame. We are happy with the handouts during campaigning and so we end up with such horrible roads. No one seems to understand the need for good roads. Can you imagine a situation where a critically ill patient needs to be shifted to a hospital in a different city? On these roads the poor chap will die in an ambulance,' she rails. 'Politicians, I tell you.'

A small bus drives in and the driver and another man walk in and ask for dinner and the two women get busy with cooking. I get ready to resume my journey but my legs hurt as I straddle the bike. I force myself to ride on. Half an hour later I am on the outskirts of Tuli which is largely on flat land with gentle slopes. Like other places Tuli is also lit up with Christmas lights but only a few shops are open in the town. There are street lights inside the town. The road gets better but the craters still appear frequently. Fortunately, there is very little traffic and I am able to ride fast and dodge the potholes.

The street lights disappear at the edge of the town. Clouds have covered the moon completely and the night turns inky black. The craters get bigger and the road seems to go on forever through forests. I finally reach the Assam border where a policeman flags me down before letting me go after asking a few questions. Lightning flashes and I can see dark clouds.

The road is finally what it should be. I am in the plains and dying to find a hotel. By 8 pm, I am in the heart of Amguri but I can't see a hotel. I stop and park the bike and decide to look around for a hotel. There is another motorcycle parked nearby and a man is heading for it. I ask him if there is a hotel nearby.

'Yes, there is one just after this traffic light. You have to take a right turn at the crossing. I am going that way and you can follow me if you want.'

I get on my motorcycle and follow him for a couple of hundred metres before he stops and points to a hotel and rides away. I dismount and walk into the reception and discover that the hotel is a relic of an ancient past. All my instincts tell me not to check in but I am too exhausted to try to find another hotel after the 12-hour ride covering 250 km from Kohima.

A steep staircase leads to the first floor where all the rooms are located. Bathrooms and washrooms are common. There are two other guests in two rooms. I take a room at the end of a corridor overlooking the road. I freshen up and rest for some time before going downstairs for dinner. But before dinner I have to park the motorcycle which I push past the reception and haul it on to its stand near the dining hall.

The receptionist tells me that dinner will take ten minutes to be served. Another man walks in and starts talking to the receptionist and then turns to me to ask where I have come from.

'You must be very tired. How long are you staying?'

'Only tonight. I am planning to go to Mon tomorrow morning.'

He sees the stickers of the cement company on the motorcycle and asks if I am employed with it.

'No. The company is one of the sponsors of my expedition,' I tell him.

He claims he knows the owner of the company. I am wary of people who drop names. When he learns that I am a journalist, he drops a few more names of scribes in Guwahati, some of whom I know. I steer the conversation to Mon and ask him for directions. He gives me a detailed description of the route and then warns me not to go ahead if it rains.

'It is bad enough in dry conditions but if it rains it will become dangerous. The red soil is very slippery,' he tells me before leaving.

I eat my dinner which is rice, fish curry, dal, and vegetables and head for my room. I go off to sleep easily and wake up at 6 am and discover that it is raining. I freshen up and head downstairs to ask how long it had been raining.

'A few hours,' the cook tells me. I return to my room and wait but the rain becomes heavier. I check Mon's weather on the internet and see that even heavier rain is forecast there. I decide to abort the trip to Mon and make up my mind to head back to Guwahati and wait for the rain to stop.

14

Heading Home

29 December 2018

The rain stops an hour later. As I load the motorcycle I feel pain on my left shoulder and biceps and realize that it is the onset of a frozen shoulder that had laid me low for a couple of months two years ago. I am glad it did not show up earlier during my journey. I push the motorcycle out of the hotel and ride to a restaurant on the main road for breakfast. A police bus and an SUV are parked outside the restaurant. There is only one table vacant and all others have been taken by a large group of armed policemen. After finishing my breakfast, I stand on the footpath and check my phone when a policeman comes and stands near me.

'Are you being deployed somewhere?' I ask him.

'No, we are going to a shooting range for routine firing practice.'

Some of them look like they are close to retirement age and completely out of shape for a policeman.

The sky is still cloudy when I start for Jorhat. The road is wet and I ride slowly. Fortunately, it is a blacktop as if compensating me for the loss of the trip to Mon. The temperature has plunged after the rain. I cross the small towns of Jhanji and Teok. Both the towns are expanding along the highway.

In less than an hour I reach the outskirts of Jorhat and toy with the idea of surprising Ajanto but decide against it just in case he is sleeping. As I exit Jorhat, the sun comes out in all its glory but even at 9 am most of the small shops are still closed.

In another 40 minutes I cross Dergaon and stop for tea at a dhaba. I am still bugged that the rain forced me to cancel the trip to Mon, but on the brighter side it meant that I would make it to Guwahati in time to pick up Sudha and Aseem who would be arriving the next day.

It is Saturday and I cross a few weekly markets along the highway. One particular market is a sprawling one that stretches over a few hundred metres on either side of the highway inside a small town where the road is narrower. Fresh vegetables, fruits, date palm jaggery, betel nut and paan, spices and bamboo artifacts are among a large number of items on sale. There is livestock also on sale including chicken, goats, pigs and piglets. The piglets which outnumber other livestock are kept in small bamboo cages and the higher demand is easily discernible with vendors selling piglets drawing the highest number of customers. A few men buy the piglets, put the bamboo cage in the carrier on their bicycles and ride away.

I continue to ride leisurely and reach the outskirts of Kaziranga National Park where I stop for an early lunch at around 11 am. Half an hour later I am in Kohora which the main entrance of Kaziranga and stop to buy souvenirs. I choose a figure of a rhino and barking deer.

Topless SUVs run up and down Kohora ferrying tourists inside the jungles of Kaziranga. Almost as a rule, each of these SUVs is a Maruti Suzuki Gypsy. Outside the souvenir shop, a Gypsy is stationary and the driver is standing by the door. I ask him if it is his own vehicle.

'Yes,' he tells me. 'Many of the drivers are owners themselves. And few owners employ drivers.'

I ask him how business has been in the current season.

'It started less than two months ago. It has been good so far. The winter is the peak tourist season. By February, tourist traffic begins to fall. And during the monsoon there is virtually no work for us because the park gets flooded.'

'So what do you do when the park is closed?'

'There is nothing much to do then. I mind my farm in the village if it is not flooded. Sometimes some people hire me to drive their cars. But no one hires a Gypsy because it guzzles too much petrol. It is only from here to the jungle that my Gypsy runs.'

'Then why do you use it? You could use a diesel SUV.'

'No. A diesel SUV costs more to own and since we operate in a limited area it makes sense to own a petrol-engine SUV. And the Gypsy is a very capable vehicle that can take you virtually anywhere.'

There has never been any doubt about the Gypsy's prowess. It has won dozens of motor rallies across the country and particularly been dominant in India's toughest motorsport event—Raid de Himalaya.

I leave Kohora and ride through the length of the highway and reach the other end of Kaziranga and stop to see a couple of rhinos not far from the road. A few other cars have also stopped and tourists are standing on the edge of the road looking at the rhinos. Among those watching the rhinos I spot Sadiq Naqvi and wave at him. He comes over and tells me that he was returning from Kaziranga with a journalist friend of his from Delhi who had come down with his wife and child on a vacation.

I ride on and make another stop outside Nagaon for tea and snacks at a large restaurant. It is crowded and waiters take orders and then relay them to the kitchen staff by shouting. The atmosphere is loud and noisy and the shouting doesn't stop. When a customer goes to pay the bill, the Marwari owner asks one of the waiters loudly about the customer's order. The waiter replies equally loudly and it seems that everyone in the restaurant must know what and how much worth of food every other customer has eaten. The restaurant is quite easily the noisiest place I have ever eaten in.

I cross Nagaon for the last time in the trip and open the throttle for some consistent fast riding through the concrete road. As I ride through Jagiroad I hear the sound of azaan (call for prayers) for the evening namaz wafting from a mosque. The setting sun has turned into an orange ball and I slow down as light begins to fade. On a bridge and across a river, few men hold up large fish enticing motorists but I don't see anyone stopping to buy or even look at them.

The volume of traffic begins to grow and the four-lane highway to Guwahati gradually gets congested. The sun sets behind the hills and I make the last stop of the day near a kiosk more out of frustration of heavy traffic than anything else. I dismount and stand near the motorcycle hoping for the traffic to ease. Two other men are also standing there, smoking. I ask one of them about the fishmongers I saw a little while ago.

'Never buy from them. The fish is usually fresh but they often increase its weight by pushing small stones inside its belly. So you end up paying for stones too,' one of them tells me.

I am amazed at this con job and it never crossed my mind that anyone would ever do something like that.

The traffic shows no sign of easing so I resume my ride. It finally gets better at a fork where one road leads to Shillong. For a few kilometres the ride is smooth before another monstrous traffic jam just at the entry to Guwahati acts as another speed-breaker. I squeeze the motorcycle through the gaps between buses, trucks, and cars and reach the last lap where I can breathe easy and reach home early evening.

I dismount and check the instrument panel of the motorcycle for the odometer reading and see that I have ridden 7,000 km across seven states. Inside my head, I exult with joy. I missed a few places like Lachung in North Sikkim and Mon in Nagaland and had to sacrifice a planned visit to Mizoram because of the initial delay in Siliguri but I tell myself that if everything had gone according to plan it would have been just too easy.

I carry my bags inside and sit on a chair in my mother's room. She has recovered pretty well and seems much better than she was when I had left for Meghalaya. I try to tell her some of the most memorable incidents of my trip, but for now, there's something else on her mind.

'When are Sudha and Aseem landing tomorrow? Are they coming on their own from the airport?' she asks.

'No. I will pick them up from the airport.'

'Okay. Now have a cup of tea and tell me your story.'

By 9 pm, I begin to feel sleepy and go to bed. The pain in my left shoulder has increased since it began in the morning and I am lucky I could reach home before it got worse. I think of the 1962 veterans in Bomdila and Tawang, Chachi Meyor in India's easternmost village of Kaho and wonder if there would be any tourists to see India's the first sunrays in Kaho in the New Year. I think of the Stilwell Road, the spectacular cloud formations and the coal miners in Meghalaya, the battlefields in Manipur, the house where Japanese commander General Sato stayed in Kigwema village. I think of Lou Majaw and in my mind I see him strumming his guitar. I regret that I could not visit Pangsau Pass despite being so agonizingly close to it but I have ticked off much of the boxes I had set for myself when I began my journey.

My back, shoulder, and neck hurt badly as I lie down and exhale. And that voice inside my head tells me again: Nothing worth having in life comes easy.

The Lohit flows fast and furious between two of India's easternmost villages—Kibithu and Kaho, a few kilometres from the Line of Actual Control with China.

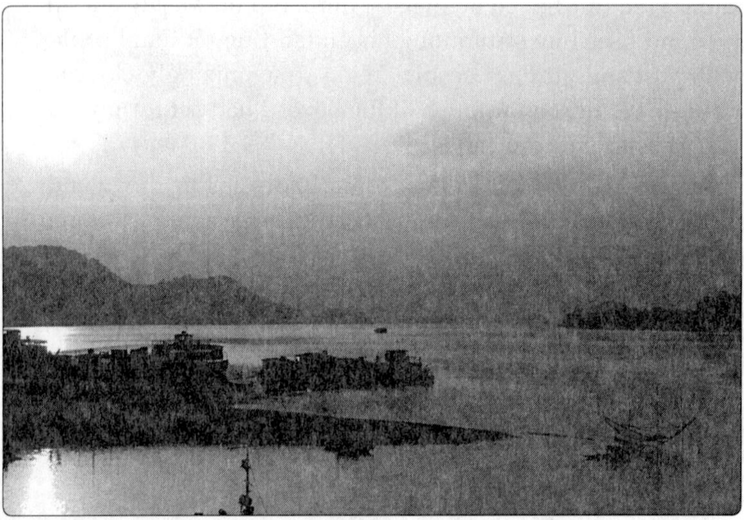

Sunset on the Brahmaputra in Guwahati.

Monks practising a dance at Tawang Monastery in Arunachal Pradesh.

A morung in Kigwema village near Kohima, Nagaland.

The double-decker root bridge in Umshiang,
Cherrapunji.

A half-frozen Sela Lake in Arunachal Pradesh.

A boat glides over a transparent Umngot river
in Shnonpdeng, Meghalaya.

Three of Kaziranga's patrol elephants raid
an Army convoy for lunch.

About the Author

Sabir Hussain has been a journalist for over three decades and now works as a freelance journalist and editor.

He has worked with some of India's top media houses and news agencies like Press Trust of India, Times Now, India Today, and most recently with *Hindustan Times*.

An adventurer at heart, he has been part of several motorcycle expeditions to Ladakh between 1998 and 2008 as a member of a Delhi-based bikers' club called Pathfinders. His first book, *Battlefields & Paradise*, published by Westland in 2016, was a motorcycle travelogue after a solo ride through Kashmir to India's northernmost place called Turtuk on the edge of Ladakh along the Line of Control with Pakistan.

He lives in Vaishali in Delhi NCR with his wife and son.

Readomania

Readomania exists to nurture, curate, and bring to you content you love. We are a publishing house that takes pride in encouraging talent, new or old, and provides a wonderful platform for awesome stories.

We make this possible in multiple ways.

The first as an independent publishing house. Readomania boasts of multiple imprints across various categories—fiction, nonfiction, children, to name a few. An eclectic mix of content for its readers, when you read a Readomania title, you enter a world that's yours, supported by unique and quality narratives.

The second, as an online publishing platform for writers—a place to share stories, poems, opinions, travelogues, a way to explore your creative talent. Available as premium, as well as free-to-read content across multiple genres, the reader is spoilt for choice.

Join us in this journey, as we explore, develop, and present stories to our readers and audiences. Welcome to the world of Readomania, get ready to craft stories that enrich lives.

You can visit us at: www.readomania.com